CROOKED PATHS

By the same author:

Radical Paradoxes:
  Dilemmas of the American Left,
  1945–1970

Peter Clecak

CROOKED PATHS

Reflections on Socialism,
Conservatism, and the
Welfare State

HARPER & ROW, PUBLISHERS
NEW YORK, HAGERSTOWN,
SAN FRANCISCO, LONDON

This book has been published with the aid of a Bicentennial Grant from the Phi Beta Kappa Society.

FIRST EDITION

Designed by Gloria Adelson

Library of Congress Cataloging in Publication Data

Clecak, Peter.
    Crooked paths.
    Includes bibliographical references and index.
    1. Conservatism—United States. 2. Liberalism—
United States. 3. Socialism in the United States.
I. Title.
JA84.U5C53 1977   320.5'0973   76–5118
ISBN 0–06–010838–X

77 78 79 80 10 9 8 7 6 5 4 3 2 1

In memory of my father
Nicholas Peter Clecak
1909 – 1975

Contents

Preface

For many of us, the two-hundredth anniversary of the American Revolution is an unnerving occasion, an anxious pause between a national past that seems increasingly less heroic and an uncertain future. Yet an event of such importance cannot be ignored: the American experiment may not be in the best of health after two centuries, but it is very much alive—more vital, I shall contend, than most of its harshest critics allow. And we live in the thick of it. Like so much else in this hodgepodge of cultures, the Bicentennial lends itself to many purposes. It ushers in a season of morally empty self-congratulation interlaced with every conceivable form of huckstering: any usable scrap of the past is for sale. But it also invites serious reflection on our genuine achievements, shortcomings, prospects.

Anticipating the event, the Bicentennial Commission of Phi Beta Kappa issued a call late in 1970 for a series of "books of broad scope dealing with the cultural crisis of our time, and in particular, with the responsibilities of the intellectual in that crisis." Finding American cultural institutions and values in "a state of revolutionary ferment," the Commission posed these questions: "What are the basic elements of this ferment? What is the essential nature of this revolution? What perspectives will enable us to distinguish them and it most clearly, to separate the ephemeral from the probably enduring? What are the most promising directions, now and later?" In the course of charting paths "from the present disruption toward a rational future order," authors of these volumes were to "suggest the new attitudes, vocabularies, and methods needed to understand the present situation and to pre-scribe for the future."

These wide boundaries of inquiry were drawn in the turbulence of the late sixties when some believed that American culture and society needed to be leveled to clear the way for a future free from the complexities, ironies, and failures of the past. In an atmosphere of self-conscious innocence, revolution came to be a catchword: it was anticipated enthusiastically by a few, feared by a sizable minority (including those in the highest echelons of government), and construed differently by nearly everyone. Although the flam-boyant hopes and crushing disappointments of that period ended abruptly—or rather, ceased being public concerns—a sense of per-vasive crisis has grown among nearly all segments of the popula-tion. Taking different, less explosive public forms thus far in the seventies, the troubles of American politics and culture persist.

Above all, the expectation of unending plenty, which informed so much commentary of the fifties and sixties, has collapsed as a reigning assumption of American social thought. It may be possi-ble still to locate the social sources of our malaise in misuses and perversions of affluence. But we no longer can predicate resolu-tions of public issues on the promise of a horn of plenty so great that it will trivialize the problem of equitable distribution. Thus, as the future becomes less and less a source of consolation, it lends a sense of permanence to the present crisis (and bends this term toward new meanings): under the rubric of crisis, we express simultaneously a curious blend of urgency, apathy, numbness, and confusion about public dilemmas which now appear to be open-ended. As we pass unprepared from a time of affluence and an-ticipated abundance into one of relative scarcity, the dominant orientations of liberalism, conservatism, and socialism all appear less durable. Each of these ideological perspectives needs to be reconsidered in the light of the long term prospect of relative scarcity.

That the charge of the Bicentennial Commission survived the moment of its origin despite the beginnings of a shift in axial assumptions concerning abundance and scarcity must be counted a minor achievement in a culture of ephemeral concerns. But the tone of the Commission's charge now seems too confident, a rough index, perhaps, of the velocity of our drift into pessimism. Long discarded by a sizable percentage of intellectuals, the idea of fashioning a "rational future order" has come to appear dubious to wider segments of the public as well. Yet I find the questions advanced by the Bicentennial Commission as intriguing now as then, when I was midway through *Radical Paradoxes,* a study of selected aspects of the American crisis from the end of World War II through the demise of the organized new Left.

Radical Paradoxes delineated the inner crisis of American—and Western—socialism through a close study of four politically unattached Left social critics: C. Wright Mills, Paul Baran, Paul Sweezy, and Herbert Marcuse. Placing them within the tradition of both classical and contemporary Marxism, I traced their responses to emerging shapes of capitalism and socialism in the early cold war setting, a somewhat different world than we encounter now. Each of these "plain Marxists" engaged the problem of envisioning an alternative society and of gauging the political means —and obstacles—to its realization. Those who lived through the decade of the sixties—Sweezy, and especially Marcuse—met their disappointments with radicalism in the United States and elsewhere by exchanging broken promises of socialism for the false illusions of communism. Badly confusing political and cultural categories in the exchange, these critics relinquished their sense of the importance of democracy in postcapitalist societies. Under the pressure of historical defeats, their social criticism yielded gradually to fanciful myths of consolation. As it developed, these myths proved spiritually unsatisfying and politically useless—even destructive when pressed too far, as the political and cultural revolutionaries of the new Left amply demonstrated.

Radical Paradoxes, then, was primarily an effort to illuminate the dead ends of utopian variants of communist visions in the American context. This critique of communism, however, was conducted from the precarious vantage point of democratic socialism. A decline of faith in the long range efficacy of liberal approaches to reform, along with the obvious utopian excesses in the ideologies of the period, seemed to indicate, almost by default, the desirability of a moderate—even conservative—version of democratic socialism as a political fiction that might help people on the Left endure the deepening confusions of American life, and perhaps carve a crooked path, a way through. I am more skeptical than ever about the theoretical coherence and moral aptness—not to mention the political utility—of democratic socialism. Though unwilling to abandon this idea, I wish to explore it more critically here, rather than employ it once again mainly as a heuristic device to clarify the utopian notion of communism.

Crooked Paths is thus a continuation of *Radical Paradoxes* in the sense that it addresses similar questions and presses the theme of conservative democratic socialism a bit further. But it represents a departure, too, for I begin here where I left off, with the idea of democratic socialism as the usable residue of communist dreams, and proceed to examine its elements from liberal capitalist and conservative perspectives. My principal intention is to reconsider three facets of the bourgeois tradition—socialism, liberalism, and conservatism—against the background of the related political and cultural crises in America, and to propose at least one crooked path. What I have written, however, is not exclusively political: there is no original program or elaborate strategy sketched out in these pages, no design to get from here to there. In fact, the political pressures of my argument keep leading me away from politics. For this is a book fundamentally about real and perceived limits—the limits of material resources as well as the limits and limitations of politics and government. Hence my preoccupation with the apolitical dimensions of the good life. In the course of composing these reflections, I have come to realize that my deepest interests are only incidentally political. That is to say, I am fascinated less by thoroughly political personalities and processes than by the individuals I criticize most harshly—the utopians who gesture wildly at but essentially in the right direction of images of the good or satisfying life. Yet politics and government remain crucial insofar as they help to illuminate the dangerous gestures of utopians and give partial form to gestures that otherwise might remain idle. These reflections, then, comprise an exercise in the public philosophy, an exercise which is concerned with ideologies, theories, and political programs, to be sure, but also with their shaping background pressures, attitudes, and inherited senses of life.

In what follows, I use elements of the received vocabularies of socialism and capitalism, liberalism and conservatism in a self-conscious way, acknowledging their inadequacies, distrusting them profoundly, but remembering also that they comprise a rich legacy, an obvious place to begin. I do not rehearse the arguments of *Radical Paradoxes* in detail, though some reiteration has seemed necessary in Chapter 2 to establish the context for subsequent discussions of liberalism and conservatism. Nor am I concerned with arranging absolute consistency of opinion between these books: too much has changed too quickly to allow me to pursue such a venal intention. I shall be satisfied if they form elements of a coherent probe.

In the course of this study, I have acquired many debts. I wish there were more, for each has represented an opportunity to learn and a chance to make an acquaintance or deepen a friendship. I am grateful to Professor Richard Schlatter and the members of the Phi Beta Kappa Bicentennial Commission for furnishing the occasion for these reflections, extending generous financial assistance, and offering just the right amount of encouragement. The Phi Beta Kappa grant, along with a sabbatical, enabled me to rediscover the pleasures of concentrated study in a leisurely ambience.

Several people have been kind enough to comment on preliminary drafts: Catherine Bowers, John Diggins, James Flink, Eugene Genovese, Richard Gillam, Robert Heilbroner, Irving Howe, Joseph Jorgensen, Jay Martin, and Arthé Anthony Shacks. I wish to thank Howard R. Bowen, Valdo Herby, Myron Simon, and David Thorburn for detailed criticisms of the manuscript which went beyond the normal bounds of generosity. I also owe special thanks, once again, to Cynthia Merman, an accomplished editor and friend. In addition to his cogent criticisms of the text, Mr. Curtis Graham, my research assistant, has spent countless hours tracking down references I never would have found (or known about).

Vivian Clecak has been a full partner. Having encouraged me to apply for a Phi Beta Kappa fellowship, she furnished many of the leading ideas, and provided close critiques of the several drafts. She has loved the author freely without always falling for the text.

Anyone fortunate enough to find friendship and love in another will know the inadequacy of a note of gratitude.

I dedicate this book to the memory of my father, a good and loving man who died too soon, but not before seeing his only grandchild. Aimée is a joy—one child in a million we like to think —his, and our, gift to the future.

P. C.

July 1976

Is there a path for us, a crooked
path for men of disciplined hope?
—Irving Howe

1 / Some Preliminaries

> For the last three decades we have felt that we were living in
> the initial phases of the greatest crisis humanity has ever
> known. It grows increasingly clear to us that the tremendous
> happenings of the past years, too, can be understood only as
> symptoms of this crisis. It is not merely the crisis of one
> economic and social system being superseded by another
> . . . , rather all systems, old and new, are equally involved in
> the crisis. What is in question . . . is nothing less than man's
> whole existence in the world.
>
> —Martin Buber, *Paths in Utopia*

I begin with three assumptions:
· America is in the midst of a sociopolitical crisis.
· America is in the midst of a crisis of culture.
· These crises are complexly related, but their resolution—insofar as resolutions are possible—will require quite different patterns of understanding, as well as separate modes of public action
(and inaction).[1]

To these assumptions I add the Kantian question, "What may
I hope for?"

These initial assumptions may be too vague to be useful and too
familiar to be arresting. My question concerning hope may be
off-key, naive, or even perverse in a time of deeply felt and widely

1

shared pessimism about chances for recovery. But such large political and cultural dilemmas cannot be finessed: they shape the ethos
of our intellectual life and, increasingly, of our national life. The
depth, intensity, and pervasiveness of what André Malraux terms
"the crisis of civilization" make it difficult to sort out the parts, and
more difficult still to assign causes or project cures. And perhaps
beside the point: we simply *experience* a desanctified and disordered
world. Initially a minor chord in modern Western culture, the
property of such figures as Swift and Voltaire, Nietzsche and
Kierkegaard, Burckhardt, Dostoevsky and Freud, the idea of civilizational malaise has become a significant public theme, for many
the orchestrating principle of our time. To some, this seems a
transitional period of turmoil between one relatively settled state
and another; to others, a period of decline, decay, regression—the
last throes of a dying civilization. But everyone experiences the
disorienting impact of change.

Critics from Karl Marx and Henry Adams to Alvin Toffler have
pursued the implications of this theme.[2] So long as the idea of
Progress remained in vogue, the general direction of change
seemed welcome, even if the accelerating rate caused a certain
confusion. Although the dynamics of Progress produced unforeseen side effects as solutions to one cluster of social problems
generated another, the growing powers of rationality, it was believed generally, would be sufficient to maintain a profitable balance between problems and solutions. Change constituted a relatively minor cost of realizing the dream of unending abundance.

Yet fear of anomie and disorder always haunted the notion of
Progress as its subversive shadow. Recently, the shadow has come
to seem more substantial than the original concept. As Henry
Adams' dynamo passes into the domain of public consciousness,
both the rate and the direction of technological and institutional
change appear ever more ominous. Assessing American dilemmas
at the outset of the seventies, Arthur Schlesinger observed that
"the basic task is to control and humanize the forces of change in
order to prevent them from tearing our society apart."[3] The
American enterprise that flourished by virtue of continuous
change, tolerating mild anarchy, maintaining its precarious stability by remaining perpetually off balance, now seems about to be

overwhelmed by a number of converging forces. Interest groups push their own ends with little regard for the public interest. Expectations of more goods, more services, and greater psychic rewards rise among all sectors of the population. And the sheer size, complexity, and interdependence of the current range of social problems promise shortly to overtax political and governmental means of defining and resolving them. Above all, conflict intensifies largely because we continue to undergo swift social change without the comforting promise of unlimited abundance. The idea of a bountiful future which assures more of everything to everyone has lost its power. Of course, popular moods of pessimism deepen in times of economic downturn or national political crisis, and give way to moderate optimism in periods of upswing and relative calm. Such rapid shifts of mood—almost manic depressive in their duration and intensity—corroborate suspicions of the underlying malaise of American civilization.

The sense of disorientation and pessimism concerning our prospects permeates the categories of politics, society, psychology, culture, and religion, lessening confidence in their analytic power and practical importance. "Our civilization is in ruins," John Lukacs goes so far as to say, *"because* our beliefs about civilization are in ruins."[4] We are tempted to surrender rationality, imagination, and will to the flux of experience. For the easiest defense against postmodern confusion is to file everything from minor personal troubles to large public issues and ultimate questions of human purpose under it. Once one yields his imagination in this way to the paradigm of total—and endless—crisis, all else falls into place. Rather, nothing need be in a special place. No new turn of events can come as a surprise. Hopes may be fulfilled, but never again betrayed. Apparently unpatterned changes only confirm fears and uncertainties, reifying the crisis and lending a sort of bogus solidity to perceptions of a weightless, protean world.

But this will not do. When it becomes so pervasive that it touches everything, the notion of civilizational malaise explains nothing. The success of the idea therefore demands that we reconsider the ideologies and structural parts that it envelops in a fog. An atmosphere of crisis may permeate our experience, but it need not conflate the categories through which we attempt to understand and direct the course of society and culture. Even if the current American sociopolitical crisis should turn out to be an epiphenomenon of a larger cultural drift that proves resistant to rational strategies of amelioration, it nevertheless ought to be considered initially in sociopolitical terms.

The dual crises of politics and culture, then, serve as primary— and partially overlapping—points of reference, a place to begin and, considering their mysterious dimensions, probably also a place to end. In between, I hope to reassess democratic socialism, liberal capitalism, and conservatism, three distinct though closely related facets of what many take to be the moribund bourgeois imagination.[5] Rather than attempt a theory of social and cultural change, I shall pursue the more modest aim of exploring these ideological resources in the new context of relative scarcity, with the hope (that word again) of delimiting a reasonable range of responses to current dilemmas. The speculative terms of this inquiry preclude the chance of drawing a reliable political map, of charting a way out of the impasse. But they may permit construction of a crude compass that points to several ways through.

The Sociopolitical Crisis

Of the several main dimensions of the present sociopolitical crisis, erosion of public confidence in the political process is in all likelihood the most widespread. Politics as a vocation has lost much of its luster. More and more people consider political animals—and bureaucrats—lacking in moral courage and social imagination, bumbling opportunists or clever operatives of powerful, organized special interests. This large scale withdrawal of confidence in the leading political agents extends to the political agencies of the system. Though various polls provide only a fragmentary—and often conflicting—record of surface opinions, they do point steadily to this conclusion. National political parties have lost much of their force as important centers of ideological and policy debate, and as sources of political allegiance: about 35% of the electorate has deserted the major parties to become independents, leaving only 21% who identify themselves as Republicans, and 44% as Democrats. Roughly 40% of eligible citizens do not bother to register; and many who do vote with little enthusiasm. This declining interest in the elective process reflects a rising sense of political powerlessness: since 1966, according to Louis Harris, the number of people who believe that their opinions do not "really count" in the public realm has grown from 37% to 67%. And those who believe that the minority exercising political power "don't really care what happens" to them has climbed from 33% to 63%.[6] Not surprisingly, then, governmental institutions, which provide links between critical debate and public policy, stabilizing the political process, have lost public favor. Less than one-third of the American public now expresses "high confidence" in the Supreme Court (the least directly political branch of government), as opposed to one half in 1966. Confidence in the Executive and Congress has dropped from about 41% to 13% in the same period.[7]

Assessing his continuing studies of American public opinion, Daniel Yankelovich concludes that the system suffers most from a crisis of moral legitimacy. The ubiquitous sense of an uncomfortable distance between promise and performance—between moral imperatives and behavior—along with increasing skepticism concerning the chances of enforcing the rules, is probably the lowest common denominator of our political malaise.[8] According to Yankelovich, the American public remains somewhat less concerned about the alleged ineffectiveness of governmental institutions than by a sense of the social injustices they perpetuate. Still, as we have seen, a majority judge the federal government—the most influential and extensive agency—less effective now than in the past. Though serious, these crises of moral and functional legitimacy do not yet amount to an ideological breakdown, a thorough questioning of essential values and ideas embodied in advanced capitalism and the American version of the welfare state.[9] Among intellectuals, of course, loss of moral and functional legitimacy are more frequently construed as signs of a breakdown of ideological legitimacy, an invitation to reconsider basic premises of current social organization. Those who explain the emergence and persistence of public problems largely in ideological terms of capitalism and the welfare state often posit such alternatives as socialism, communism, and anarchism. Whether these ideas will be debated throughout society as—and if—the moral and functional legitimacy of the system erodes further, is a central and problematic question.

There are at least interesting signs that the old shibboleths of capitalism may be losing their hold on wider segments of society. According to a poll conducted by Peter Hart in July 1975, about four-fifths of Americans believe that capitalism has already reached its peak performance. About two-fifths favor "major adjustments" in economic arrangements. And two-thirds would prefer "working for a company that is employee owned and controlled" to working for a major capitalist corporation. (But only 8% opted for a government-owned company.)[10]

From these various polls it seems safe to assume a steep decline of confidence in the idea that the public ills of American society can be resolved rationally, through various combinations of criticism and political action. In the absence of live systemic alternatives, such an erosion of confidence will add to pessimism and cynicism about chances of the system working on its own terms or generating a new set of workable terms. Though still less than an ideological crisis of legitimacy, the spreading sense of the political uselessness of social criticism represents a profound and unsettling change of attitude. Until recently, social criticism generally has been considered an important index of the nation's health and an agent of its progress.[11] A pivotal social institution in an open, democratic society, criticism enables people to develop shared definitions, analyses, and interpretations of public problems. Through discussion and debate, differences are clarified and alternative proposals emerge. Attitudes change; error is minimized; charlatans and incompetents are exposed; and through the political process some form of corrective action ensues.

Thus, when perceived disparities between problems and solutions become intense, as they did toward the end of the 1950s, the first recourse of anyone committed to the ideal of an open society is to call for more and better criticism, for appointment of commissions to study problems in depth and offer recommendations for action. (In the time of affluence, "action" came to entail public expenditures of large sums.) Until the middle 1960s, this gambit commanded general assent, even among those critics whose specific proposals had little chance of being enacted. But as problems multiplied and the volume of social criticism grew, attractive solutions appeared more remote than ever. The dreams of the New Frontier and the Great Society dissolved into the nightmare of Vietnam, intensified racism, urban violence, and student unrest. Expectations, heightened in part by the growth and dissemination of social commentary, were deflated, and faith in the value of criticism as a prelude to remedial action correspondingly waned. Even limited successes in the seventies—the liveliness of consumer action groups, significant reforms in the Democratic party, the exposures of Watergate, the FBI, and the CIA—contribute on balance to an overall sense of politics and public life as an unsatisfying (and shady) labor of Sisyphus.

Not surprisingly, this decline of confidence in our ability to cope collectively with public ills comes at a time when national problems appear to be running out of control. The issue of social justice —its meanings and applications—extends to nearly every phase of American life. In the postwar period, the egalitarian thrust acquired fresh momentum as minorities, young people, and women pressed for enlargement of their rights, responsibilities, and rewards. Indeed, throughout society, demands for higher wages and salaries, along with expectations of more and better services for everyone—security of employment, prepaid medical care, mass higher education—have accelerated, even as confidence in politics, government, and the economy has ebbed. But it is no longer evident that advanced capitalism can provide goods and services in sufficient quantity to meet rising demands and expectations. Nor is it clear that the total amount of future production can be distributed much more equitably than it has been in the recent past. Thus, to concerns for interesting, rewarding, and satisfying work expressed by a large segment of youth in the sixties has been added the more elemental question of whether this system can provide enough jobs. High unemployment, stagflation, rising energy costs, unfavorable shifts in international economic arrangements, and the decline of American global hegemony have weakened public faith in the private sector. In the past decade, according to Louis Harris, the percentage of the population expressing high confidence in major companies has dropped from 55% to 19%.[12]

At the same time, perceptions of the quality of life, insofar as it is shaped by economic and political forces, have become less sanguine. Life in rural areas and the suburbs remains less satisfying than many imagined it would be, though I think somewhat fuller than most urban critics allow. Major cities may be majestic from a distance. Close up, however, they are ugly, dirty, unsafe, in addition to being at the edge of financial ruin. For all but the very well off, life there ranges from difficult to nightmarish. Unemployment rates, conservatively estimated at around 7% nationally, and ranging up to 40% among young blacks in major cities, are unacceptably high. Millions are forced to lay aside the venerable dream of owning a home on a separate piece of territory; others despair of finding a decent place to live. In many inner cities, schools have become dangerous holding areas rather than centers of learning. Medical care has not kept pace with expectations. Even the air, which used to be free and clear, now reeks on muggy summer days.

Though serious, these immediate and medium range domestic problems might seem more amenable to solution through the combined resources of technological rationality, modern capitalist (and postcapitalist) economic processes, and representative democracy, were it not for the spate of bleak forecasts concerning outer limits. In the past decade we have been made aware (once again) of limits to human will; limits on the capacities of available social systems; limits on the ability of the international system to check the buildup—and eventual use—of nuclear weapons; limits on the future imposed by the legacy of the historical past; and perhaps most important, material and ecological limits imposed by the natural environment. Speculating on the long term global future, Robert Heilbroner concludes that the outlook for man "is painful, difficult, perhaps desperate, and the hope that can be held out for his future prospect seems to be very slim indeed." The future promises to be "a continuation of the darkness, cruelty, and disorder of the past."[13]

In America, the idea of outpacing social problems through abundance has given way to a new awareness of relative scarcity.

Recently imagined as a spacious arena where all sorts of individual and collective hopes might be realized, the American future now seems cramped, adding considerable urgency to every facet of the current crisis. It would be difficult, I think, to overrate the importance of this shift in dominant assumptions. It alters the substance, mood, and tone of social and political thought. For in the postwar era the related concepts of affluence and abundance not only have been used to characterize economic advances. They also—perhaps primarily—have served as an organizing social metaphor and a dominant expectation, a covenant with the future. Only a decade ago, nearly all major American social commentators assumed a future of at least potentially unlimited productivity, however much they disagreed over the most suitable ways to organize and release such forces. Proclaiming the advent of a triple revolution —in production, weaponry, and human rights—a number of leading left liberal and democratic socialist intellectuals, including W. H. Ferry, Michael Harrington, Robert Heilbroner, and Irving Howe, concluded in the early sixties that cybernation promised a "system of almost unlimited productive capacity which requires progressively less human labor."[14] Within the relevant future, they predicted, it would be possible to transfer much of the burden of human labor to self-regulating machines, and simultaneously to end poverty, not only in America but around the world.

No longer a utopian dream, the Western idea of plenty had become a material possibility everywhere, and very nearly a reality in America. Detached from contexts of scarcity, the concepts of work and efficiency—indeed, the concept of self—were losing their traditional meanings. These changes required a major reorientation of social thought to meet new opportunities and new problems. As David Riesman put it in a typical observation of the time, "the traditional American ideology which is concerned only with equality of economic and political opportunity and freedom from control—in other words with the major problems of scarcity alone—must readjust to face the problems that have suddenly become visible because of abundance: lack of participation in life and lack of opportunity and education for self-expression. Once these problems can be faced, a people of plenty may be able to use its power for helping other people toward economic prosperity

. . . old agendas and ways of regarding the world will have to be scrapped and new ones discovered." Riesman, of course, did not contend that the problems of scarcity had been resolved fully: "not all Americans are affluent, many are destitute, and many of the traditional issues of welfare and social justice . . . remain exigent." But the old issues associated with scarcity had become "details of the present."[15]

That present now seems a distant past, its "details" central issues once more. In the early postwar years, the idea of affluence prefigured an impending era of abundance. Now, though affluence persists among sectors of the population, the dream of general abundance is fading. We are in the midst of another reorientation of social thought. One version or another of the idea of relative scarcity now constitutes the starting point for all serious discussion of public issues. Recognition of this has quickly become commonplace, but dominant orientations toward political and social matters do not change all at once. Nor do they change altogether: I do not wish to suggest that America will revert to conditions of dire material scarcity. Elements of received ideologies that depend implicitly or even explicitly upon the older framework of abundance survive, even as we lose awareness of the connections. It is important to trace elements of political thought, ideology, and strategy back to their sources and discard formulations that do not square with new realities. In subsequent discussions of socialism, liberalism, and conservatism, I shall not assume the worst—severe scarcity occasioned by a short range collapse of the American economy. Nor shall I assume (as who would?) the rosiest forecasts of a population of 10 to 30 billion people with a gross world product of between $100 and $350 trillion in the next half-century or so.[16] I shall proceed instead on the more cautious, and I think more sensible, assumption that the American economy, with its awesome debt load of $2.5 trillion and its vast capital requirements for the next decade, must grow more slowly than it has in the past quarter-century—somewhere perhaps in the neighborhood of 2–3% per year, with, say, an average 5% rate of inflation and, at best, 95% employment.[17]

One thing on this obscure landscape of social prophecy seems clear: even if the brightest plausible economic forecasts turn out to be accurate, questions concerning equitable division of limited opportunity, goods, services, space, power, influence, and status will dominate the sociopolitical scene for the foreseeable future. The paradigm of relative scarcity and the dominant idea of limits will persist.

Small wonder, then, that the prevailing postwar liberal ideology, anchored as it was in expectations of plenty, has come under sustained attack from old and new directions. There has been continuous criticism from the Left, much of it, I shall suggest, based on outmoded assumptions concerning abundance and its implications.[18] During the postwar years of affluence, socialists of various persuasions contended that American capitalists systematically mismanaged resources, producing an undesirable mix of goods and services, wasting materiel, distributing the total product inequitably, and using increased productivity to preserve a system of political and psychic domination. Conceding that capitalism had brought about great advances in production, critics maintained that only a socialism of abundance could release the full material and spiritual potential of mankind, thereby easing the whole range of social problems that plagued people during the many centuries of scarcity and, in different ways, during the brief time of capitalist affluence. The demise of the central expectation of unlimited abundance, under *either* system, I shall argue, compels socialists to reformulate their critiques of liberal capitalism and the welfare state, to reconsider the limits and limitations of democratic socialism (the only kind thinkable in America), and to recast fundamental political strategies of transition.

Among intellectuals and among wider segments of the public as well, there also has been a resurgence of conservatisms that fit the mood of pessimism and take account of the advent of relative scarcity more conveniently than liberals and democratic socialists have managed to do. According to Yankelovich, "more than half the American people consider themselves conservative—twice as many as a decade ago."[19] As yet ill-defined and politically diffuse —perhaps it is perpetually so—conservative sentiment is shifting the grounds of American political thought somewhat, leaving recent formulations of democratic socialism and liberalism in a state of disrepair. Elements of the liberal faith survive, but precariously, in a sobering ambience of pessimism and doubt. Ambivalence about the role and limits of government in a time of fiscal crisis has contributed to a deep and multifaceted internal conflict between liberal commitments to personal liberty and to a more egalitarian society. Evident in the general drift toward a more conservative center of political thought, this tension lies at the core of moderately conservative efforts of "new liberals" to redefine their values within the paradigm of relative scarcity.

Reassessing the idea of Progress, neo-conservative intellectuals (and many new liberals) contend that in the past two decades social commentators raised expectations unrealistically, thereby adding to a mounting stock of public cynicism.[20] Postwar social criticism, in this view, constitutes a form of ideological deficit spending that parallels excessive fiscal spending, promoted mainly by liberal politicians: problems that could not be resolved through criticism, politics, and governmental activity were repressed and displaced onto a symbolic level where imagined futures, characterized by ever more government spending, blunted full recognition of an intractable present. In part, according to this general argument, liberal and Left critics misdefined the terms of what had become the standard paradox of American social life. The idea that serious public problems persist needlessly in the context of rising affluence, technological expertise, and political democracy no longer convinces. Nor do proposed solutions that depend largely upon greater generosity of middle income groups and a more extensive welfare state.

Neo-conservative critics suggest further that those who promoted contemporary versions of the idea of Progress through social criticism and a politics of incremental reform seriously overestimated the capacity of people acting through governmental institutions to optimize the moral, spiritual, and aesthetic quality of life. Rather than using social criticism as a mode of imagining sweeping change (whether gradual or sudden), neo-conservatives contend that it might be used more properly as a mode of understanding the limits of productive capacity, the strengths and weaknesses of modern bureaucracies, the limitations of government, and the boundaries of human generosity and will. With such understanding, we can adjust, as gracefully as possible, to what cannot be helped. Lowered expectations about the potentialities of the American enterprise may reduce perceived disparities between promise and performance.

The breakdown of liberal consensus is interpreted variously. Received ideologies strike a significant number of people as feeble guides to effective public action. Many believe that socialism, liberalism, and conservatism—at least in their inherited formulations—no longer serve as integrated and useful patterns of belief about the social and political environment. These perspectives all coexist in a thick ideological alphabet soup. Thoughtful people now routinely adopt conservative positions on some matters, liberal stances on others, and socialist perspectives on still others. Although individuals may carve out a sensible outlook in this way, the immediate public impact of such efforts seems disappointing: ideological confusion and political vacillation emerge precisely when unprecedented problems demand more concerted responses.

Such broad disagreements about the role of ideology occur mainly within the fuzzy boundaries of what I have termed the sociopolitical crisis. People who debate them still hope that large social problems can be managed, and further, that we ought to try, because alleviation of economic difficulties and social injustices would make a significant difference in American life. But it should be evident that this effort would not make all the difference. Political action informed by mature ideological debate may remain urgent—I shall insist throughout these pages that it does. In fact, I shall argue that the several facets of the bourgeois tradition— socialism, liberalism, and conservatism—still have more to offer than many who use them, willingly or reluctantly, usually care to acknowledge. Yet political activity based on ideological conviction no longer promises to dissolve the larger crisis of culture that permeates the social landscape and invades the individual spirit.

At the very least, such an admission probably requires a conservative revision of earlier liberal and socialist hopes. It may be possible for Americans to arrange their collective affairs so as to ensure a measure of economic well-being and social order. It may be possible also to achieve a greater measure of social justice through enlargement of liberty, reduction of inequality, deepening of democracy, and restoration of multiple modes of authority. Although they would facilitate the strong cultural drive toward self-enhancement, none of these measures guarantees fullness of life, or happiness. We lack the resources to unravel cultural dilemmas fully, for unlike political problems they cannot be settled through reallocations of power, wealth, or status.

The Crisis of Culture

Recognition of our ubiquitous civilizational malaise raises the far more disturbing question of whether cultural aspects of the present crisis impair—if not fatally, then seriously—our ability to employ ideological and political resources in the social sphere. The notion of culture eludes precise definition. In the broadest sense, it refers to a vast network of communications systems, a mixture of cognitive and affective symbols that express, compress, and often repress ideas, values, assumptions, beliefs, and moods. Cultural symbols give form to private experience, linking it with the common life and binding generations together through distinctive systems of meaning and value. Culture is the fluid medium through which individuals and communities convey their central purposes, through which they define, feel, and evaluate themselves.[21]

Without culture, individual experience would remain forever fragmentary. Traditional cultures, whose values change slowly over long stretches of time, constitute the most evident and rigorous models of coherence. Modern societies require broader, more supple conceptions of coherence, for a culture remains stable as long as people can accept and adapt to patterns of change, apprehending them as parts of a continuous historical process. Continuity often persists through perceived change, preserving a measure of stability in values, institutions, manners, and customs. But when the most deeply held and widely shared assumptions begin to lose their force, cultural patterns threaten to lapse into a chaotic jumble, subverting social purposes as in the vivid biblical parable of Babel. By these criteria, I think it fair to regard America as a culture in crisis, perhaps at the edge of a sea change.

Signs of rupture in the continuity of values are evident in every major cultural institution. Previously secure notions of personality, sex roles, family organization, child rearing, education, religion, literature and the arts, the nature of work, and the possibilities of leisure are all in disarray, challenged though not yet defeated by advocates of alternative perspectives. As in the case of ideologies, newer cultural values do not displace previous ones thoroughly; they are rather added on or mixed in, becoming further possibilities, fresh styles. Instead of shifting slowly and complexly from one predominant mode of education to another, public schools in a single city may offer a cafeteria of styles—a classroom without walls at one site, a traditional classroom (including formal dress and patriotic drills) at another, and so on. Though retaining its dominance, the nuclear family no longer constitutes the only acceptable framework for life: adults may live singly, in twos or threes, with or without children, in various combinations of sexes and sexual arrangements. Fashions used to succeed one another in parades; now everything, including nudity (the nihilism of fashion) is in, presenting compressed images of a culture in the round.

In one sense, this syncretism of cultural values and institutions represents a broadening of possibilities, their welcome democratization.[22] But it has been accompanied by confusion and a flattening of conviction, a conflation of deep categories of basic belief and surface categories of custom, manner, and style. There are thus many styles in education but no agreement on what ought to be passed along to the young; many styles of life, but little conviction about how to live. It has become possible, even easy, to select a lifestyle, but more difficult to build a life, even to know what such a project would entail. There are, then, surely more choices than ever, but probably less satisfying ones, at least less satisfying than we had led ourselves to believe they would be.

The difficulty, of course, does not lie in recognizing the enveloping cultural crisis—the signs are everywhere—but in representing it, isolating its main dimensions, assessing its changing intensity, determining its course, and relating it to the sociopolitical sphere. We are, to a considerable degree, prisoners of past success. Such

previously shared goals as self-fulfillment through material progress, greater individual freedom, and wider equality of opportunity were subordinated largely to disciplined means of personal
sacrifice, hard work, postponement of gratification—in a word, to
the rule of efficiency and rationality. Since goals in the public
sphere could be achieved only through careful effort, and then
only by a few at the culmination of a long ordeal, the difficult
means exerted considerable immediate power over individuals and
groups in America. In fact, such means as hard work and delayed
gratification served also as ends. But accomplishment of earlier
goals, their transformation into conditions of life, has loosened the
classic restraints of bourgeois culture. More precisely, it has desanctified these limits, depriving them of spiritual import and
moral authority.

Of course, American culture never has been calm for long stretches, or even unified, except in the loosest sense. This society houses
a potpourri of cultures. The current round of cultural variety,
disorder, and confusion, however, is especially unsettling because
the quest for individual fulfillment, long associated with individualism, remains and even grows in importance as the parts of
American society and culture which exerted restraint become
progressively weaker. Should self-enhancement emerge as the
only compelling norm, the social fabric will hang together by the
feeble thread of the expectation of more—more goods, more services, more freedom considered as the virtual absence of interference with individual activity.

Just when inner limits of restraint are slackening, however, we
seem to be drawing closer to outer, public limits of activity. Daniel
Bell suggests that the original axial principles of equality and the
belief in material progress have been thrown seriously off course
by more recent social changes. Growing imbalances between
rights and responsibilities, opportunities and burdens imperil social stability. The earlier American promise of plenty has encouraged a revolution of rising expectations. The promise of equality
has become a revolution of rising entitlements, "claims on government to implement an array of newly defined and vastly expanded
social rights." In Bell's view, which I find slightly pietistic and
schematic, Americans have become "hedonistic, concerned with

consumption and pleasure, lacking any moral underpinning."[23] Yet Bell is surely right in contending that expanded concepts of rights and entitlements have not been matched by a growth in individual responsibility or the development of a concept of social justice appropriate to our rediscovered sense of material limits.

Philip Rieff outlines the dilemma that this trend toward a post-Christian, postcommunal culture of permanent anomie may create. The past two centuries, which Rieff refers to as a period of "deconversion" from Christianity, have marked an antireligious, antipolitical, and anticultural revolution, "a calm and profoundly reasonable revolt of the private man against all doctrinal traditions urging the salvation of self through identification with the purposes of community."[24] Rieff then wonders whether people can survive without a culture in the received sense, without a set of controls and remissions that bind individuals to the community. Others, like Bell, who do not push their speculations quite so far, also wonder whether the subtle shift toward postbourgeois consciousness and character structure will subvert the foundations of social order. Pressed by the specter of ecological and social limits, as well as by the prospect of limitless desires, we may gradually be adopting anticultural norms that subvert efforts at controlling and directing social forces in ordinary political ways.[25]

Here the crises of politics and culture intersect. Whether the advent of relative scarcity will exacerbate tensions or lead to the formation of something resembling such classical therapies as Christianity is a moot question. Spenglerian suspicions fill the air. Lewis Mumford believes that we have stumbled into a new dark age. Announcing the *End of the American Era,* Andrew Hacker concludes that "we cannot bring ourselves to make the personal sacrifices required to sustain domestic order or international authority."[26] Even if the gloomiest commentators who project a thorough revolution of cultural values leading to the destruction of social order as we have known it indulge in exaggerated prophecies, as I hope they do, they define a significant mood that adds an important dimension to any assessment of the sociopolitical crisis.

Slackening internal restraints contribute also to more subtle changes in individuals and in the general tone and quality of life. Loss of belief and sense of purpose; alienation and feelings of inauthenticity; confusion, emptiness, drift, isolation, boredom; moods of helplessness, exhaustion, and despair; seizures of anger and rage; periods of guilt, anxiety, and depression—these have become the common coin of lamentation for Americans of all social classes. They are feeble terms for indicating personal anguish and emptiness, by now all too familiar ones. But their very familiarity suggests the depth and intensity of our malaise, the more so when measured against rising expectations of all sorts. And they call attention also to the most disturbing dimension of the crisis of culture—the decline of faith, the loss of a spiritual center that releases the energy of hope and permits a genuinely balanced moral life. Freed from older restraints, even people gravitating toward Rieff's new modal type feel the pull of the past in the form of vague guilt at the experience of narcissism and hedonism unbounded by a new structure of controls and remissions. The idea that religious sentiments would disappear as scientific models of reality displaced mythic ones now seems a dated though persistent echo of Victorian positivism and Enlightenment optimism. So does the hope that they would be satisfied wholly through reorganization of the secular city. Technology and the triumphant scientific world view have failed "to replace the moribund traditional cosmology with equally rich symbols, leaving people with 'a sense of emptiness, of a counterfeit quality to existence.' "[27] More than a century of relentless critical exposure of illusions by Marx, Nietzsche, Darwin, Weber, and Freud has left both emperors and commoners unclothed.

Rather than disappearing, religious impulses have been choked off, numbed, and often redirected into secular forms—but without much success, as the experience of the new Left suggests. Anticommunism, the last self-conscious national pseudoreligion, probably delayed recognition of the vacuum at the center of postwar American culture. But this ideology of freedom did not hold up for long, hooked as it was to a defensive variant of capitalism, and the nationalist idea of an American global destiny which amounted in practice to protecting a host of tottering, often corrupt regimes. This is no way to build a lasting empire. The inverted search for collective national purpose and meaning in anti-communism survived the sixties largely as a remnant, used goods, though ambitious political figures continue to lobby for greater defense expenditures to counter Soviet "expansionism," a less demonic characterization than we were served during the early cold war years of the satanic communist monolith. Nor have earlier positive social visions of a vastly improved, if not perfected, liberal capitalist order, of a socialist society, or of a communist community fared as well as proponents had hoped. But it seems unlikely that greater success would have filled spiritual desires and needs—or that some future success will. As Jürgen Moltmann declares, "even in the 'classless society' Christians will be aliens and homeless."[28] The lingering cultural crisis that has characterized the post-Enlightenment era now seems certain to survive all political turmoil. It follows a longer, probably deeper, and certainly rather different rhythm than the sociopolitical crisis. But they are experienced simultaneously in the middle seventies, without the softening cushion of expected abundance, or the full mediating force of incandescent sociopolitical symbols and institutions characteristic of earlier periods of scarcity. This complicated experience of crisis, along with our location in the middle of things, lends special intensity to the present historical moment.

Grounds of Hope

I have concentrated thus far on the darkest assessments of our condition and prospects. The current atmosphere of crisis is sustained by collective fears that social problems may be so large as to preclude resolution; that the ideological, political, and material resources of advanced capitalism and its projected alternative of some species of socialism may be insufficient to satisfy needs and wants; or that the cultural dynamic of individual self-enhancement alters modal character types so as to weaken the will to use our ideological inheritance and political institutions constructively.

Among intellectuals, and increasingly among the population at large, there is a growing conviction that crisis has become a permanent condition of existence rather than a historically temporary discontinuity or dramatic turning point.[29] Considering events of the past century and the precarious social situation of intellectuals, it is hardly surprising that the mood of pessimism concerning resolutions has hardened into a cultural form. As critics of the established order, intellectuals have pursued their responsibilities of seeking the truth and marshaling the courage to tell their version of it to others, acting as a conscience of society, exposing faults, and offering images of hope.[30] But during this period of intense activity, intellectuals have witnessed the collapse of hope —more precisely, the collapse of their hopes for social and cultural change. (And the current erosion of their material position and perquisites may reinforce their gloom on larger matters.) Since visions of socialism, communism, or a humane capitalism have not found ample historical space in which to unfold, they present themselves cumulatively as a series of hopes deferred and hopes betrayed. A crisis of confidence festers at the very center of the intellectual's enterprise: how is it possible to speak to (not to mention for) others if one has no more than a problematic sense of self, a dim recognition of enormously complex social and cultural forces, and a suspicion of waning influence?[31] In what public ways does the discourse of intellectuals matter?

Perhaps the nature of social reality and characteristic modes of perceiving it have changed so dramatically that the traditional methods and purposes of humanist critics are becoming obsolete. J. P. Nettl argues that the dilemma is "complete." An intellectual may "accept integration as some kind of specialist into a society too complex to be explained, understood or predicted as a whole."[32] Or he can reject the terms of modern society, become a dissenter with no capacity to posit reasonable alternatives. The first option requires acceptance of a narrower role, the promise of influence in a smaller sphere; the second casts the intellectual as an outsider dealing in abstract conceptions of society that cannot permeate the consciousness of the community.

Perhaps the best answer to such sweeping charges of irrelevancy is H. L. Mencken's customary reply to long, critical letters: "Dear Madame: You may be right." But perceptions of obsolescence must be taken seriously, even when based naively on buried assumptions of hard science as the engine of progress, and the supreme importance of winning at the historical lottery. The role of intellectuals *has* become problematic if only because so many intellectuals perceive it to be so. We may grant further that as victims and beneficiaries of a mercurial culture, intellectuals often peer into the future amateurishly, through biased and clouded lenses. So, very often, do others: generals rehearse the last war; politicians borrow tactics from the previous election; adults tend a new generation with the parental strategies (purified, of course) they experienced as children. Intellectuals serve conservative as well as radical functions. And frequently, though not always, they espouse losing, even lost causes.

We may concede, then, the problematic character of traditional intellectual activity without abandoning it. This is precisely what intellectuals continue to do despite baleful prophecies of their imminent demise. It is what nearly everyone does. The fact of stubborn persistence, I believe, constitutes the initial thread of hope: the absolutizing of despair—its reification as a cultural form —is betrayed everywhere by the robust activity of daily life. In spite of reports of the disintegration of society; the obsolescence of capitalism and socialism; the irrelevance of intellectuals and of workers (so the prophets of endless abundance had it less than a decade ago); and the death of culture, the novel, the family, and organized religion—all persist through change. Survival and persistence: these comprise the basis of realistic hope, its public anchor. Indeed, in the absence of solutions to large public problems, the persistence of personal hope should ensure another eruption of the Left before the end of the century. This disparity between a sense of individual hope and pessimism about collective affairs surely indicates the continuing need for a vital political Left.

The evidence of our history offers some reassurance as well: most of the American experiment unfolded during the first stages of the long crisis of Western culture, though we were for a time largely insulated from its European center and European circumstances. And there have been moments of sociopolitical crisis more dramatic than our own: the nation was born in revolutionary turmoil and uncertainty; in 1860, internal divisions were resolved by a costly civil war; in 1912, the two-party system fell apart; in 1929, the economy failed more extensively than it had earlier (say, in the nineties); in the late 1960s, televised domestic tensions reached dramatic intensity, spilling into the streets. And now, after Vietnam, Americans must learn to live in a revolutionary world, a neat reversal of our original role.

Considering the frustrated hopes of intellectuals over the past decades, and the phony boosterism that collected along the surface of American life, it would be unwise to ignore the dark prophecies surrounding us. I do not propose to do so. These gloomy intimations of cultural and political deliquescence contribute heavily to the ambience in which inquiry into less dramatic alternatives must make its way. They give shadowy form to our fears. Yet it seems equally unwise—or at least unnecessary—to submit wholly to the spirit of cosmic despair. Whereas despair corrodes hope, bringing on paralysis, hope balanced by fears permits inquiry and activity to proceed.

Sustained by survival and persistence, hope also sustains itself. The nature of secular hope "is to imagine what has not yet come to pass but still is possible."[33] Through mutual activity—thinking, wishing, and imagining together—we continue to project ways out, or at least ways through private troubles and public dilemmas that might not occur to us on our own. In a period of excessive pessimism, balanced critical perspectives depend upon hope. Hope permits us to accept Emerson's mandate for the scholar: "Let him not quit his belief that a popgun is a popgun, though the ancient and honorable of the earth affirm it to be the crack of doom."[34] Hope reminds us that popguns still exist, even if by itself it does not provide sufficient criteria for distinguishing them from cracks of doom.

More specifically, then, I can hope that the most melancholy prophets are essentially wrong—as wrong as those who will reclaim an uncritical optimism as their own discovery when things appear brighter. It seems reasonable to hope that the collective American commitment to social order and domestic peace will enable us to imagine and enact a decent future. And further, that the sociopolitical crisis can be managed through adoption of democratic socialism, refinement of welfare capitalism, a resurgence of conservatism, or, more probably, through some amalgam of these principles and perspectives. Moreover, I believe that the crisis of culture can be understood more fully, perhaps enlarging the chances of discovering (and rediscovering) more attractive consolations, and making our separate peace with durable features of the human predicament that remain inaccessible to rapid or conscious political alteration.

In the chapters ahead, I shall attempt to stake out this narrow ground of hope, initially through an exploration of socialism, and then through a consideration of liberal capitalism as a current reality and future prospect. I shall subject both probes to the discipline of conservative caveats, those half-forgotten values and principles that begin to seem important once again. My main concern is with what remains vital in these perspectives—with elements that have been incorporated into American life, and are worth preserving, as well as with visionary elements that remain in the province of reasonable hope. Perhaps it would be more accurate to say that I deal here with used ideologies that have become self-conscious myths. But the function of myth, Warren Susman reminds us, is mainly utopian. It offers a vision of the future without showing us how to read—and move—the social forces that might get us there.[35] Very well. This is a useful if limited function, badly needed just now. But we must ask also whether these myths—singly or in some combination—can serve as useful political fictions, parts of a revitalized American public philosophy in the decades ahead.

2 / Communist Dreams—
Socialist Prescriptions

Far away in the distant future I saw a globe resplendent, cultivated and embellished, transformed into the grandest and most beautiful work of art by the combined effort of humanity. I saw upon it a race developed, perfected by the continued influence, generation after generation, of true social institutions; a humanity worthy of that Cosmic Soul of which I instinctively felt it to be a part.

—Albert and Redelia Brisbane,
Albert Brisbane: A Mental Biography

Socialism is a perennial dream; a spacious dream; a protean dream. An adumbrated though essentially complete version of its ultimate vision of individual salvation through community may be found in the New Testament; an earlier, less vibrant, secular form is sketched out in *The Republic.* Historically, the socialist idea has taken on a variety of shapes—elaborations that turn every new social form, every revolutionary convulsion, every long evolutionary change in society, culture, and personality into a pale shadow of what might be—or what once was. Still the most sweeping response to contemporary crises of culture and politics, it has remained vital through a succession of defeats—predictably so,

24

considering the character of the dream and the hopes of consolation and salvation that periodically inspire fresh variations. On a global scale, the socialist dream has weathered even political success of sorts: versions of socialist ideology—and institutions bearing its name—now guide the thought and activity of a majority of the world's people.

Little more than a century ago, Marx offered a major scientific formulation that promised ultimately to cancel the dream by fulfilling it. But the Marxian belief in the working class as the principal historical agency capable of overtaking the dream has ceased to be a complete option in America (and even in such Western European nations as Italy and France, whose large Communist parties have dropped the idea of a dictatorship of the working class and loosened their debilitating ties to the Soviet Union). Here, the socialist idea confronts more exacting tests than mere defeat or fragmentary political success, important as these are: it must make its way also in the absence of widespread belief in its guiding, energizing communist dream. We must ask whether the socialist idea can thrive—indeed, whether it even should survive—under these circumstances. And in what form: as a regulative, critical benchmark; as a moral vision; as an approach to politics, social organization, and public policy?

Any sensible response to such large questions presupposes a plausible contemporary description. But socialism remains a fluid concept with endless nuances of acquired—and discarded—meaning. It is, to borrow Leonard Silk's phrase, a "moving target" which must be defined (better: characterized) in tension with liberal and conservative variants of capitalism, another moving target whose meanings have changed appreciably over the past century. But we must start somewhere, and I propose in this chapter to approach the problem of definition initially by composing a list of socialist dreams. I shall suggest that if we are to arrive at an idea of socialism appropriate to the American present and future, certain large features, including most of the communist core, will need to be discarded for theoretical, historical, and practical reasons. By excising the core of the dream, we may reformulate a center of meaning, a modest democratic version of American socialism that can be refined, qualified, and enriched through comparisons with liberal and conservative claims in behalf of the economic and political virtues of one or another species of capitalism. To separate socialist prescriptions from communist dreams, we must begin in Europe, for like America itself, socialism is largely a European invention.

Socialist Dreams

Until the early nineteenth century, socialism was an "unbounded dream."[1] It lacked boundaries not merely because it was a dream, but because it was above all a dream *against* boundaries, a recurrent protest against separations, divisions, distinctions. Behind every manifestation lay the wish to restore lost unities, to go beyond painful divisions within the self and conflicts with others. Socialism embodies a wish to return to a condition of wholeness that existed, or was assumed to exist, only so long as it could not be apprehended consciously—that is, before the Fall, before the plunge into history. Though ultimately psychological and aesthetic in its concern with order, harmony, and unity, the socialist dream was made visible most powerfully in theological terms, primarily through Judeo-Christian imagery. Thus, utopian myths of socialism characteristically include a re-creation of Eden—a perfect environment—and the emergence of a new Adam, a regenerated man.

From pastoral reveries of lambs mingling freely with tame lions in the Old Testament to the communist vision recorded in *Acts,* biblical embodiments of the dream exhibit a pervasive concern with ending internal conflicts arising from a sense of separation from others, nature, society, and God. The second chapter of *Acts* describes the spiritual dimensions of a community beyond alienation: "And when the day of Pentecost was fully come, they were all with one accord in one place. . . . And they were all filled with the Holy Ghost, and began to speak with other tongues, as the Spirit gave them utterance." In this passage the single conviction which bound the early Christians together—their "one accord"— transcends the multiplicity of conflicting human purposes. Their alienation is overcome spiritually by the unifying force of the Holy Spirit, which worked through them while preserving their distinctiveness: each spoke a *different* language with a *common* meaning.

This metaphor brilliantly evokes the contradictory elements of freedom and fraternity which the communist form of the socialist dream harmonizes. And it also establishes equality of spiritual and material condition as the basis of a just social order. The political economy of these early Christians (admittedly fuzzy on the production side) follows rigorously from their religious and communitarian values: "And all that believed were together, and had all things common; And sold their possessions and goods, and parted them to all *men*, as every man had need. And they, continuing daily with one accord in the temple, and breaking bread from house to house, did eat their meat with gladness and singleness of heart."[2]

This community was small, not universal; temporary, not indefinite. It was welded together by an apocalyptic conviction of the imminent second coming of Christ, an event which would complete the process of restoration by eliminating the most intractable causes of alienation—fear of death as final separation and a preoccupation with linear time as its constant reminder. Though this represents the most comprehensive form of the socialist dream in the Western tradition, secular variants of the Christian paradigm include all the features of the vision, except the essential notion of salvation. Whether located in an Edenic past or in the nowhere of More's utopia, in the City of God or in a secular city of the future, dominant images convey the urge to get beyond the miseries of ordinary consciousness produced by divisions, conflicts, separations, premature endings.[3]

Surviving the delayed second coming and the collapse of the pentecostal community of first-century Christians, the socialist dream persisted as a minor chord, a static vision in tension with historical developments that seemed to enhance its ideal character and deny the chances of its full enactment. In the Middle Ages, the notion was kept alive by the example of small communities of ascetic Christians. But its separation from social realities was observed closely, and the idea served both as a nostalgic reminder of a collective past and as a promise of a communist future outside of history.

During the early modern period, from roughly the fifteenth

through the eighteenth centuries, the idea of socialism acquired more specific meanings, changes in emphasis brought on in large part by the emergence of an alternative idea of individualism. In literary versions such as More's *Utopia* and in actual utopian experiments, the notion of socialism underwent a gradual transformation.[4] Beginning as a vision of small communities, it became a national idea with More, and by the time of the Marxian synthesis it had assumed global proportions. From a concern with consumption under conditions of scarcity, it evolved into a rational vision based on abundance achieved through unlimited, and virtually painless, automated production. Socialism thus acquired a primary economic rationale in addition to its prior spiritual, moral, and social justifications.

Gradual secularization changed the proportions and emphases of the dream without altering most of its essential characteristics. If early Christian images of socialism constitute responses to the evils of the world—the self-conscious separation of individuals that corresponds to the emergence of history—later images reflect a concern with the ideology of individualism and its mixed historical consequences. The growing preoccupation with personal freedom arising from a basic claim to individual equality has inspired a series of fitful revolutions over the past seven centuries: the achievement of civil rights (equality before the law) and political rights (formal equality to participate in government), and the restless egalitarian push for augmented economic and social rights that marks the present era. Yet simultaneous development of productive forces creates a dense social world of capitalist relations that alternately widens and threatens to abridge those individual rights which it also makes possible.

Though some utopians of the past century have clung to earlier notions of small, ascetic communities as alternatives to the excesses of individualism and the oppressive features of a social world complicated by individualism, the dominant response of socialists has been to incorporate each new advance into an enlarged vision. Modern forms of socialism in the West attempt to reconcile the growing claims of individuals to the old dream of community through the connecting tissue of affluence, the nineteenth-century promise of plenty. With the rise of historical consciousness, the acceleration of technological development, and the perfection of capitalist methods of production, the socialist dream was relocated in the future. It would unfold in a secular city opulent enough to permit the all-round development of individuals within a community characterized by liberty, equality, and fraternity. The new visions, however, preserve and extend the original concern with healing separations and erasing sources of alienation and conflict—divisions between city and country, civilization and nature, civil society and the state, mental and manual labor, men and women, rich and poor, young and old, people of all nations and races. These visions entail a cessation of conflict based on scarcity, an end to misery based on alienated labor, and a remedy for injustices rooted in systematic maldistribution of growing wealth. They promise peace and order, plenty, personal freedom, democracy, equality, and fraternity.

In its comprehensive form, then, the socialist dream still entails a new Eden and a new man. The small circle of Christian ascetics living apart from the world and in defiance of its contrary trends is redrawn democratically to include everyone in a new community of abundance. From its biblical expressions to the Marxian synthesis and beyond, the socialist dream has been enlarged, made rational, and invested with a dynamic historical consciousness. But it has been diminished by exclusion of the Christian idea of redemption, the largest human hope of victory over loneliness and death.

Socialism: Utopian and Scientific

Until the Marxian synthesis, socialism remained a dream without useful boundaries. It lacked a theory, a location in history, and a significant political movement. Indeed, it lacked even its modern designation until the early 1800s.[5] Prior to this time, socialist ideas went by other names: they were utopian speculations, essentially Christian I believe, but after More's revival of classical notions, they increasingly took the form of rational designs for the good society. Modern varieties of anarchism, socialism, and communism, including Marx's, grew from these deep roots, and were nourished in the rich utopian soil of such prophets as Owen, Saint-Simon, Fourier, and Cabet. But the Marxian tree, with its Communist and social democratic branches, came to dominate the landscape. It still does.[6] Other systemic alternatives to capitalism —and capitalism itself—inevitably are measured against it.

Even after publication of the *Communist Manifesto* in 1848—which marked a preliminary draft of the Marxian synthesis—"socialist" and "communist" led confused lives. The terms appear more or less interchangeably in the Marxian scheme of things, but in the later works they assume distinct meanings, corresponding roughly to twentieth-century conceptions of socialism and communism.[7] Although a visionary—if not primarily, then *au fond*—Marx was preoccupied with the problem of action, of finding a way to introduce parts of the utopian design into history. Thus, the distinction between "scientific" and "utopian" assumes central importance in his thought: it emphasizes the need to situate visions of the good society historically. Marx insists that "scientific" versions of socialism or communism be anchored to a theory of history; that they be materially and technically possible; and that they be at least politically plausible outcomes of current trends and conscious movements for change. Every serious socialist after Marx has been aware of the need to distinguish "scientific"—or plausible—specifications of the dream from utopian formulations. Indeed, this imprecise distinction informs many critiques of what Marxists consider scientific in their own tradition.[8]

The chief contemporary importance of Marx, then, resides as much in the fact as in the character of his attempt to set boundaries on the collection of fragmentary socialist and communist dreams. Though Marx did not originate the dream, formulate the idea of history, or invent the concept of political economy, he brought them together in an original and important way. Discarding its expressly Christian character and its ahistorical rationalistic forms, Marx provides an initial approximation of socialism as a distinct historical vision removed from his own larger, and, I think, thoroughly utopian, version of the limitless communist dream. He imagines an order that preserves the character of the vision and establishes a historical sequence through which its elements might be enacted. For the first time, utopian dreams come into historical focus and take on apparently plausible forms: secular features are grouped together in the political foreground around the theme of exploitation, whereas quasi-religious elements of the communist dream of ending alienation are pushed into the background of the future.[9] Socialism emerges as a distinct if limited sequence of the dream, imaginatively subordinate to the image of communism but politically and morally nearer the existing system of capitalism and its liberal and conservative political ideologies. Indeed, the *Manifesto,* which paints the long range future in bold, sweeping strokes, emphasizes also the next steps—political aims such as steep progressive taxation and free public education that may be pursued prior to full achievement of socialism.

Partly in reaction to their contemporaries' disposition to draft elaborate social blueprints without considering the suitability, or even the availability, of historical space, Marx and Engels devoted very little energy to imagining the contours of future societies. They concentrated rather on understanding the origins, evolution, current status, and prospects of capitalism. In fact, as Werner Sombart remarked, capitalism "has . . . remained one of the key concepts of socialism down to the present time."[10] It fascinated and repelled Marx, for in his view capitalism simultaneously facilitated and prevented realization of socialist and communist values. It harnessed science and technology, revolutionized techniques of production, and extended itself into every part of the globe, establishing for the first time the outlines of a universal, world history. It produced the technical means to ameliorate the physical misery of the masses, and to permit them to become the democratic subjects of history rather than its passive objects.

Under capitalism, the historical drive toward greater personal freedom, democracy, and equality gathered momentum. But the system was organized around an unending contest among classes for shares of a growing surplus product. Divided into warring classes, governed by an oppressive state apparatus representing mainly the interests of a ruling minority, capitalism eroded civil society. And according to Marx, it produced fragmented individuals, pushing them toward the extremes of physical misery through systematic exploitation, and toward spiritual desperation through alienation in its several modes. Capitalism was a ritualized, social version of the Hobbesean war of each against all.

Though positing only two final outcomes—socialism or barbarism—Marx projected several paths through this wilderness. Capitalism engendered a growing class of miserable proletarians potentially capable of destroying oppressive, irrational elements of the system, preserving its achievements, and releasing its full productive promise in the construction of a new society and a new culture. Conflicts between the increasingly social character of production and the anarchic patterns of private ownership ensured cycles of boom and bust. Victimized by these cycles, and pressed into a common mode of existence by the spreading factory system, a self-conscious working class might stage a successful political revolution through some combination of democratic politics and spontaneous mass action. Even if capitalism survived its own sharp rhythms and the workers did not form a class-for-themselves, Marx reasoned in the *Grundrisse,* it theoretically would collapse when automated production thoroughly undermined the social rationale of distribution based on outmoded obligations to produce and superfluous entitlements to consume. One way or another, capitalism would meet the historical fate of all social systems.

In the Marxian scheme of things to come, the chief aim of socialism was to end exploitation through establishment of a new mode of production based on social ownership of basic industries and planned production for use rather than socially unplanned production for profit.[11] This is the classic minimum definition of socialism. Marx remained deliberately vague about its specific character, and he took more than one view of the mode, timing, and circumstances of the transition to postcapitalist societies. In his mature writings, however, the two stages of socialism and communism are projected serially. Briefly describing them in the *Critique of the Gotha Programme* (1875), Marx observes that the broad outline of the completed communist society cannot be projected as if it would develop "on its own foundations," but rather must be projected as it *"emerges* from capitalist society; which is thus in every respect, economically, morally and intellectually, still stamped with the birth-marks of the old society from whose womb it emerges."[12] Socialism not only intervenes between capitalism and communism; its specific contours depend upon the presocialist society from which it evolves, the moment of its birth, and the character of the human agents and the class agency of revolution.

Marx then sketches in the essential continuities and differences between bourgeois and socialist societies. As long as most people live under the domination of material scarcity, he argues, the fundamental bourgeois form of quid pro quo (the principle of equivalent exchange) must loosely govern individual behavior as well as social production and distribution. In fact, this is the most civilized principle, the signal moral achievement of presocialist society. Capitalism, however, applies the concept only on "the average." Dominant classes still control mechanisms for extracting huge portions of the surplus. But socialism extends the principle of equivalent exchange to the "individual case," because each man can contribute nothing except his labor and can receive in return only "individual means of consumption." The bourgeois principle of quid pro quo is thereby transformed from an essentially ideological notion that conceals an exploitative reality into the working principle of the transitional society: "from each according to his ability, to each according to his work."[13]

In contrast to exploitative, multiclass societies of the past, socialism was to have been essentially a single-class society, a democratic dictatorship of the proletariat. This seemingly contradictory notion of democratic dictatorship makes sense only in the context of Marx's leading assumptions concerning the nature and circumstances of the transition in advanced technological nations.[14] He believed that by the time political power changed hands, the proletariat would be a democratic majority. Until lingering bourgeois elements disappeared, of course, democratic methods of government could not be extended to the whole of society. But in the interim, the vast majority of citizens would establish a socialist democracy.

According to this paradigm, democratic socialism brings scarcity and the most egregious forms of economic exploitation to an end, and with them, grossly inequitable distributions of power, status, wealth, and income characteristic of capitalist society in its several historical forms. Democratic socialism promises full realization of bourgeois individual and democratic rights, excluding, of course, most rights to private property. And it permits democratization of culture in two essential directions: diffusion of the achievements of the bourgeois imagination throughout the population, and release of cultural energies previously inhibited by the class structure of capitalist society. But a democratic socialism does not establish community, and hence it cannot overcome fully every source of alienation. This is the promise of communism, a later and fundamentally higher stage of human civilization beyond capitalism and socialism. Socialism in an advanced industrial society may enlarge slightly the sum of liberty and equality. But since it promises mainly to enable democratic alteration of the ratios between liberty and equality in favor of somewhat greater equality, the essential moral structure of socialism bears a far closer resemblance to capitalism and its political ideologies and institutions than it does to the ultimate vision of communism. The seeds of communism that Marx envisioned in socialism require the soil of abundance.

Marx's sketch of socialism is "scientific" in the sense that it represents a possible alternative to capitalist society and culture rooted in analyses of the social forces of his time. Without providing a rich description of its content, Marx bounded the socialist dream and situated it historically, just beyond capitalism. But he regarded socialism as no more than a temporary stage, a transitional period during which the notion of communism—for centuries only a utopian reverie—would become historically possible.

In contrast to societies divided into antagonistic classes and alienated individuals working at cross-purposes, communism represents a *Gemeinschaft,* a "voluntary association in which the free development of each is the condition of the free development of all." Based on the real material, technological, and moral achievements of capitalism and the projected accomplishments of socialism, such a community theoretically fulfills the goals of ending alienation and of establishing genuine equality and full personal liberty.

Marx's vision of communism depends upon creation of material abundance *and* virtual abolition of work as an externally imposed activity, divided endlessly into more specialized functions, and rationalized by the overlapping criteria of efficiency and profitability. These assumptions enable him to imagine a resolution of tensions among the concepts of liberty, equality, and fraternity implicit in their meanings under capitalist and socialist conditions. And they permit him to project a community marked by a congruity of proclaimed values and social performance. (Communism does away with tensions between sincerity and authenticity.) Once the conditions of abundance with a minimum of compulsory work have been approximated in the transitional period of socialism, society can evolve into a vast communist community. Genuine equality becomes possible when abundance removes the social necessity for measuring either individual performance (ability, in the communist equation) or individual need against related external standards. Under communism, all people could realize their differing capacities equally, through creative activity (labor as opposed to work), while satisfying their unequal needs by drawing goods from a full storehouse. "Only then," Marx declares, "can the narrow horizon of bourgeois right be fully left behind and society inscribe on its banners: from each according to his ability, to each according to his needs."[15]

True liberty, then, presupposes the communist notion of equality. And alienation, which in Marx's view arises from scarcity and the division of labor into narrow specialties, disappears under communism. Purged of distortions created by the rise of the powerful modern state, civil society is restored, ending forever anxious separations between man's personal and collective existence.[16] Democracy—the preferred method for resolving differences among alienated people—also becomes obsolete, though its essence of liberty, social justice, and tranquility is preserved in a harmonious, well-ordered community. An entirely new outer world reflects and reinforces man's changing consciousness and moral vision. Indeed, communism makes every form of traditional morality obsolete, completing in a secular way the triumph of at least one Christian version of community over more legalistic Judaic and Roman codes.

The Communist Heresy

Marx, then, goes far beyond previous utopian thinkers by demonstrating the need to set boundaries on the socialist dream, to divide it into stages, and to locate it historically through an analysis of current social forces. But he departs from the Western tradition of utopian fictions only to return to it. In the midst of an age of exposure, of preoccupation with the decline of religious faith, he rekindled the communist dream of ending conflicts, divisions, and separations. Connected as it is to an analysis of capitalism and a projection of socialism, Marx's version of communism appealed to a range of sensibilities: it could be entertained by people who rejected formal Christianity, accepted the assumptions and methods of science, believed in History as the main agency of progress, expected the advent of abundance to eliminate much misery, and considered themselves schooled in the ways of power. Marx thus revived the ancient vision of communism by surrounding it with modern materials, imagining it not as an ascetic alternative to individualism but rather as the culmination of modern social development, a community spacious and flexible enough to accommodate the autonomous flowering of every individual.

It has been suggested that Marx's reluctance to sketch out socialism and communism in greater detail contributed to subsequent failures of the radical imagination: "the vision of socialism had a way of declining into a regressive infantile fantasy."[17] Perhaps. But Marx's own imaginative achievement depends upon his steady refusal to draw blueprints for the new society. He creates and sustains an illusion of credibility by surrounding the myth of communism with an edifice of analysis and polemic composed of thoroughly modern materials. Offering oblique glimpses of postcapitalist social orders rather than attempting to articulate a fantasy that lies beyond language, he sustains an illusion of credibility by concealing the vision.

The radical imagination, I think, falters in part because the idea of socialism now seems prosaic in comparison with impossible communist dreams and unremarkable in comparison with earlier American dreams. Equally important, however, is that the core of the dream—its communist essence—remains what it was from the beginning: an impossible and politically debilitating fantasy. In its secular forms, it is fundamentally an ahistorical myth of consolation for the way of the world after the fall. Utopians who advocate going beyond Marx's vision of utopia, then, miss the point: his version of communism is essentially complete. It may be elaborated endlessly, but not revised. We cannot improve upon the ideas of perfection, unity, wholeness, and harmony that inform the communist dream. We can only retreat from them.

Surely any contemporary American version of socialism must begin here, with an unequivocal rejection of the communist dream. It is, I believe, flawed in theory and oppressive in practice. Though it embodies such primary social values as freedom, equality, and fraternity as ends, the communist dream contains no provisions for limiting them or resolving conflicts among them. It merely includes a vague vision of a community *beyond* society in which serious conflicts can no longer arise. But the minimal historical preconditions for its enactment—abundance and the virtual elimination of compulsory work—obviously do not exist in America.[18] Nor do these essential preconditions seem apt to be realized in the foreseeable American future, much less in other parts of the world. And even if through some miracle they should materialize, the communist vision of ending alienation would remain flawed, in my opinion, because it does not allow sufficient room for tension, growth, and conflict in the new order. It is essentially a myth, not a social theory or even a useful political fiction. As critics from Dostoevsky on have observed, the image of a vast community beyond alienation should be recognized as a hollow caricature of the Christian vision of salvation, purged of its theological center. It should not be posited as a goal of political action or as a vision of social salvation, but rather assessed on its original grounds, as a doctrine of spiritual liberation, or as the basis of regulating the conduct of small, voluntary knots of believers. In my judgment, then, elements of communist vision—including the dominant principle, "from each according to his ability, to each according to his needs"—remain admirable as norms governing behavior in families and in voluntary communities, but not as the visionary basis of a Left politics.

Nor does communism serve well as a normative idea against which to measure current American realities. Since no actual or plausible social order can measure up to the dream, all systems appear utterly corrupt when compared to it. Hence, such facile comparisons often precipitate misleading critiques of present conditions: through the lens of total equality, all modes and degrees of inequality become blurred; through the lens of perfect liberty, all democratic institutions and norms appear feeble, corrupt, even repressive. When apprehended as a utopian goal—an end never to be achieved but rather gradually approached—the idea of communism may be of some critical value, but not much: it suggests no useful way of assessing the relative importance of intermediate steps toward its ultimately conflicting ends of total equality and complete freedom in a harmonious community. By raising expectations, the communist vision may move people to political action, even to reasonable political action; more frequently, at least in the American context, I suspect that it serves as a powerful inducement to political cynicism.

Historical evidence suggests sadly that those who proclaim communism as an ideology either fail to attain power, or perhaps worse, attain power only to fashion caricatures of the dream. Under conditions of scarcity or even of relative abundance, efforts to enact communist ends invariably require oppressive means: those unwilling to sacrifice personal desires to the collective ends of equality and fraternity must be compelled to do so. Though frequently it is denied officially or rationalized as "nonantagonistic," conflict persists in these societies. Democratic machinery, which communist ends allegedly make obsolete ultimately, is either too inefficient or too risky to be employed as means: hence the resort to totalitarian practices. The subordination of individuals to the collective purposes of establishing modern economies and ameliorating severe poverty, ignorance, and disease can be justified in a number of ways and in various settings—the question is live—but not, I think, on the basis of communist visions of the future. In any case, such justifications are beside the point in this technologically sophisticated society: barracks communism clearly cannot be considered a medium range American alternative.

In both their expressly religious and their quasi-religious forms, visions of a communism of abundance in America were doomed from the outset as models for the larger society.[19] The attempted incarnations of the communist vision in the eighteenth and nineteenth centuries were ephemeral. And the reasons for early failures seem clear: as a political vision, communism was the very antithesis of the developing trends and possibilities of industrial capitalism, their simple denial. It counterposed an image of an integrated community (or a federation of communities) to ideas of robust individualism and to the realities of an increasingly stratified, though mobile, society. Nor did those who held the vision most passionately make much headway: they simply withdrew, having concluded that some combination of the presence of evil and the absence of good made life in society intolerable.

Whether they considered spiritual, psychological, or material fulfillment as central, communitarians wanted, above all, a second chance to redeem the utopian hopes which animated the first European settlers. Whereas religious communitarians wished generally to remain separated from the world, some nineteenth-century utopian reformers—for example, followers of Owen, Fourier, and Cabet—wanted to be separate in order to construct models others might emulate. But Fourier's quixotic search for the perfect capitalist willing to finance a new social order ended in failure, as did attempts by Cabet's followers to establish utopia on the plains of Texas. None could challenge successfully the rise of industrial capitalism. From religious, therapeutic, and personal frames of reference, variants of the communist vision may have registered partial, local successes. As a persistent element in the popular imagination, fragments of the myth may have offered the consolation of momentary release from the burdens of daily life. But as the visionary basis of political solutions to social problems accumulated over the past two centuries, it must be considered a thorough failure.

The most recent eruption of the Left in America illustrates even more clearly the persistent appeal of the communist dream and its pernicious political consequences. Coming into political existence in the space between old Left sects tied to Stalinist and Trotskyist pasts and what Michael Harrington calls the "invisible social democracy" which the Kennedy Administration attempted to revive after the comparatively dormant Eisenhower years, new radicals of the early sixties found both points on the Left spectrum unpalatable. The sectarians were ideologically rigid and politically inconsequential. And the vision and politics of Camelot did not match the scope and urgency of national and international problems.

Politically minded new Leftists began as radical reformers—semianarchist in spirit—committed to peace, civil rights, student rights, and the extension of democracy through redistribution of wealth and decentralization of political and economic power. Without explicitly positing socialist aims, or placing socialism at the top of their political agenda, they adopted elements of a socialist program that included a simultaneous enlargement of liberty *and* equality through an aggressive politics of radical reform. By 1967, many new radicals, having encountered the perennial strategic dilemma of powerlessness, abandoned the eloquent if somewhat naive goals outlined five years earlier in the Port Huron Statement in favor of revolutionary perspectives imported from China, Cuba, and Vietnam rather than from the Soviet Union, which had inspired much old Left rhetoric. The results of substituting an apocalyptic vision for genuine politics and the rudiments of a useful social theory were predictably disastrous. Students for a Democratic Society and the Black Panthers (chief organizational centers of white and black radicalism) took on the sectarian, authoritarian cast of their old Left predecessors; splintered into even less effective organizations; lost whatever support they had among students, workers, professionals, and minority communities; and finally disintegrated following a period of nihilism in the late sixties and early seventies.

From the welter of events of those densely packed years we can rather easily abstract the dominant pattern of failure and indicate its relationship to the romantic communist dream. Beginning with elevated hopes, political activists quickly lost their innocence in a series of encounters with forces of the larger society. Predominantly young white students, these children of affluence sank rapidly from grandiose hope into a sort of nihilistic despair. Those who remained within the movement required a new myth of revolution to match their disenchantment, which came to encompass every institution, symbol, and lifestyle of the old order. Within less than a decade what began as political dissent ended in radical despair. Those who abandoned the search for a sociology of change to pursue a dialectic of liberation freed neither themselves nor their countrymen.[20] The substitute proletariats in this pop art revival of Marxism—the new working class, various minorities, students, the young, women, a coalition of bums, criminals and outcasts, the masses of the Third World—all failed to act as the new lever of revolutionary change in America.

A tiny minority took up terrorism as a last resort. An international phenomenon in the seventies, terrorism, sabotage, and political assassination add an unwelcome, though seemingly long term and largely uncontrollable dimension to postwar American life. The dynamics of left-wing terrorism and the responses (often, the initiatives) of government agents unfold within a growing netherworld populated by crackpots, dedicated zealots (many schooled in Vietnam), some FBI and CIA personnel, and a network of informers who cross easily from one side of the law to the other. In this blurred moral world, terrorists and dirty tricksters inhabit both camps, periodically confronting their spiritual doubles without ever recognizing them. Eroding sources of civil authority and reducing the scope of democracy and personal liberties, such activists can neither posit nor achieve reasonable political aims, though the net result of criminal activity in and out of government may be to raise somewhat the level of political morality.[21]

Of course, few people attracted to the politics of the new Left went over the revolutionary brink into terrorism. Most simply became disillusioned with radical politics or lost interest before disillusionment could set in. It is too early to imagine a gathering of fugitives, but some of the prominent pop revolutionary figures of the sixties have sought new, and probably representative, radical modes of ending aliention (their principal, if not always acknowledged, agenda from the outset): Abbie Hoffman went underground; Rennie Davis became a disciple of Maharaj Ji, the young perfect master (later pronounced less than perfect by his mother); and Jerry Rubin, once ostensibly committed to social revolution, now seeks to revolutionize his own consciousness through a smorgasbord of ancient and modern therapies from Fischer-Hoffman Psychic Training to Tai Chi.[22] Many movement people now engage in Left political activity at or near the fringes of the Democratic party: Tom Hayden, a principal architect of the Port Huron Statement, returned to California to run for the Senate as a Democrat after a stretch as a "warrior" of the people.[23] Still others devote their considerable skills and energies to community politics, single issue causes, or political activity connected with the service professions. But a majority, I suspect, has become generally disenchanted with politics.

One obvious reason for the decline of interest in politics was the difficulty of achieving visible results immediately. Since all social problems seemed needless considering American affluence and know-how, even such important accomplishments as unseating a President, contributing to the partial reversal of a disastrous foreign policy, and exposing some of the most enervating myths of American capitalism did not match larger ambitions. Progress toward the modest domestic aims of the Port Huron Statement was at best uneven and slow, at worst, virtually nonexistent. And the stakes of radical activity rose more rapidly than most activists really anticipated: the shootings at Kent State and Orangeburg in 1970 removed any residual doubts about the willingness of government officials to take violent action against young Americans. More important, the political goals of the new Left themselves came to seem modest, especially to the young who were seeking the communist promise of ending alienation. In retrospect, the widely publicized political dimensions of the new Left eventually may be regarded as secondary surface phenomena in comparison to the cultural revolt beginning with the Beats in the middle fifties and surviving the turbulent sixties. Indeed, the quest to overcome alienation from self and others, so evident in the nearly endless variety of political, social, and religious moods of the period, was a fundamental impulse of the new Left.[24] When encased in a rigid political ideology, this search sooner or later results in subversion of political aims: the socialist goal of more liberty and greater equality within a framework of democratic social order recedes before the ends of communism—a *Gemeinschaft* which harmonizes the needs and desires of each with the general will.

In this communist view, individuals can be freed from the sources of alienation only after the structures and values of societies characterized by relative scarcity, a strong state, bureaucratic hierarchies, social stratification, excessive division of labor, and inequalities of rewards have been swept away—that is, only after abolition of capitalism *and* socialism. Hence the stress on the revolutionary act, the decisive event prior to the millennium. (Though imagined often in the theatrical imagery of modern revolutions, from the French to the Chinese, the idea of such an event recalls also the imminent second coming, a dramatic reversal in which the last become first.) But the high price of this utopian heresy includes political failure, personal disillusionment, and, within the new sects, submission to authoritarian structures of power, frequently personified by a political guru. Renunciation of democracy as a mode of protecting the one (or the few) against the many may be taken in the name of a mythic community: more often than not, however, it ends in the destruction of the organization, or worse, in its survival as an authoritarian sect.

When not encased in a political ideology, the urge to achieve happiness by ending alienation assumes limitless forms. In the past two decades, we have witnessed a proliferation of moods and attitudes that make up the counterculture, or at least comprise elements of the wider cultural revolt in which the radical politics of the sixties finally was enveloped. The revival of pentecostal, or charismatic, Christianity and the popularity of Eastern mysticisms, the countless modes of instant therapy, the search for sexual liberation and liberation of the sexes, and the return to pastoral communes testify in various ways to a quest animated by the communist myth of a new person in a free, abundant, and supportive environment. All are symptomatic of the lingering crisis of culture.

There are, to be sure, important differences: some seek release from alienation through intentional communities; others explore the teachings of mystics to achieve inner peace. Reflecting a conservative turn in the seventies—a partial eclipse of the counterculture hedonism paralleling the decline of abundance as a central expectation in the larger culture—recent modes of therapy emphasize self-control and personal responsibility. Some of these probes represent serious attempts to come to terms with the crisis of personality and culture, whereas others amount merely to fads, some of them harmful ones.[25] But ginger groups do introduce (or revitalize) important ideas into the larger culture. Freed from their crackpot excesses, the renewed concern with spiritual life, meditation, and a heightened awareness of the importance of diet and fitness may bring major benefits to a significant portion of the population. Yet to one degree or another, most of the counterculture ideologies involve rejection of the various political forms of modern society, actual or imagined, as oppressive structures which deny full realization of personality. They often define self-realization as submission to a nonrepressive Other—the will of Christ, the will of a Perfect Master (preferably under eighteen), or the will of a small group. And most still emphasize feelings and sensations rather than reason and intellect as the most vital and prized media of communication, the grounds of unalienated existence. Some posit a form of communist community; others do not. In either paradigm, however, religious, therapeutic, and private impulses tend to eclipse public, political ones.

In the recent past, then, the socialist vision seems to have been short-circuited on the Left by a minority seeking more transcendent ends, as well as by others pursuing personal well-being in more routine, apolitical ways. An inverted image of existing states of affairs, communism now appears in the guise of a vision of the future when in fact it is primarily a nostalgic image of a badly recollected past. It is a dead, sometimes deadly political end, a bad political dream. The Marxian idea of communism has not been achieved because it is impossible under any conceivable circumstances. The democratic socialist vision has not been realized for more complex reasons. It remains a possible sketch of the future. Yet when measured against current realities, it remains an ambitious vision.

The Democratic Prescription

Though there are overwhelming reasons for consigning the communist vision to the realm of bad social dreams, the costs of surrendering it are high and the risks considerable. Insofar as communism represents a proposed solution to the problem of evil, it mobilizes powerful hierophonic energies in the service of social goals. The dissipation of such spiritual energy augurs at worst a kind of social torpor, and at best a restrained disposition to participate in public affairs. Moreover, abandonment of the communist dream virtually precludes the chance of imagining any sweeping vision adequate to the political *and* cultural crises in America. Marxism was the last grand synthesis in the West, the most comprehensive secular response to what remains the major problem of ideology: the need for a plausible and compelling vision of the future that connects visible trends toward (perhaps beyond) various modes of collectivism with the growing desire for individual autonomy and the felt need for community.

But it is not immediately clear whether socialism, once severed from its organic connections to the utopian dream, can—or should —become a guiding American political vision. Although I have characterized communism as an ideal type, conceptually and logically separate from socialism, elements of these two notions mingle in most nineteenth- and twentieth-century versions. The Marxian design wove everything together imaginatively: on the far side of history, it was hoped, all of the claims of all individuals would be satisfied in the matrix of a nonrepressive community. In the meantime, there would be progress toward the final goals through socialism, and progress toward socialism within the bowels of capitalism. In this view, aspects of the communist vision typically provided an escape hatch, a symbolic realm onto which current tensions, or conflicts that promised to arise under transitional modes of socialism, might be displaced and resolved imaginatively.

They still do. This mechanism of displacement is used, predictably, by utopians and antipolitical visionaries; it is used also by such sophisticated commentators as Michael Harrington, a principal American spokesman for democratic socialism. After advising socialists to work within the Democratic party in lieu of genuine institutional alternatives, Harrington offers a vision of the far future largely unconstrained by political or structural considerations. The battle against nature has been concluded successfully, on socialist terms: technological advances ensure a high level of continuous productivity without compulsory work; such abundance permits distribution of goods and services on a communist basis, without money. Under these conditions, Harrington suggests, "a psychic mutation takes place: invidious competition is no longer programmed into life by the necessity of a struggle for scarce resources; cooperation, fraternity and equality become natural."[26]

Harrington's version is neither messianic nor naive, but restrained and hedged about with self-conscious caveats. Communism will not eradicate every source of human misery, only those traceable to economic, political, and social causes: " 'Under Communism, man ceases to suffer as an animal and suffers as a human. He therefore moves from the plane of the pitiful to the plane of the tragic.' "[27] Nor can communism now be regarded as the inevitable outcome of History, only the best possible one whose improbability Harrington underscores by invoking Pascal rather than Hegel.[28]

Despite all this, Harrington feels compelled to serve up a vision of the far side of socialism, similar to what I have termed communism. Without some version of the communist dream, he seems to imply, socialism is either insufficiently distinguishable from current modes of capitalism and possible developments of the welfare state, or insufficiently arresting, to attract a sizable American following. Rather than considering the possibility of readmitting elements of the communist dream into a political conception of socialism, however, we should ask whether, and in what form, the idea can stand on its own, as a distinct vision, ideology, and theory relevant to the American present and future. To what is democratic socialism an answer, and for whom? More precisely, what aspirations require a democratic socialist organization of society as a condition of their fulfillment? Without the distracting communist vision, we may reconsider, here and in the chapters ahead, the extent to which socialism has been absorbed by American ideology, preempted by the achievements of American capitalism, and made problematic by events elsewhere. We may in this way see what remains of the idea and what needs to be added.

If socialism has a future in America, it will be, I think it safe to say, a democratic version similar in fundamentals to the Marxian scenario for economically advanced Western nations, but informed by more than a century of historical experience and thickened by a conservative awareness of such new problems as proliferating bureaucracies and ecological limits that neither Marx nor most of his epigone could foresee. The differences will be decisive. For one thing, as I have suggested, socialism can no longer be apprehended as a fleeting historical moment between the capitalist present and a communist future. It is rather a "final" set of possibilities beyond which we should not pretend to see. Any pro-jected faults, then, should not be finessed by appeal to some imagined resolution in a postsocialist era: democratic socialism is simply the end of this speculative line.

For another, most of the twentieth-century social experiments bearing the "socialist" name provide negative examples, instructive in their way, but not very helpful in imagining a positive alternative to advanced capitalism. Some elements, of course, may be transposed, adopted piecemeal, but it seems to me as unrealistic to project the cooperative ways of a kibbutz onto the diverse American continent as to advocate some form of authoritarian socialism—perhaps more so. America thus far has been the great exception, the only major nation in the world without a sustained, explicitly socialist movement. If we are to adopt a socialist alternative now—under whatever name—it will differ importantly from others emerging throughout most of the world, especially those in less developed nations.

But the negative, or inapplicable, cases deserve to be mentioned briefly, for they remain important to an understanding of how democratic socialism received its current emphasis on democracy as the indispensable element. Insofar as there has been a public debate over socialism in America, it has been influenced heavily by the turn of events elsewhere: revolutions in the less developed world and the convoluted course of European social democracy.

The circumstances of the two major revolutions of our time— the Soviet and the Chinese—did not match Marx's preconditions for transition. In neither place did a self-conscious working class majority voluntarily proclaim socialist ends and achieve power in a technologically ripe modern economy. To account for this disparity between preconditions and actual circumstances, defenders of the Soviet experiment deliberately took a step back from Marx's notion of a transitional democracy, offering in its place a minimum definition of socialism as public ownership of the decisive means of production and comprehensive planning for the benefit of all citizens. That the planning was to be undertaken by an elite party without sanctioned political opposition rather than by the people themselves seemed to many at first only a temporary measure. It was dictated by the exigencies of underdevelopment, the aftermath of an exhausting civil war, the lack of strong democratic traditions, and the absence of a working class majority (not to mention a socialist one). Once these circumstances had been overcome, and the Marxian preconditions satisfied, authoritarian socialism would become democratic, and in time the Soviet Union would achieve communism, redeeming the full vision after a long, unavoidable detour.[29]

In its several variants, this mixture of a minimum definition of socialism and an ideological commitment to a maximum conception of communism appealed to many Western intellectuals during the twenties and into the thirties.[30] Abstracted from Soviet particulars and distilled for domestic consumption, the minimum definition decisively affected the course of the American Left after World War I. Using the general Marxian idea of a sequenced transition, sectarians claimed that the first stage of socialism was being realized in history. Identifying their fate with the Soviet experiment, they could project an American version that would be democratic . . . at least after the revolutionary seizure of state power: according to such interpretations, it is important to notice, democracy serves as a floating element rather than as a fixed centerpiece, desirable but finally subordinate to political opportunities that may dictate its suspension. The Bolshevik victory, then, not only served to vindicate the basic idea of socialism: it also encouraged unremitting opposition to developments within capitalism (except on the many occasions when Soviet foreign policy required support), and preserved the illusion of a minority pattern of transition—a revolutionary conquest of power in America under the auspices of a small party. These basic images haunted the imagination of the far Left, contributing significantly to its sectarian cast and enforcing its isolation from the mainstream of American political and ideological life.

The minimum definition of socialism affected others on the Left as well, though less directly. With the emergence of Stalinism in the late twenties, the rise of fascism and the rapid growth of the American welfare state in the thirties, and the onset of the cold war in the late forties, moderate versions of socialism in the West came to seem politically inadequate and conceptually deficient. Socialism remained a forbidden word in the American political lexicon.[31] But the minimum definition was consistent at least with basic aims of European and American socialists in the tradition of social democracy, the noncommunist modern branch of the Marxian tree. Those who imagined an essentially peaceful transition through democratic means posited public ownership and planning as necessary if not sufficient conditions for realizing socialist aims in economically advanced nations. Democracy would be preserved, even deepened, under socialism. Yet when socialists have taken office, though not complete power, in England and on the Continent, it frequently has been hard to tell how their policies differ appreciably from those of others on the democratic Left.

Several alternatives emerged in the postwar years: many Western and most American intellectuals abandoned the idea of socialism altogether; some disillusioned intellectuals of the old Left and a sizable segment of the new attempted to reclaim the socialist idea by reemphasizing the communist vision; others remained in sectarian parties; still others tried to rescue the socialist vision from failures and distortions by stressing its democratic components. The success—or rather the survival—of the minimum conception in the Soviet Union forced those who followed this democratic option to reconsider the idea of socialism itself, to take seriously the critiques of anarchists, liberals, and conservatives—indeed, to take seriously critiques that maverick socialists had anticipated.[32]

In an important sense, then, the history of the socialist idea in America over the past five decades can be understood as a series of attempts to get beyond the minimum definition without relinquishing its distinctive essential elements or lapsing into communist fantasies. Though unique, the Soviet example helped to demonstrate that in democratic societies public ownership and planning without democratic controls may yield results worse than those of the emerging welfare state. Indeed, mere public ownership and planning proved to be at least compatible with ends that socialists had long opposed and opponents of socialism had deduced regularly from the idea: greater concentration of economic and political power exercised by a ruling elite rather than democratization of power and majority rule; emergence of a

large, unwieldy state bureaucracy which discouraged active participation in social life, and a secret police apparatus which discouraged autonomous participation in political life; a decline in
liberty not offset appreciably by advances in equality of opportunity and rewards; and finally, a withering away of fraternity resulting from a heavy-handed emphasis on competition for higher
education, jobs, and income.

At the height of the Stalin period (say, in 1936, when he proclaimed the advent of socialism in one country), the Soviet Union
exhibited the worst features of an undemocratic socialism. But the
experience helped to convince socialists elsewhere that any system
based solely on the minimum definition would display authoritarian and elitist tendencies. Public ownership and planning remained socialist goals, but they came to be regarded as potentially
far more ambiguous than had been supposed previously: "Without socialism," Howe declares, "democracy tends to wither, to be
limited in social scope, to apply its benefits unequally, and to
suffer from co-existence with unjust arrangements of social
power; but without democracy, socialism is impossible."[33]

The central socialist prescription, then, came to be more—and
more effective—democracy. It serves as the basis of responses to
liberal and conservative critiques of the socialist idea. It is proposed also as an immediate remedy for many of the ills of advanced capitalism (which displays collectivist tendencies of its
own). After outlining a lengthening list of American social problems, Harrington contends that "the answer is not to retreat from
democracy, but to deepen it, to give it social and economic content."[34] Finally, democracy constitutes the only acceptable mode
of transition: considering the tendencies of socialism without democracy, there can no longer be any question of a minority revolution in America. Even if it were to become politically possible,
such a dialectical course would be morally self-defeating.
Thoroughly so: the democratic socialist position undercuts traditional moral quandaries of revolutionaries who weigh immoral
means against desirable ends. To suspend democracy in the quest
for socialism amounts to moral suicide, at least in a developed
nation with a strong tradition of political freedom. Within the
contemporary framework of democratic socialism, such an option
has become unthinkable.

Recent developments in Western Europe also suggest the indispensability of democracy as a goal and as a means to socialist goals. In Italy, to take the ripest example, socialists—principally the Communist party (PCI)—hold the key to political stability and possess the power to challenge if not destroy capitalist economic hegemony. But even in such circumstances, serious Leftists stress the importance of democracy and the danger of imagining violent shortcuts to the assumption of state power. Though paths to socialism remain uncharted and perilous even in nations where socialist ideology and organization are strong, one thing has become clear: democracy is the principal means by which a vast majority of people must be persuaded gradually to support a socialist transformation of the political economy in relatively advanced nations. Nothing less than a decisive majority—not even a narrow electoral plurality—will do. When challenged abruptly, directly, and totally under politically ambiguous circumstances, the powers of capital can be expected to respond by disrupting the economy, and bringing on political reaction, as in the case of Chile. In technologically advanced societies, these powers will prevail in the absence of overwhelming socialist political opposition. The socialist course thus requires patience, not recklessness; structural reforms, not revolutionary histrionics; and democratic procedures, not authoritarian actions by minorities, even if they are sizable ones. The ideological and organizational strength of socialism in Western Europe and America differ obviously and decisively, as do their immediate problems and prospects. But differing degrees of influence and power should not alter the socialist commitment to representative democracy as morally desirable and politically indispensable to socialist survival.

Distilled in part from its Marxian origins and in part from the twentieth-century experiences of the Communist and social democratic movements, the idea of democratic socialism thus establishes a basic logic of its own, disciplined further by American circumstances. The ends of establishing order and security, expanding liberty and equality, and reversing the present stress on competition over cooperation still require socialist means: abolition of capitalist modes of production and distribution; development of flexible overall planning; and the strengthening and deepening of democracy. Moreover, socialist ends apparently presuppose growing abundance, the elaboration of technology, and a democratic majority favorably disposed to the idea. In the absence of any one of these means and preconditions, it has been customary to maintain, there can be no socialism appropriate to America. Using this sort of argumentative structure, Harrington presents socialism as a regulative idea, locating it once again in the future, as a possibility beyond present compromised conceptions, and beyond the framework of the welfare state.

Putting the question of the intrinsic merits of democratic socialism aside for the moment, we can pose the problem of its usefulness as a speculative theory connecting the American past and present to a politically viable future. Harrington's delineation of the ends, vehicles, and preconditions of socialism permits him to interpret what others have taken to be mere failures of the socialist enterprise as partial successes, openings onto the present and intimations, perhaps, of the future. Following the lead of Leon Samson and others, Harrington suggests that "America's receptivity to utopia, not its hostility," was a "major factor inhibiting the development of a socialist movement."[35] The proliferation of social panaceas in the nineteenth century, along with the dominant ideology of equality of opportunity and the myth of classlessness, enabled every man to imagine himself a potential capitalist (itself a socialist notion of sorts). But Harrington argues also that the elements of socialism—"the social democratic impulse in American life"—struck deep roots despite the misfortunes of socialist organizations. It is a mistake, in his view, to deduce the failure of ideologies from the collapse of organizations. Exceptional in many ways, American capitalism nevertheless gave rise to formidable class struggles over the division of wealth and income, over working conditions, social security, education, and other forms of welfare. But the social democratic impulse, which we may equate roughly with the intermediate aims of the old Socialist party and many immediate goals of significant left liberal forces within the Democratic party during and after the New Deal coalition, assumed different forms and went under different names in America than in Europe. Rather than leading to the formation of a mass socialist movement with a strong party, as in the case of Germany, this social democratic impulse worked its way through the trade union movement, following more or less the English pattern.

Harrington characterizes the American social democratic movement as "invisible" because it has wrapped itself in antisocialist symbols while pursuing many medium range socialist aims (short of reorganizing the economy under the democratic control of the working class). Organized labor gradually became political despite the contrary intentions of its founders, and beginning with the New Deal, the Democratic party served as the principal organizational medium of American social democracy. By the middle sixties, the AFL-CIO formally endorsed the idea of extensive democratic planning, a move which closely resembled the program of the socialists defeated by Gompers in 1894.

Thus, in the past century a potential popular base for what might yet become a democratic socialist movement has emerged slowly and fitfully from the long struggle to establish a welfare state within the expanding perimeters of corporate capitalism. Including parts of the traditional working class, a new majority coalition of the democratic Left would be composed also of elements of the service sector, the conscience constituency of professionals, women, minorities, the young, the old, parts of the underclass, consumers—all those who should be concerned with preserving popular gains and extending them.[36] Harrington admits that this coalition is only a potentially effective majority at the moment, that it remains inherently unstable and prone to internal conflict, subject to powerful opposition, and far from explicitly socialist in orientation. But it does represent a genuine American political option, one situated in the political history of recent decades; in fact, it apparently represents the only sane political direction open to socialists in America. Though moving beyond the sterile antinomies of revolutionary versus evolutionary change, Harrington does not pretend to solve the problem of transition. He rather suggests more modestly that it is neither hopeless nor self-defeating as so many on the American Left have been compelled to conclude.

Dilemmas of Democratic Socialism

I have brought the logic of American democratic socialism into partial relief by placing limits on the idea which exclude maximum utopian versions and minimum conceptions. When we eliminate the utopian overtones—both full and partial variants of the communist dream—it becomes evident that democratic socialism must be imagined as a "final" social vision: it cannot be justified in terms of a future beyond itself, though its achievement obviously would not mean an end to history. To be worth the political trouble it would take to bring this long shot off, rather than to trust the slow process of structural evolution, democratic socialism needs to be ideologically distinct from the current system and superior to it. Not only must the socialist ends of preserving order, guaranteeing security, expanding liberty, advancing equality, and ameliorating the competitive ethos seem desirable: the vehicles of social ownership and planning under democratic control must be more conducive to these ends than other social arrangements. Or at least they must appear so. Otherwise, it is difficult to see how the crucial preconditions of a decisive democratic majority favoring socialism ever can be met.

Freed from its communist moorings, however, the idea of democratic socialism is apt to drift, for it is a partial vision, resembling contemporary strains of liberalism in many respects. Whereas communism posits complete liberty, total equality, and full fraternity in a community beyond scarcity, democratic socialism acknowledges their limited character and tendency to conflict in any finite social world. Thus, it is not clear on ideological grounds alone whether socialists who advocate a society of maximum feasible equality with a minimum of social control over groups and individuals differ importantly from others claiming the same ends. In an appraisal of the socialist idea, Leszek Kolakowski suggests hopefully that "what we lack in our thinking about society in socialist terms is not general values which we want to see materialized, but rather knowledge about how these values can be prevented from clashing with each other when put into practice and more knowledge of the forces preventing us from achieving our ideals."[37] In contrast to communism, socialism is a matter of more or less, of some, not all. Its superiority to current modes of capitalism becomes a complex and in many ways moot issue, a cluster of empirical questions which can be tested only gradually, through political trial and error.

These difficulties emerge even more pointedly when socialism is approached from the opposite direction. I have already noted the insufficiency of the minimum definition of nationalized ownership of major economic functions and comprehensive social planning. By making democracy the centerpiece of a revised definition, it may be possible to minimize the authoritarian potential inherent in public ownership, while preserving the other essential elements of the socialist idea. Yet this resolution of the authoritarian dilemma, implying as it does commitment to the notion that any genuine socialism must grow democratically out of the American past and present, entails also a deep, perhaps fatal socialist ambivalence toward the nature and value of the welfare state.

Democratic socialists have advocated progressive expansion of the American welfare state principally for two reasons. As Robert Heilbroner notes, "the 'welfare' state, however inadequate in actuality . . . brings with it a considerable degree of 'socialism' in the form of guaranteed incomes, family allowances, public health assurance, educational subsidization of lower income groups, and the like."[38] Moreover, expansion of the welfare state sustains the central hope for a democratic politics of change that ultimately will become socialist. The welfare state sets in motion a continuous tension between rising expectations and the benefits it can confer.

Contributing to progress of sorts under capitalism, this tension also makes visible the inherent limitations of the present organization of society. "There are," Harrington maintains, "three basic reasons why the reform of the welfare state will not solve our most urgent problems: the class structure of capitalist society vitiates, or subverts, almost every such effort toward social justice; private corporate power cannot tolerate the comprehensive and democratic planning we desperately need; and even if these first two obstacles to providing every citizen with a decent house, income and job were overcome, the system still has an inherent tendency to make affluence self-destructive."[39]

If a majority of Americans ever comes round to the socialist idea, then, it presumably will do so as a result of successive political encounters with the welfare state, through a dynamic pattern of gains and losses. It is a delicate balance, for a revolution of disappointed expectations set off by a failure of the welfare state to sustain a productive tension between expectations and benefits probably would lead to a contraction of democracy and to the utter collapse of socialist hopes. Democratic socialists, then, have supported the welfare state provisionally, arguing all along that liberal visions can be redeemed only through their partial fulfillment, when a sufficient number of people come to understand the inadequacy of the economic and political assumptions which underpin them. Thus, the fragile fate of democratic socialism has been bound up intimately with a certain liberal vision, with images of the welfare state, and, by implication, with the system of corporate capitalism that presently sustains them both.

We may conclude provisionally that democratic socialism does not seem self-evidently to provide an ideological resolution to the two American crises. Without the communist core, democratic socialism offers no visionary response to the lingering crisis of culture. All right: we should not ask more of social visions than they can deliver. By virtue of its ambiguous relation to the liberal vision and to American realities, democratic socialism seems also increasingly problematic as a guide through the political crisis. This is so for three reasons, each revolving about the central idea of democracy.

1. DEMOCRATIC SOCIALISM MAY NOT BE DEMOCRATIC ENOUGH: Basing their hopes partly on the enlargement of material plenty, democratic socialists find it difficult to imagine realistic alternatives to powerful governmental agencies and the proliferation of large, hierarchically organized bureaucracies. Though these institutions tend in obvious ways to reduce the scope of liberty and discourage maximum participation of citizens in public affairs, they seem necessary, at least for the foreseeable future, to sustain a measure of economic well-being and to enable a more equitable distribution of opportunity and rewards. But libertarian socialists, as Gar Alperovitz notes, contend that the transition from welfare capitalism to socialism requires a primary stress on decentralization of economic and political power as a way of expanding liberty and encouraging initiative, even if this means reducing inequalities at a slower rate.[40]

Democratic socialists also favor as much decentralization as possible, sharing as they do the ambivalence of liberals toward big government. When "we make power and therewith politics a part of our system," John Kenneth Galbraith observes, "we can no longer escape or disguise the contradictory character of the modern state. The state is the prime object of economic power. It is captured. Yet . . . remedial action lies with the state. The fox is powerful in the management of the coop. To this management the chickens must look for redress."[41] By virtue of their commitment to extending the material base of the welfare state through a democratic politics of reform, however, democratic socialists acknowledge this ambivalence, accepting life within its difficult terms, rather than placing decentralization at the center of their vision. It may be, then, that democratic socialists have not revised traditional conceptions of the forms of representative democracy and government—of power and the state—sufficiently to allow enough space for individual growth, expression, and participation in public affairs. This suspicion is apt to become the basis of a permanent critique of democratic socialism from the Left. It will be important as a moral perspective, and useful potentially as a ballast to the structural drift of democratic socialism toward excessive concentrations of power, but tiresome when pressed zealously.[42]

2. THERE MAY NOT BE ENOUGH DEMOCRACY: Should present economic trends persist, the delicate balance between expectations and productivity may be disturbed in new ways. Prior to the seventies, when social theorists of all persuasions predicted an endless horn of plenty, many radicals feared that the productivity of corporate capitalism and the new possibilities for more equitable distribution through the institutions of the welfare state would bury the socialist idea, possibly in a sea of junk. Moreover, completion of the welfare state, it was supposed, might corrode the socialist idea of participation. Now, it appears that this sort of burgeoning productivity is unlikely, and perhaps not even desirable. But if slower growth and persistent inflation come to characterize the economy for long periods, we may expect intensified struggles over shares of wealth, income, and opportunity. Postwar liberal visions, of course, are predicated largely on the notion of secular grace, of new increments of production as the means of satisfying new

claims by individuals and groups. Without large quantities of this social lubricant, there may be no set of generally acceptable democratic criteria by which to settle conflicts over relatively more scarce goods, services, and space. Should the mechanisms of rising expectations and expanding material plenty, on which socialists also have come to depend, malfunction seriously, we may expect a decline of hopes for Left coalitions of working class, poor, and upper middle income professionals, as well as a deliquescence of consensus democracy. The further erosion of democracy may be demanded by a majority concerned more with order and economic stability than with any enlargement of liberty or reduction of inequality.

3. DEMOCRACY MAY NOT BE ENOUGH: As I have suggested, democratic socialists maintain that preservation of political democracy is essential to its extension and deepening, to the achievement of greater economic and social democracy. And further, that its immediate precondition is a continuous flow of ever greater productivity. But we must wonder also whether democratic socialism—considered as a vision and as a political ideology—includes a moral center with principles that might help to clarify, qualify, and limit the traditional liberal and Left justifications of the claims of all but the very wealthy to more of everything. In what way, that is, does democratic socialism contribute to a public philosophy that may help to control and humanize the forces of change, rather than merely irritating them? In his appraisal of the present American crisis, Thomas C. Cochran asks whether democracy or egalitarianism, even if accepted fully, "is . . . the kind of value or belief that can by itself cure antisocial behavior and loss of social morale?"[43]

Thus, the present cultural and sociopolitical crises in America serve to sharpen the old question of whether democratic socialism would be a desirable public philosophy if it were accepted by a decisive majority. And it raises a new issue of more immediate importance: is the general democratic socialist approach to transition through a thickening of a liberal politics of democratic reform in need of fundamental revision, not on the basis of arguments offered by far Leftists that it is too slow or that it betrays socialist and communist ends by suppressing "revolutionary" options, but on the more urgent, or at least prior, grounds that democratic socialists in America only reinforce a liberal vision grown stale, self-destructive, and politically fragile in a new time of relative scarcity? A full assessment of the value of democratic socialism and its place in the American ideological spectrum thus requires an examination of liberal and conservative views of capitalism, the other moving target.

3 / The Liberal Connection

> What the democratic parties of the developed nations have
> done, in short, has been to use the state to force capitalism
> to do what both the classical capitalists and the classical
> Marxists declared was impossible: to control the business
> cycle and to reapportion income in favor of those whom
> Jackson called "the humble members of society."
>
> —Arthur M. Schlesinger,
> *The Vital Center*

Although it has enjoyed moments of prosperity, socialism remains
an unpopular idea in America. Before the turn of the century,
Edward Bellamy observed that it "smells to the average American
of petroleum, suggests the red flag and all manner of sexual novel-
ties, and an abusive tone about God and religion."[1] By now, the
burden of such cultural overtones has become slight in comparison
to the more fundamental objection that socialism augments state
power, and thwarts rather than facilitates the values associated
with self-enhancement. While tracing flagrant abuses of individualism to capitalist roots, and arguing the case for cooperation as a
primary social virtue, proponents from Wilde to Sartre and Harrington have insisted also that full expression of individuality
requires a socialist transformation of society. Whatever the merits
of these varied arguments, they have not persuaded most Ameri-

cans. The largest ideological spaces continue to be held by liberal and conservative defenders of capitalism. Conservatives who oppose the welfare state, or at least fear its extension; liberals who wish to maintain, augment, or go beyond it; even social commentators who believe that new realities have drained received ideological concepts of meaning all agree upon this final line of defense: despite its many faults, capitalism (or the mixed American system) still offers individuals the best chance to fashion a full life.

This minimal rationale suggests that capitalism, too, has lost much of its authority during the past decade. Whereas opponents utter the word with cold assurance—and scorn—defenders frequently identify the system hesitantly, as if reluctant to speak the name of a social god, not out of misplaced reverence but out of fear of its inadequacy. This diffidence stems partly from the untidy history of "capitalism" and its symbiotic connections with American liberalism and the welfare state. But it issues also—perhaps primarily—from the deep fear that the economic engine of capitalism may no longer be powerful enough to advance the interests of liberal politics and the welfare state. Or even worse, that the welfare state may have reached a stage where it fatally compromises liberal ends.

The chance that the welfare state is approaching economic and political limits in America revives important philosophical and political questions about modern liberalism. And it threatens to invalidate reigning assumptions concerning the delicate balance between the idea of democratic socialism and the prospects of liberal capitalism. Historically, the fortunes of American socialism have been tied in sundry ways to the progress of liberalism. The socialist movement of the early twentieth century rode the tide of progressivism; the Left of the thirties developed in the larger currents of the New Deal; and the new Left was an aspect, however distinct, of the resurgence of reform liberalism in the Kennedy-Johnson years. This reciprocal relationship is, of course, both complicated and ambiguous: some socialists claim to have drawn liberal movements leftward, whereas others contend that liberal advances (and tepid socialist responses) have absorbed and blunted more radical initiatives.[2]

In any case, advocates of a gradual, democratic transition argue that socialist prospects still depend upon the ideological and political vitality of liberalism. And they hope that a steady tension between rising expectations and rewards, facilitated by the welfare state, will heighten the demand for democratic socialism. As Erazim Kohák puts it, "the welfare state represents easily the most appealing program socialists have ever offered. Its success in alleviating both the specific costs and existential anxiety of industrialization, together with its proven compatibility with liberal democracy, make it an ideal basis for a coalition capable of appealing both to industrial workers and to the middle sector of the self-employed, small entrepreneurs and service employees with hopes of independence. A broadly conceived program of social security, covering employment security and medical services as well as old-age pensions, housing, transportation, and municipal services —though perhaps not under the name of 'welfare,' in deference to American sensibilities—is clearly the most effective program democratic socialists can present in the United States."[3]

Considering the beleaguered state of liberal thought, the fractured condition of liberal politics, and the uncertainties of the economy, however, prevailing assumptions about liberal-socialist connections invite reconsideration. In his reflections on the welfare state, Irving Howe wonders why it should "be so difficult to preserve a balance between the struggle to force the present society to enact the reforms it claims to favor and the struggle to move beyond the limits of the given society. . . . Tactically, to be sure, this creates difficulties; but conceptually, as a guiding principle, I think it our only way."[4] Perhaps so, but it seems an increasingly tangled path. For the difficulty which Howe traced to a lack of conceptual suppleness nearly a decade ago takes on new complications as malfunctions in the capitalist engine and diminished expectations of future growth under any system coincide with the waning of a period of liberal political experimentation and a resurgence of conservative sentiment. If the democratic socialist idea in America depends upon a measure of liberal success, then we had better understand the changing character and contexts of liberalism, and if necessary, seek other ways.

Liberal Capitalist Dreams

I should like to summarize the claims usually advanced in behalf of classical capitalism and liberalism, for despite serious challenges and major revisions, these concepts remain leading elements of American political and social mythology. Both terms raise definitional problems that I shall only indicate here. "Capitalism," for example, is an economic theory (indeed, several) and an ideology, a mixture of descriptive and prescriptive elements used to identify the business system and to designate important parts of what may be termed vaguely the bourgeois ethos.[5] Its range is immense. Capitalism has operated with success in different historical periods and geographical settings. It has managed to thrive in such diverse political arrangements and cultural contexts as Germany under Hitler and Willy Brandt, and the United States under Lincoln and Gerald Ford. At times—in the early part of this century and after World War II—capitalism appeared to many destined to become the dominant model for world civilization, most nearly approximated in America and the West, and less perfectly realized throughout developing areas. Yet in a mere quarter-century, attention has turned once again from grandiose hopes to more immediate problems of survival. Even in America, capitalism has come to seem a problematic foundation of a just social order, rather than the commonly unquestioned framework of social reality.

Capitalism, then, is not only a historically moving target; it wears several faces, ugly and benign. Reduced to essentials, it is a way of doing business whose main features are private ownership of capital, a system of contract or wage labor, and production for profit coordinated by a relatively free market. Because of its historical associations with liberal and conservative political philosophy, this minimal definition stirs European and native elements of the American imagination: it may evoke nostalgic images of the Enlightenment past, of a rational, orderly world projected in *The Wealth of Nations,* a late Haydn symphony, or a Mozart sonata.[6] Or it may awaken ideas of rugged individualism, the homesteading spirit, everyman chasing his own pot of gold at the

end of the American rainbow. In the popular imagination, however, capitalism remains above all a system of free enterprise
which sustains a wide range of individual liberties.

That these images now lack much descriptive value does not
deprive them of imaginative force. Within the domain of American values, classical free enterprise capitalism furnished the tidiest
answers to the central problem of ideology—the orchestration of
public and private spheres. Synchronizing the activity of people,
the invisible hand of the market directed private ends toward the
common weal. Those unable to satisfy consumer wants at competitive prices were displaced by more able entrants. The discipline
of the market thus distributed opportunity equally insofar as everyone had the chance to become a capitalist. By coordinating
countless voluntary decisions, the market mechanism also guaranteed a large measure of consumer democracy, obviating the need
for much coercive regulation. Thus, capitalism maximized efficiency, material prosperity, and the general welfare—in a word,
progress. And it contributed to a benign social order.[7]

The essential outlines of competitive capitalism imply the sa-
lient features of the equally difficult term "liberalism." Similar in
many respects to contemporary strains of libertarian conservatism,
nineteenth-century liberalism surrounded the idea of capitalism
with a theory of government and political life, investing the social
whole with an elegant philosophical rationale. With antecedents
in Hobbes, Locke, and Mill, classical liberalism began with a rational defense of personal and property rights against the arbitrary
claims of illegitimate power—whether of the crown or of a repressive central government. Ensuring a measure of political cohesion,
especially in the upper registers of society, the institution of private property lent substance to the central liberal values of equality of opportunity, material prosperity, and liberty in all spheres
of life. It established a sound basis for responsible citizenship and
the exercise of republican virtue. And it facilitated the quest for
personal happiness and rational cultivation of what John Stuart
Mill called "the inner life," without pretending to guarantee their
achievement.

Assuming that the health of private property depends upon a
policy of laissez faire in the economic sphere, classical liberals

arrived easily at their most general principles of government.[8] With a curious blend of optimism and pessimism concerning the character of human nature, they argued for a minimum state charged primarily with defense against foreign assaults and protection of civil rights and liberties—tasks that private citizens could not manage themselves. Its range of domestic concerns was narrow. Insofar as government was necessary, liberals favored representative forms of democracy as the surest means of discovering sound social policy and of resolving disputes. They encouraged wide participation and many centers of popular initiative as well as an intricate system of checks and balances against the use of excessive power by minorities or majorities.

I am dealing here with complementary strands of a single myth of liberal capitalism: it is an unretouched image, a simplified interpretation of old ideas and faded realities. Contemporary capitalism and the several strands of liberalism cannot be deduced wholly from these thin propositions, yet this bare summary suggests the intense power of the myth and its strong hold on our political imagination. Intellectuals and artists often draw attention to the comic, pathetic, grubby, and excessively rationalistic sides of the bourgeois spirit. But liberal capitalism is also an extravagantly hopeful, elegantly simple vision, anchored in what still strikes most Americans as a realistic estimate of the competitive, self-interested character of human nature and a fair conception of social rewards. The ideal of service that emerged as a ballast to the competitive features of American capitalism may be less fulsome than the communist idea of community, but it remains consistent with the elemental bourgeois dream of a secure, fulfilled private life supported by a well-ordered political economy. Americans donate more than $25 billion annually to philanthropic causes; and nearly fifty million people give some portion of their leisure time to such ventures, far more than the citizens of any other nation.[9]

Although the liberal capitalist dream appears to be in decline, it continues to illuminate areas of the American landscape. Partly because of its obsolescence, the idea retains power as a dominant cultural and political ideal. It serves also as the basis of perspectives on current confusions, having become a key element in modernist modes of political perception characterized by irony, ambiguity, paradox, absurdity—and uncertainty. We return to it even as we deny its relevance. Like socialist dreams elsewhere, the liberal capitalist vision has been complicated and compromised by history. Of course, we must pay attention to significant variations in elements and emphases of the vision over the past century, notably a deepening of the idea of equality and a widening of the concept of individual fulfillment beyond the confines of business ideology. But the economic forces, institutions, and class structures of society have changed even more dramatically. The historical evolution of the American system—notably the ascendancy of huge corporations, the rise of organized labor, the creation of new technologies, the emergence of a large service sector, and the augmented political role of the state—has shattered the socioeconomic, political, and cultural frameworks which originally animated the powerful values of liberal capitalism. Sanctioning individual initiative, the ideology of laissez faire justified a system that sabotaged itself in the brief space of six to seven decades: between 1850 and the end of World War I, competitive capitalism evolved into corporate capitalism, a profoundly different species.[10]

The present confusions, tensions, and uncertainties of American liberalism issue primarily from this central irony. In a simplified but important sense, the crisis of liberalism, which amounted to a public concern by the middle sixties, comes at the end of a series of programmatic adaptations of the old bourgeois dream to new realities that challenge and subvert some of its principal tenets. From the origins of the contemporary welfare state in the thirties, liberals have retained their strong commitment to civil rights and liberties. They have advocated pluralism as the political mode most apt to ensure a dynamic balance of power among contending groups in society. Yet by and large they have come to assume a benign attitude toward the expanding role of government as orchestrator of economic growth and stability, facilitator of more equal opportunity, and promoter of a spate of welfare measures.

Though nearly everyone now accepts some version of the welfare state as a fact of mature capitalism, many liberals have pursued it eagerly—perhaps too eagerly—as a matter of utilitarian principle, or at least as the chief modern means of enacting old values.[11] Progressive legislation from the New Deal through the

Great Society is largely a result of successful political coalitions forged to realize as much of the liberal dream as possible within the perimeters of corporate capitalism and through the vehicle of the burgeoning welfare state. To the extent that voluntary public action molds the contours of society, then, modern liberals can claim major responsibility for the current size, shape, and direction of the welfare state. It is the institutional monument of our "invisible social democracy," the American substitute for socialism.

Until the late 1960s, economic growth and the promise of rising prosperity energized the liberal vision, stabilizing its inherent tensions and evoking a large measure of public confidence in its piecemeal approach to social change. The widening economic base of the welfare state provided some continuity of vision, linking past values to future options: disparities between elements inherited from the old liberal capitalist dream and present American realities comprised the political agenda, an opening onto a future of salutary change without major social conflict. There was substantial faith among such liberal thinkers as John Kenneth Galbraith, David Riesman, and Robert Theobald that these values might be enacted in their deepened form under new, unforeseen, even inhospitable social circumstances. Few denied that the enlarged scale and complexity of social life created unprecedented problems. Few denied the potential dangers of a ubiquitous state. But liberals claimed also that leading social problems could be solved democratically with time, patience, technical skill, goodwill, *and* a broadening base of affluence. Rising prosperity was welfare capitalism's secular equivalent of grace.

There were melancholy strains of philosophical conservatism in postwar liberalism, too—a brooding fear of nuclear disaster, a sense of ideological isolation from the larger world, and a suspicion among certain intellectuals that issues of moral and spiritual purpose soon would overshadow the social question. David Riesman's "Abundance for What?" typified fears concerning the potentially enervating effects of unlimited prosperity.[12] But these somber variations did not overwhelm the prevalent tone of tempered optimism concerning the American future. Since unending abundance can no longer be projected with such nonchalance, however, the odds on the liberal project of completing the welfare state have lengthened considerably, bringing the varied philosophical and political strains of pessimism together. The old liberal capitalist dream now seems a nostalgic—and mythic—reminder of a better past, a high point of reference which casts current options into bleak relief. In recent years, the vision has become for many more a source of irritation, even of anger, than a source of hope. But it continues to haunt us.

Liberalism and the Welfare State

To bring current liberal dilemmas into sharper focus, let us review the main dimensions of the welfare state, taking note of its historical development, its present American contours, and its immediate prospects. It is a difficult notion. Since any action performed or coordinated by the state for the benefit of individuals or groups in society can count as an act of welfare, the idea of the welfare state may be traced back nearly as far as a historian wishes to go, though the term itself is of quite recent vintage. The problem of definition thus becomes largely a matter of judgment and convention, even of ideological and political preference. At minimum, however, a welfare state entails considerable governmental involvement in collecting revenues, redistributing income, and administering an expanding range of services that may (or may not) lie beyond the powers of individuals or voluntary associations. Once these tendencies establish themselves as prominent features of the sociopolitical scene, it becomes useful to speak of a welfare state.[13]

In America, the welfare state has emerged within the changing economic perimeters of capitalism, the political traditions of representative democracy, a variety of ethnic cultures, and a cultural spirit of individualism. These stamp its ambiguous character and bring us closer to a usable description. The expansion of capital that accompanied the transition from laissez faire to corporate capitalism established the material groundwork for a sizable welfare state. This process also compounded the need for such a state because the calculus of economic growth within business firms largely discounted the rising social costs of crime, poverty, unemployment, inequitably apportioned income and wealth, urban sprawl, pollution, wasted resources, and discrimination in all its forms. Far from developing as a mere reflex of economic forces, however, the American welfare state is an intensely political creation. Its current size, shape, and character have been forged through a long succession of political encounters. Though federal, state, and local expenditures for domestic purposes have grown steadily if unevenly since the founding of the Republic, the most spectacular advances have occurred in this century, especially since the early 1950s: it took 163 years, from 1789 to 1952, for governmental expenditures on domestic services to reach $34 billion. But in the ensuing twenty years, the totals rose dramatically by a factor of eight, to $257 billion.[14] Between 1950 and 1974, GNP rose from $284.8 billion to $1,397.3 trillion, and federal expenditures, including defense, climbed from $63 billion to more than $400 billion, or from 22% to more than 30% of GNP.[15]

The welfare state is kaleidoscopic, serving many interests simultaneously and perhaps for this reason satisfying nearly none. In one sense it may be viewed as an instrument of capital that modifies an evolving economy through state action. To an unprecedented degree the state now intervenes routinely in the interest of preserving the market system and ensuring stability and growth. The government regulates economic activity and fiscal policy, purchases about 22% of the national product, exercises broad powers of taxation, and transfers billions annually in purchasing power. In fact, the connections between government and corporations in areas of defense and welfare have been close enough to justify terming them "military-industrial" and "social-industrial" complexes. For these reasons, many radical detractors of the welfare state regard the invention as a mere palliative, even a design on the part of enlightened owners of capital to preserve as much of the system of wealth, power, and privilege as possible. But the welfare state has served other interests as well. An instrument of public policy regulated by the political process, it has advanced to one degree or another liberal goals of economic security, eradication of poverty, full employment, equality of opportunity, a fuller measure of economic democracy, health care, urban renewal, public education, and assistance to the disabled, the elderly, and children.

Most thoughtful liberals regard the capacity of government to serve many conflicting interests at once as essentially an asset. However much they differ over other matters, liberal supporters of the welfare state agree generally that it requires a strong and growing capitalist sector: this remains the first, if not the most cherished, priority of government because it enables progress toward other goals. Although this assumption does not lead to elimination of conflict over the distribution of society's benefits, or even to consensus on the most desirable size, scope, and social role of corporations, it does set fairly clear outer limits on expansion: the political managers of the welfare state may nibble at the corporate hand, and even bite it occasionally, but they may not cut it off. The principal owners and managers of capital continue to regard democratic socialism as an unacceptable mode of extending and completing the welfare state. Thus far, this extensive limit of mature capitalism has been enforced thoroughly by American public opinion.[16]

It is therefore the space between present configurations of the welfare state and the outer boundaries of corporate capitalism that becomes the most contested political ground and the primary social locus of liberal dilemmas. In a period of slower growth, rising governmental costs, and the frustration of previous expectations, conflict deepens within this contracting space. After four decades of social experimentation, large numbers of Americans are wondering whose interests have been served by the welfare state and how well. And they are asking whether liberal goals ought to be pursued through expansion of the current welfare state—indeed, whether such goals ought to be pushed much farther at all. These are legitimate questions which most liberal and Left commentators have brushed aside far too cavalierly.

In his appraisal of contemporary capitalism, Leonard Silk observed that by the early 1970s, "many Americans seemed to have lost faith in the ability of government to improve their lives or anybody else's."[17] At first glance, such pervasive dissatisfaction with the quality of public services seems curious. From a broad historical angle of vision, the gains are appreciable. The gradual formation of the democratic welfare state has accompanied and facilitated recognition of masses of people, granting them a public identity previously denied.[18] Scarcely one hundred years ago, blacks, women, small farmers, and working people of all races and both sexes lacked much political visibility. Though the state intersected with their lives at various points, it did not attempt to meet a broad range of human needs. In the course of winning public identity through political activity, people have learned to think of the state less as a remote object shrouded in mystery than as a set of dynamic institutions accountable to them. The state thus attains unprecedented legitimacy as people who previously lived apart or in fear of it begin to perceive it as a responsible agent of their welfare.

This process establishes the open-ended character of the current American welfare state and guarantees its considerable size. When people develop a measure of dignity as citizens, their expectations rise, and the state expands to fulfill them, periodically taking on new functions and deepening others. As a consequence, the proper nature and degree of state activity become matters of continuous public debate, though material gains affecting large numbers of people tend to be cumulative, making it progressively difficult for Congress to enact specific cutbacks. Important pressures for reform existed early in this century, but the framework of the modern American welfare state emerges most clearly in the variety of measures designed to alleviate the misery of life in the thirties— from social security and workers' relief to extensive labor legislation.

The most recent, and in many ways the most spectacular, episode of reform began slowly in the second Eisenhower Administration, reached its peak around the middle sixties, and then leveled off somewhat in the Nixon and Ford Administrations. The spirit of liberal reform permeating the political atmosphere during the Kennedy years established a new direction for government: in the thirties, the state took on the task of creating "normative economic policy;" in the fifties, it supported science and technology on a generous scale; but in the sixties it took on a spectacular mission, setting out *"to redress the impact of all economic and social inequalities."*[19] Though more rhetorical than substantive, this new egalitarian thrust reached its first legislative fruition under Johnson, especially in 1964–1965, before his intensification of the Vietnam war interrupted progress toward the Great Society. In this brief moment, Congress passed legislation to augment federal aid to education at all levels. It approved a major civil rights act. It enacted medicare and medicaid. And with the passage of the Economic Opportunity Act of 1964, poverty became more than ever a direct concern of government. Between 1965 and 1970, the level of federal spending on education, health, and welfare rose from $7.6 billion to $29.7 billion (from 6.4% to 15.1% of the federal budget). But if the spirit of reform languished, the costs of the welfare state mounted steadily: by the end of the first Nixon Administration in 1972, the total had soared to $43.3 billion, which represented an increase of $35.7 billion since 1965.[20] Indeed, federal spending for all domestic purposes rose from $13 billion in 1952 to $133 billion in 1972, and it reached nearly $170 billion in 1975.[21]

Though impressive, the gains registered through liberal politics and the welfare state now strike many as less significant than the actual and potential liabilities of this thrust. The manifestations of current displeasure are evident to the most casual observer. From complicated problems of mass education, Aid to Families with Dependent Children, and control of crime to the comparatively simple task of delivering mail, public services seem progressively less adequate, and the distribution of burdens and benefits increasingly unjust. Efforts to advance the egalitarian ideal appear feeble to some and unfair for various reasons to most. Huge governmental bureaucracies that reduce the scope of personal liberty and constrict the exercise of democracy have grown partly as a by-product of this egalitarian quest, producing a deep popular revulsion against the public sector and leaving nearly everyone from corporate executives to students with a sense of powerlessness and frustration. No one appears satisfied: welfare recipients find it difficult to express gratitude for small favors, often thoughtlessly, even cruelly, administered; working people frequently resent the burden of such payments; and welfare professionals feel underpaid, frustrated, and unappreciated. Such vicious circles circumscribe every public activity.

Meanwhile, as the perceived character and quality of services declines, expenses of government rise dramatically, underlining the chief economic liabilities of the democratic welfare state—its tendency to exacerbate rather than control inflation; its failure to promote balanced growth, equitable distribution, and full employment; its slowness in ensuring an ample supply of reasonably priced energy, or in effecting wise use of resources. But its tendency to grow like Topsy probably troubles people most. Totalling more than $400 billion, governmental expenditures now account for about one-third of the national product. Roger Freeman estimates that a "straight projection of governmental trends of the 1952–1972 period would produce results by the year 2000 that seem absurd. There would then be one person working for the government for every 1.75 persons in private employment—compared with a ratio of 1:4 at the present time—and governmental spending would equal 70 percent of the GNP—compared with 36 percent in 1972. It is hardly conceivable that this could happen. Expansion of domestic public programs is therefore unlikely to continue at the 1952–1972 rates for much longer."[22]

Yet political advocates of the welfare state continue to propose elaborations of current programs and establishment of new ones, despite these impending material limits and the growing popular sentiment for less government, less spending, less federal manpower, and less government regulation of citizens' activities. In the sixties, disparities between liberal promises and governmental performance were mitigated somewhat by an inflationary—at times inflammatory—rhetoric of progress. Whatever its harmful side effects, such rhetoric at least connected a range of liberal values to the vehicle of the state. Now, many citizens hold the state responsible for reducing the quality of their personal lives through inefficiency, economic mismanagement of resources, excessive and inequitable taxation, unconstitutional invasions of privacy, and clumsy bureaucratic attempts to enact humane principles. And they identify liberals as the main philosophical, ideological, and political culprits.

Of course, such sweeping charges against American liberalism are in many ways unfair. Though compounded by the memory of extravagant promises and a recognition of the approaching fiscal limits on government, the growing public irritability over the welfare state must be traced to certain patterns of tension and conflict that mark its development as a central form of mature capitalism, despite the philosophical predispositions of groups in office or their fundamental policy biases. I have alluded already to some of these conflicts. Because the welfare state serves multiple interests partially, it satisfies none completely: indeed, both success and failure breed various forms of discontent, some of them desperate. As the state becomes less an object of mystification, it ceases to inspire strong loyalties. As it turns into a rational instrument of public policy, the state opens itself to endless claims, beginning with modest demands of economic, racial, and ethnic groups for minimal inclusion, and extending to more elaborate claims for a series of broad economic, political, and social rights for everyone. These tendencies encourage grandiose rhetoric and heightened expectations on the one side, disappointment and disillusionment on the other.

At least in periods of extended prosperity, the political price of augmented benefits to groups of citizens appears to be a cumulative loss of control over the size and shapes of the state. Though invading groups resort to political insurgency in the opening rounds, victories generally are consolidated in the form of permanent bureaucracies charged with administering benefits. Once established, such measures as social security, unemployment compensation, and veterans' benefits require only minimal political participation to be maintained, even though their costs mount spectacularly. Because of their broad base of popular support and the continuing efforts of strong lobbies, they evoke little sustained opposition in Congress and the Executive, and no more than sporadic public controversy. New groups demanding entry or further benefits and opportunities—minorities, women, and poor people are obvious contemporary examples—may arouse deep passions and provoke strong opposition. But it is usually not concentrated sufficiently to prevent some sort of accommodation which, while leaving everyone less than satisfied, contributes to the expansionary drift of the welfare state. Mainly the property of conservatives and right-wing ideologues, essentially negative appeals to curb the scope of state power thus far have lacked sustained majority support; and they have not been translatable into specific policies.

Until recently, most liberals found these stresses and strains tolerable. The welfare state had effectively foreclosed the possibility of revolution (or rather, of a *coup d'état*) by the far Left or the far Right. The mixed American economy combined the productive virtues of capitalism with the democratic and humane virtues of a minimal welfare state. Although the idea of melting various groups into a harmonious social pot receded into a nostalgic recollection or a distant vision, the immediate prospect of stability based on a grumbling consensus seemed both realistic and politically acceptable—indeed, it seemed the only way. Contending, discontented forces provided dynamic motion, preventing stagnation; and the capacity of the political process to contain rival claimants by financing the winners of each round out of new increments of wealth ensured orderly, progressive change.

The plausibility of forecasts of long term stability and reasonable progress toward full social justice depended upon what now appears to be a highly problematic prescription of an expanding welfare state, managed under liberal auspices: this prospect kept conflict in motion toward a brighter future. In his sanguine appraisal of liberal progress to the early 1960s, Arthur Schlesinger observed that as the welfare state passed through several stages, each success engendered new problems: in the thirties, "economic recovery" dominated public attention; in the forties, the project was "full employment"; in the fifties, it was "economic growth"; and in the future, he predicted, the main concern would shift to "allocation of resources." Casting the history and prospects of the welfare state in linear rather than syncretic terms, Schlesinger identified allocation as the main issue of the seventies; but he failed to realize that within this decade the problem of allocation would be exacerbated by the simultaneous recurrence of all the others—recovery, full employment, and growth.[23]

The charges against liberalism already summarized suggest that the old socialist path toward social justice—a path which presumably led straight through the expanding territories of the welfare state—may be neither economically nor politically traversable in the next decades. The allegations also challenge the root promise of modern liberalism—the enhancement of private life through active promotion of public policy. At bottom, then, the dilemmas of liberalism are philosophical and ideological. But they have been compounded by political and structural developments in the postwar era. Floating on a tide of imagined abundance—a metaphysic fashioned by liberal and Left social critics in a mere two decades of postwar prosperity—liberal principles moved easily in the sea of political rhetoric. But the *modus operandi* of postwar liberalism has produced waves of illiberal consequences. And the new prospect of slower economic growth and limits to government expansion make it impossible to finesse difficult choices among competing social goods. Liberals are left high and dry, without a unifying set of principles governing hard choices, a coherent approach to public policy, or a solid political majority.

Let us look more closely at the liberal impasse. For several decades, the liberal enterprise managed to thrive politically on a set of unresolved misunderstandings. Spheres of liberal philosophical discourse, liberal ideology, and the actualities of coalition politics overlapped without immediately serious consequences. The shifting coalitions of trade unionists, white collar workers, big city ethnic machines, racial minorities, the poor, Dixiecrats, and elements of the corporate and financial worlds that composed Democratic majorities from the middle thirties through the middle sixties came together primarily for reasons of self-interest. But mere self-interest—hardly an arresting political motive—does not account wholly for liberal successes.[24] The competing claims of various groups were integrated into the dominant ideological pattern inherited from the liberal capitalist past, and for the most part accepted by a majority of the electorate. At its center was the bourgeois dream of a better private life, extended to as many as possible in this instance of a broad coalition. A vague utilitarian ethic linked private and group purposes to the larger coalition, and by inference to some version of the public good.

There were, of course, important differences in this unstable majority coalition, elements of serious tension and conflict between, say, skilled workers seeking higher pay and poor people seeking a base of economic survival through the state; between cosmopolitan reformers committed to Victorian cultural values and white working class ethnics (Poles, Italians, Greeks, Slavs, Russian and Eastern European Jews); between pragmatic politicians and idealists intent upon completing the welfare state.[25] But differences between Democratic regulars and reformers were contained politically through a network of fairly settled power relationships. And they were managed ideologically under the wide umbrella of liberal capitalist mythology which accommodated orthodox and left liberals. If only because it was supposed widely that liberal policies would promote gains in productivity, the values of liberty, equality, and service became staples of majority political ideology. As the economic cake grew, there would be more for everyone, extending the freedom of productive citizens and the freedom of disadvantaged people to enjoy private life. The Democratic coalition thus broadened the bourgeois ideal of service to ensure a decent standard of living for people temporarily or permanently sidelined by age or ill health. At the same time, it advanced the idea of equality of opportunity, justifying state intervention to guarantee every citizen a fair chance—even several chances—to compete for society's rewards.

This coalition delivered the goods, though hardly in such lavish quantities as its main postwar defenders had imagined or projected. And since all their goals could be pursued simultaneously in periods of affluence, left liberal social critics and activists stayed generally within the ambience of the Democratic party, at least on issues of national import.[26] The present belonged largely to political realists; the future, perhaps to left liberal idealists.

I would suggest, then, that the modern American welfare state began in earnest during the thirties with a loose fit among philosophical principles derived from classical liberal capitalism, a popular ideology of orthodox liberalism, and a sufficient number of immediate, shared concerns to nourish a stable political coalition, principally within the Democratic party. Most important, members of this shifting coalition were at least willing if not eager to use the state freely as a vehicle of social change; no alternative instrument presented itself. The welfare state thus grew within these perimeters, and by the early sixties it seemed on the way to permanent stability. Propelled by the exigencies of World War II and the temporarily unifying ideology of the prosperous cold war years, the state grew. Everything was expected to move fairly smoothly under this ideological consensus so long as productivity rose, so long as the state managed to improve the lot of the less privileged without disturbing seriously the interests and lives of other citizens, and so long as entering groups proceeded cautiously, hats in hand. By the early seventies, however, each of these conditions of stability had been undermined. The welfare state, as I have noted, was approaching a fiscal crisis. It seemed to many to be following a pattern of development that burst the confines of the ideological consensus which had permitted its early growth. Finally, in the sixties, previously excluded or neglected groups—victims of poverty and discrimination and also new victims of alienation—demanded inclusion or augmented power and benefits on substantially different terms.

The growth of the welfare state—and now its apparent fiscal limits and the limits of its political acceptability—heightened the conflicts of material interest that fractured the old Democratic coalition and exposed the dominant ideological set as inadequate. To these conflicts have been added a range of cultural issues— from drugs and abortion to styles of leisure—which cut across traditional class lines, ethnic divisions, and political ideologies. For a time, the expansionary trajectory of economic progress and the inflated ideology of expectation permitted establishment of new institutional configurations. Now that these enlargements of the state require fresh justification, a serious philosophical controversy over liberal commitments to liberty and equality—a tense balance in the easiest of times—is shaping up. For instance, as left liberal proponents of the welfare state extended the promise of additional benefits, the idea of equality of opportunity was stretched beyond acceptable ideological limits (indeed, far beyond its original meaning). However vigorously proposed by liberal social philosophers, advocated by members of insurgent groups, or prosecuted by reform-minded liberals, new, expanded conceptions of equality of access and of result do not command anything like majority assent. In fact, they provoke wide, though as yet politically diffuse, opposition. Hence, there is at the moment no consensus on how to determine what a citizen needs to lead a decent life, or to decide what children require in order to compete for society's rewards and to experience life's satisfactions. Are all children entitled to an adequate diet, housing, clothing, medical care, and schooling (from the moment they can lift a bottle) that compensates for inherited or acquired handicaps? If every child is entitled to a decent family life—a far more radical notion—to what lengths should the state go to ensure it? Or is all this merely desirable, a social hope that must yield before political priorities disciplined by stubborn economic and institutional limits? As a determinant of social policy, the egalitarian quest begins to appear endless, and even to threaten or collide with other democratic principles and commitments.

The failure of the conventional liberal ideology under which the welfare state emerged now assumes crucial importance. This ideological set includes a fairly clear hierarchy of values. The welfare state must ensure rising prosperity first. Its political managers must keep big business within reasonable bounds so as to prevent large corporations from taking excessive profits and violating the competitive sensibilities of ordinary people. The state also must offer fair opportunities and rising rewards to currently industrious citizens, extend chances to others as finances permit, and, finally, assist the rest. This hierarchy of values rests solidly on the work ethic: those who produce goods and supply services (or who possess wealth based on past labor) are unambiguously entitled to consume. Others have a right to live, but their claims on society's resources rest precariously on a confusing mixture of attitudes and assumptions: generosity and compassion for the underdog; expectations of abundance; the pragmatic economic need to raise effective demand and the equally pragmatic political need to avert civil disorder; and finally, the implicit belief that state assistance should be a temporary expedient for most, not a way of life.

But the intense pursuit of greater economic and social equality by large sectors of society threatens to overturn other priorities and to weaken important values: the scope of personal liberty contracts as the state intervenes even more extensively in the affairs of those it purports to assist as well as of those whose private existence it must restrict in order to finance further increments of social justice. Ideological confusions run deep here. The poorest citizens are assisted by welfare payments from the state. In order to gain such assistance, however, they must tolerate a means test and other invasions of privacy which would have shocked traditional liberal philosophers. Other citizens whose tax load rises to subsidize the underclass and the supporting bureaucracies of middle class professionals consider their liberty—in the concrete form of disposable personal income—confiscated involuntarily. In effect, many proponents of the welfare state argue that everyone has a *right* to a certain income, even if he chooses not to work. But old attitudes hang on: income from the state, which does not require every able person to work, is still regarded widely as a *privilege,* and, ideally, only as a temporary one. This confusion of values engenders dissatisfaction among all groups, eroding traditional sources and centers of authority and legitimacy. The concept of merit blurs as the work ethic is applied unevenly among middle and lower sectors of the population, and among the active working class and the unemployed. Orthodox liberal ideology comes to appear an insufficient guide to social perception and political judgment, but there is as yet no adequate philosophical substitute that can claim the allegiance of a democratic majority.

I believe that the conventional liberal ideological set, though not nearly so entrenched as it was half a century ago, still comprises the central mode of political perception for millions of Americans, probably for a decisive majority. These liberal notions are no longer the source of sure standards, having been challenged in a variety of ways. Too often, these standards are inapplicable to public affairs, and hence become an infectious source of cynicism and apathy. But they serve nonetheless as standards of last resort, especially on matters affecting immediate interest. Thus, for example, many American academics who defended the rising claims of disadvantaged people as a matter of philosophical principle and political conviction in the sixties fell back to an old meritocratic line of defense when confronted with demands to alter the racial, ethnic, and class composition of the student body on their own campuses. Liberals who participated in the civil rights movement in its early days—and still consider integration an admirable social goal—find themselves opposed to busing as a means of enforcing the law, or at least are in deep conflict over the matter. People who once supported higher welfare payments to the poor and augmented public services for everyone are having second thoughts —and second feelings. Small wonder: middle income families now pay between one-fifth and one-quarter of their earnings in taxes, as opposed to one-eighth in the early 1950s.[27]

The postwar changes reviewed thus far suggest the main causes of disorder within liberal circles. But if I am right in contending that orthodox liberal ideology persists as a perspective of last resort—serving as a sort of ideological superego—then new coalitions within the Democratic party will display a more conservative cast than left liberals and democratic socialists had become accustomed to expect. Futhermore, levels of anxiety and guilt will become progressively more intense throughout society as new values jostle old ones. We are, it seems evident, in the midst of a realignment of political ideas and political sensibilities. It is not merely the deepening of the idea of social equality that subverts previous ideological convictions and political coalitions, but also rising demands on the part of most citizens for fuller personal development and expression. New conceptions of self imply changing valuations of self-interest. Bound by the discipline of the work ethic, the idea of individualism that animated various factions of the New Deal coalition did not include the expectation of happiness, the assumption that private life would consist of progressively more—and more satisfying—leisure. These were mere hopes, consistent with Jeffersonian ideals. Now, nearly everyone expects not only a freer life, but a more satisfying one, made felicitous by some combination of more income, less work, and better public services (roughly in this order of importance). But we have as yet no full philosophical rationale or ideological consensus on how to integrate new conceptions of individualism into the framework of a workable public philosophy. And so, the content of the notion of self-interest expands and deepens. Everyone expects to have more and to be more. But the political realities of interest group democracy force awkward divisions of personal interest: equality is pursued by categories of age, race, and gender that often do not match individual profiles. In the absence of a balanced social component, then, the only widely accepted ideological mold—the old, individualist liberal capitalist one—leads many to regard the heightened expectations of *others* as excessive or unjust, and their own as unfulfilled. It may be, then, that as the expectation of happiness grows, the hope of it wanes.

This divisive pattern of unseemly self-interest cuts through all spheres of American life. And it forces submerged liberal conflicts between libertarian and egalitarian impulses to the surface, as central elements in a lively and seminal, if not very well focused, philosophical debate over social and political ideology. This debate is at bottom an effort to articulate changing sensibilities and to account for rapidly shifting social options. Finding the old liberal categories drained of meaning, or filled with meanings that are no longer acceptable, people begin to seek new bearings. Because it is most compatible with the orthodox liberal ideology, a drift into a moderate conservatism, stressing individual initiative and responsibility, as well as opposition to uninhibited expansion of the welfare state, forms the political line of least resistance. We shall explore these conservative and "new liberal" options in the next chapter. But an influential minority of intellectuals has edged toward the Left in search of philosophical moorings and an ideological framework that might sanction further extensions of the welfare state and yet command the political allegiance of a democratic majority.[28] This philosophical search has a significant though comparatively small social and political counterpart among some elements of the old New Deal coalition—minorities, the poor, women, young people, echelons of organized labor—as well as among the growing stratum of people associated with the media, administrators, consultants, educators, public advocacy lawyers, urban planners, social scientists, and mental health professionals whose personal interests and ideological convictions are tied to an expanding public sector.

John Rawls' highly regarded *A Theory of Justice* offers an especially good example of this diffuse intellectual trend toward the Left. It is the most ambitious contemporary effort to establish a democratic philosophical foundation for the shift to the idea of equality of result implicit in the institutional thrust of the welfare state and in the ideology of those who would push it toward (but not to) completion. Through a series of complicated arguments Rawls defends his general conception of social justice as fairness: "All social primary goods—liberty and opportunity, income and wealth, and the bases of self respect—are to be distributed equally unless an unequal distribution of any or all of these goods is to the advantage of the least favored."[29]

Rawls' quasi-liberal, quasi-democratic socialist ethic, I should think, furnishes a useful philosophical basis for thoughtful left liberals who continue to press for massive extensions of the welfare state, even under conditions of relative scarcity. Maintaining that his conception of justice can be enacted under capitalist or socialist schemes of political economy, rather than identifying freedom with capitalism and excluding other possible forms of political economy, Rawls provides the essentials of a left-wing solution to the ideological inconsistencies between traditional liberal notions of liberty and left liberal defenses of the welfare state as an agent of greater equality. Rawls' first principle guarantees the priority of political liberty: "Each person," he asserts, "is to have an equal right to the most extensive total system of equal basic liberties compatible with a similar system of liberty for all." In social conditions of relative abundance, liberty ought not be traded off for other social goods; it can be restricted only for the sake of other liberties. Rawls' second, or "difference," principle concerns the arrangement of social and economic inequalities: "The intuitive idea is that the social order is not to establish and secure the more attractive prospects of those better off unless doing so is to the advantage of those less fortunate."[30]

Though difficult to apply in the easiest of circumstances, this notion of social justice becomes especially elusive in a context of relative scarcity, as the problem of equitable distribution becomes increasingly a matter of *redistributing* goods, services, and opportunities. Consider, as an example, the Full Employment and Balanced Growth Act of 1976, supported by such liberal leaders as Henry Jackson, Hubert Humphrey, Fred Harris, and Morris Udall. It seeks to guarantee a job for everyone who wants work—preferably through private industry but also through regular channels of government and, if necessary, through a permanent Job Corps—and to liquidate poverty, substandard wages, and substandard working conditions, all within a decade. Proposing an enlarged planning role for the federal government, the Humphrey–Hawkins bill envisions major improvements in American life over the next ten years—"a decent home in a greatly improved environment" for every family; "adequate health care for all at costs within their means"; "educational opportunities for all"; improvement of cultural life.[31]

It may be suggested that these goals—seventeen altogether—are merely a staple of postwar left liberal rhetoric, nothing new. So they are: ten years ago a group of liberal and Left intellectuals and public figures proposed a "Freedom Budget" with the same intention of eliminating poverty, etc., by 1975. Then, however, such proposals were framed carefully in a rhetoric of generosity, moral obligation, and self-interest consistent with norms of orthodox liberal capitalist ideology and the prevalent tone of public discourse in the early sixties. The proposals were to be financed out of anticipated increments in productivity ("economic growth dividends") that could be set aside without seriously affecting corporate profits, or the rising fortunes of working people and professional elements of the Democratic coalition. (Those who endorsed the Freedom Budget were prepared, at least for the occasion, to waffle on Vietnam, suggesting—naively, it turns out—that domestic programs and dubious foreign adventures could be pursued simultaneously, so great was the horn of plenty.)[32] Now, though they have broad support in Congress, in organized labor, and even in the 1976 Democratic party platform, such expensive domestic programs presuppose a more explicit ethic of redistribution, a leveling down toward equality that would affect middle and working class people who already have been pushed as far as most wish to go.

Before the crisis of liberalism assumed its current proportions, such critics as Arnold Kaufman sorted out the most important pieces of the puzzle. In the late 1960s, Kaufman argued that an enfeebled liberalism would expire without an infusion of radical energy. He sought more extensive welfare measures, contending that meager liberal programs retarded reasonable progress toward egalitarian goals. But he proposed also a deepening of democracy —wider participation and an invigorated politics of coalition—to expand the scope of liberty and to offset growing concentrations of state (and corporate) power.

Kaufman's admirable effort to clarify ideological puzzles and establish political space for a radical liberalism depended upon the assumption of sharply rising productivity that lies at the center of all postwar liberal social criticism: "Confronted by the sordid reality of American affluence," he observed, "it is impossible . . . to be authentically liberal without turning resolutely toward radicalism."[33] Now, in the context of relative scarcity, it may be impossible to be authentically liberal without renouncing a socialist ethic and opposing an enlarged welfare state—that is, without retreating to the more conservative ground of traditional liberalism. The clearest alternative to creeping conservatism is an explicitly socialist ethic. But if we take this step, why not go further than Rawls and Humphrey and reconsider socialism as an American possibility? There are still obvious reasons of political expediency for not doing so. These considerations may help to account for the willingness of some pragmatic liberals to dispense with the subject of political ideology altogether, and perhaps also for the impatience often displayed by left liberals at the suggestion that socialism may be after all a useful idea. It may be that in deference to American sensibilities, "socialism" cannot become the name of our desire. Its essential features of democratic planning and partial redistribution of wealth may nevertheless become the object of our political desires. As Michael Harrington observes, "socialism must . . . be put [forth] as the logical next step for liberalism, indeed as the only way to assure the actual achievement of liberal values."[34] By virtue of the changes in American sensibilities and institutions, and the new prospect of slower economic growth, policy positions taken regularly by such liberal organizations as Americans for Democratic Action and proponents of the Full Employment and Balanced Growth Act have come to depend upon a largely socialist rationale, however much advocates shy away from the name or from a consideration of the political economy of socialism. New fiscal and ideological contexts are changing the meaning and political implications of old proposals. People on the Right who have been calling reform liberals "socialist" for so many decades finally have a point.

If democratic socialists cannot persuade left liberals to take this tentative step of discussing adoption of what is becoming their proper name (or else reformulating their political outlook), the gathering force of conservative public opinion should. Left liberals will be labeled increasingly as socialists, not merely because politicians on the Right find it to their convenience, but also because their commitment to extending the welfare state in a time of relative scarcity and their acceptance of versions of the idea of equality of result seemingly have foreclosed other coherent options. Moreover, should left liberals be unable to imagine genuinely democratic alternatives to burgeoning state power and hardening arteries of political participation, they will be identified also as corporate or state socialists, misguided democrats seeking antidemocratic courses.

Thus, democratic socialist critiques of welfare capitalism assume fresh importance as responses to the deepening crisis of liberalism. They should interest those who have edged (or been drawn) toward the Left over the past decade as well as those who have traveled so far to the Left that they now wish to return to firmer ground.

Democratic Socialist Critiques of the Welfare State

The suggestion that troubled liberals adopt a socialist view of American political economy to match—and to justify—their implicitly socialist ethic has much to recommend it. This advice does not proceed merely from a perception of disparities between promise and performance, which reasonable people expect to find everywhere. Nor does it issue from a discovery of conflicts among social goods: these, too, mark every society. It rests instead largely on a compelling socialist critique of welfare capitalism. With the revival of American socialist scholarship and social commentary in the past two decades, we are, I take it, well past the need to pause over exaggerated indictments which begin inevitably with a laundry list of past, present, and impending problems; then proceed to trace them all to capitalist sources; and finally imagine socialism as something on the order of a superdetergent. A summary of the more modest case against the welfare state as the last word on the social question will do nicely here.

In the long run, socialists argue, the welfare state cannot establish a framework for realizing liberal values because it operates within the constraints of a system of capitalist power and privilege that generates massive irrationalities and promotes widespread injustice. Of course, as we have had occasion to note, serious socialists maintain that the appearance of the welfare state has softened the harshest features of Spencerian capitalism. They take account also of the changing character of work, of alterations in the class structure, and of shifting aspirations of various groups that accompany the movement from an industrial toward a postindustrial, or largely service, economy. Despite full allowances for crucial changes, however, critics maintain that the organization of production and distribution of goods and services in American society remains capitalist in essential ways.[35]

A system characterized by large blocs—principally the corporate sector, government, and organized labor—welfare capitalism may accommodate a multiplicity of interests, but it exists ultimately for profitable enterprise, for the welfare of the rich first, and for others thereafter. Maintaining stability and preserving a system of wealth, power, and privilege, government spending generally benefits the very well off first. As the bailout of Penn Central, Lockheed, and the Bank of America in New York suggests, the federal government is prepared to subsidize the rich openly, in dramatic ways, as well as routinely through massive tax expenditures amounting to tens of billions of dollars each year. It also benefits a small upper range of bureaucrats and public servants, as well as overlapping elements of what Galbraith calls the technostructure. Providing some sort of employment directly for approximately sixteen million people (roughly 20% of the work force), government finally grants the surplus population small allowances through transfer and in-kind payments. Socialists contend that the functional organization of capitalism supports patterns of privilege which frustrate orthodox and left liberal, socialist, and even conservative goals and processes, subverting their related conceptions of social justice and individualism.

Capitalism responds slowly and fitfully to new problems of stagflation, energy, environmental deterioration, and allocation of scarce resources. Though liable to serious charges of productive inefficiency, wastefulness, and social irrationality, it fails most intractably in the area of distribution. Especially in times of economic slowdown, capitalism retards solution of the perennial problem of a just distribution of goods and services. It always inhibits a just distribution of opportunity, power, and privilege. But capitalism is no longer immune to coherent planning, as socialists earlier thought it always must be. To meet major social problems, it surely will have to incorporate comprehensive modes of planning in the next decades. The interesting questions, however, concern the kinds of planning that will be adopted, the character and composition of the planners, and the real beneficiaries of the plans.[36]

There are, then, two essential touchstones in the democratic socialist critique of the welfare state. First, in the course of its evolution the welfare state should register progress toward a more equitable system of opportunities and rewards. Though socialists define equality variously, they agree generally that equity in the American case requires elimination of the extremes of severe poverty and tasteless opulence, movement toward a more even distribution in the middle ranges, and, equally important, full employment, for people without jobs in this culture lack both purchasing power and self-esteem. Second, socialists advocate reallocation of power in the direction of a democratized social order whose citizens take charge of their own lives at work and in their communities, participating more or less as equals in important social decisions. Both sorts of redistribution are necessary. Without a more equal division of wealth, and work for everyone who wants it, individuals cannot exercise fully their share of political power. Lacking this capacity, they must pursue other liberal and socialist ends under severe handicaps.

It is now evident, to socialists and liberals alike, that despite the growth of the state, American progress toward both touchstones has been disappointing. In periods of rising prosperity, many Left social critics conceded too easily that the potential productivity of welfare capitalism eventually might obviate the need for a socialist redistribution of goods and services. They concentrated on the fear that at some point along the path to limitless abundance, citizens would find the idea of democratizing power not worth pursuing. Though often criticized as a kind of philosophical spoof, Herbert Marcuse's speculations on one-dimensional society were well grounded in the general, quasi-official belief in the endless horizons of American prosperity. More sophisticated and less well known Left critics such as Michael Walzer maintained that abundance within a greatly enlarged welfare state would allow the socialist bid for democratic power to begin in earnest.[37] Both sorts of projection now belong to a familiar but distant social universe. Under present circumstances of relative scarcity, the full socialist case concerning redistribution of rewards and opportunities must be pressed, if a convincing socialist case is to be made at all. To concentrate the case for socialism merely, or even mainly, on the issue of maldistribution of an endlessly growing stock of social goods is no longer tenable.

Socialists contend that the priorities of capitalist economy largely influence the comparatively puny size, distorted shapes, and semidemocratic processes of the American welfare state. They challenge the popular notion that the American state already bestows excessive benefits and opportunities on poor people and minorities. In fact, transfer payments account for much of the growth in the welfare sector since the Roosevelt era. Such forms of social security as unemployment insurance, retirement insurance, veterans' benefits, and assistance payments, as well as parts of the bloated defense sector, characterize the main lines of our welfare state, not government programs that attempt, however ineptly, to help impoverished people change substantially their lot in life or improve their share of the national wealth. Though federal activity in housing, education, manpower development, and community improvement has been comparatively slight, and not terribly effective, vigorous efforts to redress injustices through the courts, which must be counted as part of the thrust of the welfare state, have met with more success.[38] Moreover, it may be suggested—and justly so, I believe—that transfer payments, along with such programs as medicare and medicaid, do retard the growth of inequality which in any case remains a central dynamic of corporate capitalism. Doubtless matters would be far worse without these measures.

On balance, however, the benefits of the welfare state are parceled out antisocially, reinforcing the main patterns of inequitable claims on income and wealth in America. This becomes especially evident if we recall the total impact of state activity on society. Neither the mildly progressive tax structure nor the patterns of government spending has affected seriously the basic priorities of capitalist distribution, though government intervention has contributed obviously to the upward spiral of income, employment, and profits. Over the past quarter-century, the distribution of income has changed little: the poorest 20% of all families continue to receive about 5% of the cash income, whereas the wealthiest 5% claim about 15%.[39] Even greater inequalities of total wealth persist: if the top 1% claim about 10% of the income, the richest 5% hold 26% of the wealth—a share roughly equal to the entire holdings of the bottom 80%. Poverty diminishes the lives of millions. And the goal of full employment has been abandoned quietly as a viable public policy by the Nixon and Ford Administrations.

What has changed significantly is the size, distribution, and relative weight of burdens. In the postwar era, the percentage of the federal tax bill paid by corporations has declined from 33.6% in 1944 to 14.6% in 1974, while the percentage for individuals has risen from 48.5% to 73.9%.[40] As the surplus population grows, the total of small allowances to individuals adds up to rising taxes which hit lower and middle income people hardest. High rates of inflation eat up the discretionary income of these groups and draw them into higher tax brackets. Poor and middle income groups are the most distressed victims of an elaborate, government-managed shell game over which they exercise little control.

From the vantage point of low and middle income working people, the welfare state is grossly unfair. Those who perform the least interesting and lowest paying jobs are asked to contribute most heavily to support those who do not work at all. Such responsibilities to what has become a permanent underclass cannot be justified by the old liberal capitalist work ethic. Nor can they be rationalized through a genuine socialist ethic—from each according to his ability, to each according to his work. They require a caricature of the communist ethic of distribution on the basis of need. But the full needs of the underclass cannot be met satisfactorily, and their abilities remain largely untapped. The surplus population lives miserably with its own resentment, while kindling resentment among those above. Upper middle class families with incomes of more than $30,000 survive tolerably, dispensing with some luxuries, and the very rich, as always, manage very well. All this compounds social divisions and makes left liberal political coalitions of have-nots, working people, and the conscience constituency of upper middle class professionals more fragile than ever.

Socialists maintain further that the fantastic explosion of transfer payments reflects the failure of the private sector and government to generate sufficient employment. Corporations exert considerable political pressure for additional tax benefits to solve the alleged capital shortage problem. The circle becomes vicious, and the main liberal political response within advanced capitalism has been to encourage more unbalanced growth in order to achieve the bigger economic pie upon which the whole enterprise has come to depend. We prime the economic pump by giving tax credits to corporations and barely feeding an ever larger surplus population, rather than owning up to the issue of redistribution of opportunity, wealth, income, and power.

Without denying the value of the welfare state, or the long political campaigns required to achieve even its present modest contours, reasonable socialists contend that past and present injustices embodied in the American state are due primarily to the larger economic and political climate in which it must function. They maintain that over the long haul, efforts to reform the welfare state—to move closer toward the goal of a better distribution of wealth and income—are subverted ultimately by antisocial forces governing capitalist production and distribution. Surely, nothing in the history of the past quarter-century would lead socialists to abandon this working assumption.

By preventing significant reallocation of power—the other major area of socialist concern—such enormous imbalances in income and wealth also retard progress in democracy. Democratic socialists have accepted a growing state as a ballast to inequitable economic power that tilts the political ship in the direction of already advantaged groups. They have done so reluctantly, though in retrospect perhaps not reluctantly enough. Within the expanding welfare sectors, some new political power is created and shared. But not much, and even this becomes congealed quickly in bureaucracies. Within government, political power tends to shift toward administrative agencies. Legislative bodies become increasingly defensive and ineffective, reflecting popular divisions and the absence of direction. At the same time, the processes of representative democracy harden, popular power remains diffuse, and levels of participation apparently decline. Candidates are bought and sold, merchandised like household items. Political favors go to the highest bidders. Of course, moderate levels of disreputable practice are inescapable in any free political process created by people animated by some mixture of ambition and idealism. But the degree of dishonesty symbolized by Watergate, which goes beyond acceptable limits of corruption, is by no means endemic to advanced capitalism. Nor is it even representative of the deep professional commitment of most appointed and elected public officials. Indeed, such corruptions of power only reinforce the importance of surviving elements of democracy. Without these—and some fantastic luck—Watergate would not have been exposed, nor would the various efforts to restore (and augment) integrity in business, politics, and government have been launched. What has been clear, before, during, and after Watergate, is this: the economic biases of the American system—especially the fantastic power of large corporations—inhibit citizens from achieving the sort of political and personal power they require to create and sustain a fully vital democracy.

In theoretical and moral terms, then, the new American context of relative scarcity strengthens the ambiguous socialist case against welfare capitalism. But it does so perversely, forcing democratic socialists, as well as left liberals, to reconsider their most fundamental political values and approaches to social change. It is one thing to recommend that left liberals accept what has become their philosophical lot—this would augment the socialist voice somewhat—but quite another to do so just when the old economic bridge to a significantly broader American audience may be nearing political collapse. Both democratic socialists and left liberals have clung to the idea of lavish growth as the precondition for progress toward their various goals. For left liberals, it constituted the material basis for a larger welfare state. For democratic socialists, a growing welfare state, with its long term disparity between rising expectations and rewards, promised to ferment a genuine socialist politics. Even if we assume a steady rate of growth through the rest of the century, though perhaps slower than the 3.3% that prevailed from 1929 through 1972, both positions begin to seem utopian.

Those of us who retain a commitment to democratic goals and processes need to rethink socialist aims and instrumentalities in the context of uncertain economic prospects, the high probability of further political polarization, and the certainty of limits. It is, of course, no simple matter to sort out the limiting factors that cramp future space, and to define the mixture with any precision: the impending limits on growth result from a combination of stresses on the natural environment; international reallocations of wealth and power; inefficiencies and injustices of capitalist economics; the sluggish, Madisonian structure of our governmental institutions; and widespread voter dissatisfaction with the apparent trends of the welfare state. Taken together, these factors compel left liberals and democratic socialists to imagine the future in far less spacious terms than both have grown accustomed to.

In the preceding chapter, I concluded provisionally that for democratic socialism to emerge as a serious political alternative— deliberately imagined and pursued—it must be judged distinct from the present system and superior to it on several counts: the ends must be more just and more desirable; the means or vehicles of social ownership and democratic planning must be more conducive to these ends than present arrangements. I proposed further that the process of transition presupposes abundance and requires democratic procedures. These, in any case, are the preconditions customarily invoked by democratic socialists. Since both preconditions seem dubious now, it is difficult to hope for a widespread public demand for democratic socialism. At the very least, we need to define new grounds for hope. This is the nub of the matter: though a clear majority continues to believe that their chief values may be approximated most closely (or violated least often) through some altered version of capitalism—a return to laissez faire, a deepening of the welfare state, or a widening of ownership (people's capitalism)—there is also considerable apprehension that we may fall into the wonderland of bureaucratic or state socialism by default, through the fiscal sinkhole of the welfare state. Socialism names a collection of American fears, as well as a collection of American desires.

Disclaimed as a positive vision by nearly everyone, especially by democratic socialists, the prospect of merging large business firms into even larger governmental structures nonetheless looms as a path of last resort, an alternative to decline and social chaos. This possibility of a gray, in-between American state socialism (or state capitalism) presents a far more subtle challenge than images of a clumsy, Byzantine, red bureaucracy or a black Orwellian collectivism that haunted American minds in the fifties and sixties. In fact, the importance of a socialist presence and the chances of a successful socialist politics rest largely on the capacity of socialists to show convincingly that enriched democratic institutions and practices can provide sufficient counterweights to the long range authoritarian, collectivist tendencies in the structure of such a planned system. They must argue that socialism and planning can be democratic, and that democracy may yet provide a path to socialism.

The full case for democratic socialism now requires an even more vigorous critique of welfare capitalism, one stressing its material, fiscal, political, and structural limits—especially its lack of capacity to redistribute wealth significantly—than democratic socialists have offered in the recent decades of prosperity. It requires also more attractive images of socialism than most Americans currently hold. Most important, I believe that the democratic socialist case must be reformulated through a sympathetic examination of the moral claims and the political exigencies of an emerging centrist conservatism, rather than through nostalgic reliance on outmoded strategies based on discredited economic fantasies. It seems to me especially important that left liberals and democratic socialists abandon the revered, often smug, practice of grouping conservative opponents of an extended welfare state with reactionary forces of the Right. For the turmoil in American sensibilities—with its many conservative cross-currents—deeply affects precisely those large sectors of the organized working class and the new technostructure that democratic socialists have long recognized as the fulcrum of democratic change. Barrington Moore, Jr., advances the modest suggestion that the task of the Left remains one of keeping "radical fire" under liberal reforms.[41] But the confused meanings and confusing directions of postwar liberal reform imply the need to reconsider the uses of the small democratic socialist flame. Left liberals should entertain the idea of becoming socialists. Both, I shall propose, need to become more conservative.

4 / Conservative Caveats

> Society is indeed a contract. . . . [But] as the ends of such a partnership cannot be obtained in many generations, it becomes a partnership not only between those who are living but between those who are living, those who are dead, and those who are yet to be born. . . . Changing the state as often as there are floating fancies . . . no one generation could link with the other. Men would be little better than the flies of a summer.
>
> —Edmund Burke, *Reflections on the Revolution in France*

Let us take stock of the argument to this point. Beginning with characterizations of the main features of the political and cultural crises in America, I turned initially to the idea of socialism as a source of illumination and remediation. To suggest what remains morally appealing and politically vital in this melange of traditions, I sorted out the utopian dreams and political nightmares of communism, noted their intimate connections, and rejected them as false hopes and dead ends. And I isolated the more modest notion of democratic socialism as the most plausible medium range American guide from the Left. But in the course of delimiting this idea, it became clear that it is also a problematic guide: the ends remain contested, the means or vehicles appear more dubious than ever, and the customary preconditions probably are not attainable.

That is to say, the socialist goal of enlarging the scope of liberty through egalitarian measures taken in democratic ways apparently lacks the imaginative and motivating power of more radical, communist schemes. In the absence of utopian overtones, the aims of socialism may not differ sufficiently from liberal ends to warrant the arduous political effort to institute its vehicles. Moreover, with the growth of the welfare state, the ends themselves seem less firmly anchored to the socialist means. This dissociation occurs partly because achievements of the capitalist welfare state have entailed some use of socialist means, and partly because a majority of citizens continue to regard the vehicles of large scale public ownership and flexible planning as subversive of democratic socialist ends. Democratic safeguards, it is feared widely and with some justice, would be too weak to offset full socialist concentrations of economic and political power.

Recognizing the importance of these well-established reservations concerning the character and relationships between socialist ends and means, I nevertheless have concentrated thus far on the prior matter of the preconditions for socialism in America. For it is here that the usual strategic assumptions of democratic socialist thought have been challenged most severely by the events of the seventies. As long as left liberal political coalitions seemed likely to gather strength and advance the interests of the welfare state, it was reasonable for socialists to work toward establishment of their values and vehicles through activity largely within the Democratic party. This was—and is—the principal American form of revisionism: no other basic socialist political strategy has ever made better sense. As we have seen, however, the liberal connection frayed badly over the past decade. The idea of endless abundance, which sustained both democratic socialist and liberal hopes, has collapsed as a reigning assumption of social thought. Although the decline of the notion of abundance may strengthen the philosophical case for socialism as the surest (and perhaps the only) means to egalitarian ends, it also subverts the second major political precondition—the hope that a democratic majority favorably disposed to the socialist idea would emerge from continuous tensions between a progressive welfare state and the even more rapidly rising expectations of its citizens.

The crooked socialist path leading through the regions of a liberal welfare state appeared difficult and problematic in the best of times. It is now an obstructed path. Altered economic conditions and the prospect of relative austerity accentuate tensions between the egalitarian and libertarian impulses within American liberalism. I have explored the left side of this fissure—the option of incorporating the egalitarian impulse to redistribute power and wealth into a democratic socialist framework. Noting such political obstacles to this course as the weakening two-party system, the growing difficulty of establishing viable left liberal coalitions, and the rise of conservative sentiment, I concluded with the hypothesis that democratic socialists need to examine attempts to recast ideological positions around the libertarian, or individualist impulse.[1]

Left liberals, I proposed, should consider adopting democratic socialism, and then, along with democratic socialists, they ought to reconsider varieties of conservatism in a sympathetic spirit. The immediate reason for doing so, of course, is the spreading revolt against further extensions of the welfare state articulated by politicians and publicists traditionally associated with the right wing of the Republican party (and its fringes). It would be short-sighted, however, to dismiss the latest conservative turn as another politically suicidal exercise conducted by neo-Goldwater-ites. It may be that in part, but it is more. Moderate variants of such basic conservative themes as opposition to big government, excessive welfare spending, and proliferating bureaucracies—all perceived as unjust infringements on personal liberty—now appeal to millions who inhabit the shifting center of American political thought. Serious people who have long considered themselves essentially liberal (or even socialist) in outlook are drifting into a centrist conservatism without knowing quite why.

Evolving fitfully during the postwar period and gathering momentum in the late sixties and early seventies, this collection of conservative moods, which includes the "new liberalism," needs to be understood if socialists are to chart new democratic paths. But there are equally compelling reasons for exploring conservative themes once more. Since Burke, conservatism has been a major Western mode of accounting for political and cultural crises of the modern era. It is also a deep, if periodically obscured, part of American experience, driven underground after 1933 and largely unacknowledged among politicians, intellectuals, and journalists until the middle 1950s. Because of its intrinsic value, conservatism demands periodic review and redefinition, not only by its self-conscious exponents, but also by those outside the tradition. This seems an apt occasion, not merely because the socialist path is obstructed and the socialist destination indistinct, but because the liberal center no longer holds. Or should I say, it no longer holds for the same reasons which have prevailed over the past half-century.

I shall not contend, however, that American conservatives possess the resources to produce convincing analyses of the contemporary crises *and* to imagine a politically sensible way out. Indeed, few serious people in this mode would pretend to offer so much more than they can deliver. Rather than attempt a comprehensive analysis of the varieties of American conservatism, then, I shall be content here to borrow freely from them, to highlight conservative caveats in the hope that warnings and reservations from this fertile tradition will illuminate, enrich, and qualify socialist and liberal perspectives. In any case, the exercise should be refreshing, for as John Stuart Mill remarked, "even if a Conservative philosophy were an absurdity, it is well calculated to drive out a hundred absurdities worse than itself."

The Forbidden Faith

Despite a substratum of habitual or temperamental conservatism extending back to the founding of the Republic, Americans have been ambivalent about acknowledging this bias, especially in recent decades. Just after World War II, liberalism seemed to have triumphed as the dominant American philosophy, ideology, and public rhetoric. In 1950, Lionel Trilling concluded that liberalism is our "sole tradition."[2] At about the same time, Raymond English, a British interloper, characterized American conservatism as a "forbidden faith," noting that nearly every prominent figure, including such men as Robert Taft and Thomas Dewey, identified himself as a liberal. Even the National Association of Manufacturers, sensing no doubt the importance of public relations in the postwar period, issued a pamphlet entitled "Be Glad You're a *Real* Liberal."[3]

It has been suggested often enough in defense of the liberal tradition that this schizoid disposition to proclaim liberal values and behave in conservative ways (and on occasion, to proclaim conservative values and act liberally) expresses the genius of American politics. It preserves our capacity to form coalitions and to effect compromises. We muddle through when the clear, hard edges of ideology threaten to splinter the body politic into hostile factions. Such arguments carried great force when the major factors of American exceptionalism—ample land and natural resources, the frontier spirit of individualism, security from foreign interference, a stabilizing two-party system, and a pervasive optimism—were in fuller play.[4]

Because there is still some urgent truth—and more than a touch of conservative wisdom—to various liberal theories of balance, the lack of a fully articulated conservative presence among a people so habitually conservative yields unfortunate consequences. It confuses political debate and narrows political choice. It weakens intellectual life, retarding the ripening of conservative and socialist ideas, and trivializing liberal thought. Thus, for an example, political figures currently espousing a moderate conservatism in tardy response to the groundswell of public opinion were taken lightly at first by media journalists and characterized with only partial accuracy as "new liberals." Proposing restrictions on the burgeoning public sector for serious economic, ethical, and political reasons, they nevertheless were dismissed offhandedly by left liberals and liberal realists as either utopians or cynics on the ground of the alleged impossibility of enacting such schemes. Perhaps these "new liberals" are in some measure both, but I think it unwise to minimize the importance and block the public articulation of conservative sentiments that have managed to become a massive force without the sanction of the national media or widespread support within the academy.[5] In fact, considering the collapse of the premise of expanding abundance which until recently lent an air of inevitability to the direction if not to the destination of liberal reform, it is simply foolish (not to mention philosophically illiberal). The most persuasive reasons for liberals to encourage a lively and self-conscious conservative presence, then, may be pragmatic.

But there are large difficulties, too. For decades, critics of all political persuasions have recognized the desirability of a strong conservative presence, including a vital conservative party. And they have delineated the obstacles to such developments. As Tocqueville noted, the democratic and egalitarian American context complicates the search for authoritative sources of continuity —a body of doctrine such as the Constitution, Christianity, or Judaic ethics *and* some equivalent of an aristocratic class fit to rule by virtue of long experience and ripened judgment. The idea of a government of laws, not men, requires both a good Constitution and essentially virtuous people. Despite their insistent attempts to establish a system of institutional restraints, American conservatives from Hamilton and Madison on have known this. But the search for wise governors has never been easy. Such recent standard-bearers of the conservative cause as Barry Goldwater, Richard Nixon, Gerald Ford, George Wallace, Ronald Reagan, and James Buckley surely do not strengthen the case for a natural *aristoi* of right-minded governors. This collection of leaders, so uneven in talent and probity, only complicates relationships between conservative philosophy and politics, adding to the confusion between reasonable conservatives and sectarians of the far Right.

Nor have conservatives devised sure tests for certifying one another. Disagreeing intensely among themselves, they debate endlessly the credentials of individuals and groups along the Right side of the political spectrum. The perpetual confusion arises in part from regional, cultural, and class differences: at least according to popular stereotypes, conservatives are drawn from (or identify with) upper social echelons. Tweedy and from the East, they are generally affluent, well-educated professionals, whereas right-wingers tend to be less educated, less affluent, more likely to be found in ethnic, urban centers and along the southern rim of the nation from Florida to Southern California. (Among those on my previous list, only James Buckley qualifies as an authentic conservative.) But these stereotypes, which never were very accurate, have come apart in the seventies, as elements of the once forbidden faith spread.[6]

The confusion arises also from the disposition to transpose the "more revolutionary than thou" gambit from Left to Right, so that, for example, advocates of lower tax rates who appear conservative by conventional standards are discredited as crypto-liberals by the Liberty Lobby that campaigns for full abolition of the federal income tax. The search for ideological purity and cathartic relief from complexity leads to a scramble for position at the right edge of the political spectrum.[7]

Though politically significant, neither socioeconomic differences nor the extremist dynamic kept in motion by right-wing ideologues accounts fully for the disorientation among conservatives. It has a deeper source. As Karl Mannheim observes, conservatives discover their idea only ex post facto.[8] Lacking a commonly accepted source of authority, tossed about by changing public contexts, American conservatives live in turmoil, constantly having to adjust vague and disputed principles to changing issues and options. Partial to the claims of tradition, conservatives in this protean culture do not easily discover a usable and defensible past. In fact, they often are compelled to defend older modes of liberalism whose dominant assumptions frequently conflict with their own. There is therefore not one conservatism but many. The phobic anticommunism of a William Buckley, whose callow early cold war response to the slogan "Better Red than Dead" was "And if we die? We die," has little in common with the concerns of neo-conservative intellectuals and such "new liberals" as Governor Jerry Brown of California, Governor Michael Dukakis of Massachusetts, and Senator Gary Hart of Colorado.[9] That the American context ensures a continuous emergence of conservatisms—different, often divergent positions on a range of public issues—does not vitiate the phenomenon. It rather challenges anyone intent upon using the tradition to recover enduring conservative styles of reflection from yesterday's conservative or right-wing pronouncements on domestic and foreign policy.

To determine what ought to be recovered, let us begin by elaborating the simple taxonomy of conservatisms advanced by Raymond English.[10]

Temperamental Conservatism: According to English, "instinctive," or what I should prefer to call temperamental, conservatism is "the profound, socially indispensable, and frequently cowardly human impulse to cling to the known and accustomed."[11] It is this and more. In its least attractive but historically crucial manifestations, this elemental conservative instinct furnishes a major source of support for personal and class privileges against what often are just counterclaims of those with less power. It also moves people with very little to cling to the known, accepting the burdens and discovering the satisfactions of relatively secure arrangements in preference to new and untested ones. The proverbial saw, "A bird in the hand is worth two in the bush," draws attention initially to the risks of change: in the quest for more, we are cautioned, everything may be lost. But habitual acceptance of the status quo out of unexamined fear of the alternatives represents only the prerational dimension of temperamental conservatism. Though reflexive aversion to change may be reasonable in many instances, it is so for insufficient reasons. Thus, instinctive conservatism degenerates easily into irritable reaction, especially in America, where the "status quo"—a relative and confusing term at best—tends to be so dynamic.

Temperamental conservatism has a more subtle and more ambitious side to it. Born of the strong, perhaps instinctive, disposition to conserve—to minimize risk—it edges toward a dialectical style of reflection: those two indistinct birds in the bush may be elaborate plastic decoys (we are well accustomed to talking dummies); they may be poisoned (paranoia is fashionable, and as sex roles become more androgynous, poison may turn out to be as American as handguns). Or upon further reflection, it may be that only the bird in hand is needed. A temperamental disposition to conserve suffuses the deliberate search for principles governing acceptance (or even pursuit) of the new, as well as grounds for resisting it. Aware of accelerating change, temperamental conservatives nevertheless approach it always as a problematic rather than a welcome relief from an oppressive past. Questioning the new as intensely as radicals examine received institutions and systems of thought, conservatives stand in a dialectical relationship to modern history, cautioning others about what may be lost in the search for better social arrangements.

Libertarian Conservatism: Temperamental conservatism, then, is the common source of more articulate political and philosophical modes. Following the fashion of intellectuals who espouse philosophical variants, English considers "economic," or what I shall call libertarian, conservatism the dominant—and virulent—American type. It is, he says, essentially "the desire to cling to one's economic privileges if one is fortunate enough to have economic privileges."[12] In its popular manifestations, native American conservatism often does sink into mere rationalization of material privilege (there are, after all, considerably more ominous shaping motives in public affairs). Among the most put-upon right-wingers—whose economic privileges may be as slight as they are tenuous—conservative clichés can be the vehicles of such ugly forms of self-deprecation as prejudice on grounds of race, ethnicity, sex, age, region (even neighborhood), and physical appearance. These crude imitations of genuine signs of status come to substitute for more tangible economic tokens and psychic satisfactions. In its extreme forms, this mode of conservatism rests on a caricature of nineteenth-century liberal images of man the economic animal, moved by selfish, material desires and constantly threatened by treacherous social forces, including oppressive governments.

In its more moderate dress, libertarian, or what might aptly be called liberal conservatism were it not an even more confusing designation, has become the dominant type for the evident reason that it expresses central American themes associated with individualism. It is in my estimation neither so virulent nor so different from philosophical conservatism as English and others would have us believe, though the differences, as we shall see, are critical. The cornerstone of this species is a libertarian stress on liberty, evident in varying degrees among the Republican Right, neoconservative intellectuals, and "new liberals." Sharing the major premises of classical liberal capitalism, most libertarian conservatives believe that a vital system of free enterprise best ensures the preservation of liberty. In this general view, acquisition of material goods (and defense of privileged access to more) may function merely as an end in itself, in which case business becomes the secular religion so often caricatured in American life and letters. But it need not: the pursuit of property often goes well beyond the Midas syndrome. Wealth may be considered mainly a vehicle for expressing human skills, talents, and energies. Or it may be regarded primarily as a means of enacting other elements of the bourgeois dream (in which case the economic arena assumes secondary importance). In any event, libertarian conservatives regard a system of private property as the central precondition to personal and political liberty.

Liberty is enhanced further by limited governmental regulation of personal, family, and local life; by full protection of civil rights; and by the guarantee of equal opportunity rather than active governmental promotion of equality of result. A classically bourgeois view of individual liberty as the absence of coercion disposes contemporary political conservatives and "new liberals" to oppose —to one degree or another—extensions of the welfare state into ever wider spheres of economic and social life, and to be nervous about the growing influence of multinational corporations.

On social and religious matters, conservatives tend to be somewhat more conventional than others, favoring comparatively stringent legal and moral regulation of public behavior. But the libertarian stress fits well enough with offbeat modes of behavior and dress, most of which are new only to those with little historical sense. (It is harder now to identify members of the Young Americans for Freedom by their appearance: they used to look like dentists, when dentists looked like dentists.) What renders their attitudes politically and socially conservative in the American context is finally the passage of time and the emergence of new institutions and new liberal attitudes which compromise older values: the rise of corporate capitalism, the growth of the welfare/warfare state, the decline of nostalgic images of community (especially the ligatures connecting individuals in voluntary groups), a shift from the norm of equal opportunity toward more egalitarian interpretations of the idea of social equality, and the quickening of the cultural drive toward individual fulfillment.

Philosophical Conservatism: This third type aims at bringing the dialectical style of reflection inherent in temperamental conservatism to maturity. Some philosophical conservatives attempt to bypass libertarian conservatism; others do not. Despite their differences, such postwar American conservatives as Peter Viereck, Russell Kirk, Will Herberg, Robert Nisbet, and Richard Weaver usually return to a cluster of related themes. They are interested above all in refining the basic problematic of conservatism—the relationship between stability and change. They seek principles for evaluating change brought about by the movement of natural and societal forces, and change sought consciously through political activity. As aware of the pervasive emphasis on novelty in modern cultures as they are moved by their disposition to question it, conservatives reflect intensely on the problems of defining limits, estimating the effects of violating them, and prescribing governmental, cultural, and individual restraints.

With its modern origins in Burke's reflections on the French Revolution, philosophical conservatism emerges as essentially a series of responses to the breakdown of traditional feudal and aristocratic modes of social organization, the entry of the masses into history (at least as partial subjects), the triumph of capitalist economy, the acceleration of technological change, and the general crisis of bourgeois culture. Indeed, from a longer historical view, philosophical conservatives may find other political conservatives embarrassing at times, though in some ways the others must seem the least obnoxious minority of the invading forces composing modern history. But intellectuals need to come to terms with popular bourgeois variants, either to demonstrate the consistency of conservatisms or, as in the case of such figures as English, to reveal the dominant American type as a disguised liberal heresy.

As I have noted, libertarian conservatives proceed from a more or less Lockean conception of liberty as the absence of external constraint. Without ignoring the problem of material, moral, and psychological limits, they conceive liberty rather narrowly, mainly as an imperative to defend individuals against collectivities. Taking a more organic view of society and a longer view of Western as opposed to merely American traditions, philosophical conservatives usually imagine liberty positively, as a function of authority.

Without legitimate social order, they maintain, there can be no genuine liberty, no vital culture, and hence no depth, fullness, or meaning to individual experience: men in this state would be little better than Burke's "flies of a summer." This mingling of positive and negative views of liberty works against philosophical consistency, but it thus far has rescued American conservatism from a strong bias toward varieties of fascism that still plague sectors of the European right. "Somehow," Russell Kirk observes, vaguely though reassuringly, "our conservative leaders must contrive to reconcile individualism . . . with the sense of community that inspired Burke and Adams."[13]

In the movement from temperamental to philosphical conservatism, we can observe the evolution of a distinctive style of reflection. Though its practitioners caution against hardening pronouncements issuing from this antitheoretical mode into theory or dogma, they do venture rough formulations. In *The Conservative Mind,* Kirk proposes six canons of conservative thought which, if we alter their form and sequence slightly, summarize nicely the dominant themes:

1. Society rests on religious and/or moral authority, which links all the generations in a continuous tradition. These are the ultimate sources of secular authority and wisdom, the bases of truth, order, liberty, and purpose in human existence. And they constitute also the foundation of moral equality and spiritual fraternity.

2. Philosophical conservatives hold to a restrained view of the character of human nature, emphasizing some religious or secular version of original sin. They stress the need for controlling baser instincts and dispositions by prescription, "those ways and institutions and rights prescribed by long—sometimes immemorial—usage."

3. Because of their pessimistic views of human nature, and their desire to preserve certain inequalities among people, conservatives assume that society requires "orders and classes." Seasoned over time, such groups produce leaders in every sphere—government, education, science, and the arts. When such an order is destroyed or seriously weakened by egalitarians who would level all distinctions, government becomes tyrannical, the plaything of despots: people yearn for public direction, and in the absence of wise

governors, they settle for strong leadership. Cultural life slackens, and variety withers as pluralism and merit give way to uniformity and mediocrity. Science may survive, but only to stage a succession of hollow triumphs.

4. "Property and freedom are inseparably connected." Property rights—including the right of inheritance—nurture tradition, establishing the material substratum for continuity among authoritative orders and classes. Moreover, in contrast to other forms of ownership, private property constitutes the surest defense against tyranny.

5. Philosophical conservatives celebrate the "proliferating variety and mystery of traditional life." They find the concrete and inarticulate elements of the past that merge into the present a far richer source of wisdom than the threadbare abstractions of rational modes of discourse which flatten history and caricature tradition. They distrust intellectuals who cut abstract systems of thought from whole—or new—cloth, and attempt to tailor institutions and people to them.

6. Finally, as a consequence of these interrelated canons, conservatives prefer slow, organic, and evolutionary to rapid, violent, or wrenching change, at least in the comparatively narrow realm of public affairs where some degree of initiative or restraint may be exercised. As Burke puts it, "a state without the means of some change is without the means of its conservation." Since the whole of human experience is complexly related, and the primary sources of constructive change lie beyond the control of any single generation, people ought to seek an understanding of what little can be altered profitably, estimate the probable social costs, and only then move ahead at a deliberate pace.[14]

Conservatism and the Crisis of Culture

In sorting out the main strands of American conservatism, I came across several of the tensions and paradoxes which critics in and out of this tradition customarily explore. Though important, these dilemmas become decisive only to those hoping to discover a high degree of philosophical consistency (or inconsistency) and an exclusive political vision in conservatism. But I am not concerned here with bringing neatness to this disordered philosophical house, nor am I interested in proposing a political strategy centering on restoration of competitive capitalism or a return to traditional social forms. I wish rather to pursue the more modest intention of suggesting what remains vital in conservative styles of reflection and conservative canons of thought.

This mode seems most valuable as a perspective on the moral and spiritual dimensions of the crisis of culture. Let me begin with three related caveats—one spiritual, one moral, one traditional— distilled from Kirk's canons. (1) Above all, the conservative vision reminds us that our deepest discontents have spiritual sources and require spiritual amelioration. (2) With their traditionally pessimistic assumptions concerning the character of human nature, conservatives remind us also of the need for balanced moral vision, a set (or complementary sets) of norms that individuals (and communities) may use to restrain passions, to discipline will, and to guide the process of forging a coherent, humane, and significant identity. (3) Finally, the dialectical mode of temperamental and philosophical conservatism persuades us to exhaust traditional sources of spiritual consolation and moral vision—in the Western instance, Judeo-Christian—before revising them, to recycle dying cultural symbols rather than attempt to catch new ones out of thin air.

These three related caveats strike me as crucial despite the several telling objections they immediately raise. Some further comment and qualification should provide an occasion to consider the most familiar reservations. My suggestion concerning religion surely appears ironic in the light of modern developments that undercut the institutional bases and legitimacy of a continuous Judeo-Christian tradition. After the triumph of the scientific outlook and the terrible political events of this century, Christianity does not seem the most likely source of spiritual fulfillment and cultural renewal, even in the West. No doubt, but I would not be so rash as to advocate restoration of New Testament Christianity —especially in its communist variants—as a dominant cultural project: it rather remains the most obvious mode available to many individuals and small communities within American society.

Still less would I welcome a convergence of theological and political spheres under the auspices of representative American fundamentalists of the caliber of Billy Graham who, if not an embarrassment to the Christian cause, certainly add little to the substance and tone of our political discourse. At the same time, it should be noted that in recent years evangelical Christianity—a broader term than fundamentalist—has become a dominant religious force in America, rivaling Catholicism in numbers if not in political influence. With something like forty million adherents from various regions, ethnic groups, social classes, and denominations (including a segment of Roman Catholic pentecostals), this gathering social force generally displays conservative political sentiments. At least it has until now, by virtue of its predominantly white, middle class, and suburban-rural composition. But millions of its adherents are serious people, who have yet to be taken seriously by cosmopolitan critics. Evangelical Christians and fundamentalists share Luther's concern with personal salvation through faith in Christ, as outlined in the New Testament. Both value the authority of the Bible over that of any organized church. But fundamentalists, who stress the spectacular miracles of the ministry of Jesus and take scripture literally, are usually more conservative than evangelicals in both theological and political matters. Many fundamentalists are simply reactionary, of course. But evangelical Christianity (and the moderate elements of the new fundamentalism) needs to be understood sympathetically by liberal and socialist critics, rather than dismissed ignorantly as if it were only a rehash of the fundamentalism of the 1920s, a social disease which Veblen labeled a collective case of "nervous prostration."

Those of us unable to believe fully must see nevertheless that Christianity presents the most complete image of hope, at least in this culture. That relatively few find it possible to accept the idea of salvation does not detract from its importance as a paradigmatic response to the deepest level of the cultural malaise and as a caveat against surrogate solutions. Christianity casts a pale light—and properly so—on the enigma of origins and endings, and on the ambiguities of history. It preserves the moral vision of Judaism and completes the spiritual longing within Judaism for a Messiah, a deliverer. Offering spiritual hope, the life, death, and resurrection of Christ provide relief from guilt and isolation, and deliverance from sin. A celebration of the idea of personhood, the incarnation of Christ permits individuals to be twice-born, to gain spiritual identity by yielding up the petty aspects of self. It admits individuals into the community of believers—the body of Christ —and establishes grounds for spiritual fraternity. Finally, by promising victory over death—the prince of terror—salvation gives spiritual meaning and dignity to life.

At the very least, then, Christianity shows us what a genuine and total solution to the crisis of personality and culture would look like. Knowing this, we can learn not to confuse the vision of salvation with pseudosolutions spun around political, social, sexual, or psychological schemes of liberation. Reinforcing distinctions among related realms that have become blurred, the conservative remembrance of the central Christian vision helps us to reject, as cruel and debilitating illusions, utopias based on a conflation of theological and political categories. Life may be impoverished vastly or enriched greatly through social activity, but the sickness unto death that Kierkegaard so brilliantly dissects—and that our less intense souls experience fleetingly, in dark, solitary moments—requires healing that lies beyond the range of socioeconomic, psychological, and political symbols and institutions. "The radical error of the modern democratic gospel," Walter Lippmann observes, "is that it promises, not the good life of this world, but the perfect life of heaven. The root of the error is the confusion of the two realms—that of this world where the human condition is to be born, to live, to work, to struggle and to die, and that of the transcendent world in which men's souls can be regenerate and at peace. The confusion of these two realms is an ultimate disorder. It inhibits the good life of this world. It falsifies the life of the spirit."[15]

Even if it is rejected, then, the Christian paradigm demonstrates the somber fact that the cultural crisis is likely to survive all attempts at full resolution. A conservative recollection of this vision shows nonbelievers that they must learn to live morally on less, if they are to live decently at all.[16] Conservative thinkers debate the question of whether justification of various modes of authority must reside in a religious vision, or whether a moral outlook alone may be sufficient. For people immersed primarily in Western traditions, this concern turns initially into a consideration of whether Judaic ethics, suitably revised in the light of Christian experience, can serve as a moral lodestar in a post-Christian culture. Critics of conservatism identify this ambivalence over religious and moral authority as a serious dilemma, a barrier to philosophical coherence, and a source of political division.[17] It is also, I believe, a fruitful ambiguity.

Even—perhaps especially—if the Christian idea of salvation lacks plausibility, the Judaic moral framework that preceded it and inhabits its theologies in altered forms ought also to survive it. Critical thinkers from Freud to Lionel Trilling call attention to pessimistic views of human nature at a crucial moment in the crisis of American culture. And they insist on the need for moral norms as a means of achieving balanced individual life within reasonably ordered communities. Some conservatives of a more fundamentalist bent hold to a thoroughly pessimistic view of human nature, projecting a mirror image of light-minded optimistic caricatures. According to this view, man is sinful by nature, ruled by passion and self-interest, fundamentally irrational, irresponsible to self and others, unchanging despite the procession of social systems and cultural contexts, and hence not perfectible. Even this stern view, which I do not share, might serve as a useful corrective to glibly optimistic images of human nature, or what is worse, to neutral images rooted in the assumption of infinite plasticity. Nietzsche prophesied the nihilistic consequences of mingling pity and contempt. And in the horror of Nazism we had glimpses of the extent to which men can degrade themselves and others. It should be clear that activity which includes the premise of discovering the furthest extremes of human nature—good or evil—must be shunned.

"Men are not angels," Madison observed, and in this lies the basis of more dignified views. Reintroducing the pessimistic voice into the endless antiphony over the character of human nature, thoughtful conservatives insist upon balance. People are both good and evil, selfish and generous, capable of reason and prone to destructive passions, cruel and kind, individual and social. Though changes in values and typical behavior do occur over centuries, we still understand the earliest philosophers, prophets, and moral teachers. And we still learn from them. There is, then, sufficient continuity in human experience to convince the most casual observer that the mixed character of people requires strenuous cultivation of the moral life. We know that the mixture of good and evil dispositions varies among individuals. Though some embody one extreme or the other, most of us combine admirable and despicable traits less flamboyantly, clinging usually to the middle range. If only because of the presence of what might be termed a damning remnant, however, strong moral (and legal) restraints have been socially necessary, and will continue to be so for the politically imaginable future.

The need for renewed emphasis on moral vision assumes additional weight in a culture whose central dynamic over the past two centuries has been the project of individual fulfillment, at first in narrower economic and social arenas, and more recently along the frontiers of heightened consciousness and feeling. As old modes of restraint loosen, and traditional spiritual consolations lapse into ironic memories, individuals seek to liberate themselves from the past, from institutions, from all structures of authority, and from the responsibilities involved in close associations with others. The full expression of self becomes the goal and measure of activity, its blurred center and circumference. In this search, as Daniel Bell observes, "there is a denial of any limits or boundaries to experience. It is a reaching out for all experience; nothing is forbidden, all is to be explored."[18]

Foreshadowed in the themes of modernist fiction, painting, and music (as well as in Genesis, for that matter), this dynamic has spread carelessly beyond the boundaries of art, which after all may exert aesthetic discipline on the chaotic materials of the modern apocalypse, investing them with form. Transposed from art to the wider culture, the quest for self-fulfillment requires a moral equivalent of aesthetic discipline that alone can lend form, balance, and proportion to individual life. Or else it becomes grotesque. Just when a moral anchor becomes the chief means to establishing a modicum of order and meaning in a larger culture shaken by multiple crises, however, many take it to be merely an oppressive weight, an impediment carried over unnecessarily from the past.

The end of this tether is nihilism, a bid for everything that yields nothing. Without a moral matrix to control the symbolic creation of a self, we are defenseless against dissolution into mindless subjects who make politically manipulable objects. There are signs, however, that this dynamic of undisciplined self-realization may be losing force. They are feeble signs when set against larger social forces, for in its extreme forms the main American cultural dynamic represents the most grotesque mutation of the still vital drives for power and profit, so powerfully shaped by modern capitalism. But as people discover once again that old sins pay about the same wages, they move tentatively toward some version of the conservative moral caveat.

The idea of restraint, self-control, and revulsion against all sorts of excess is in ascendance everywhere. It clearly lies at the center of all efforts to recast and balance the implicit cultural assumption that more and bigger are always to be considered better. We begin to realize that less and smaller often are better—and that in any case quantitative criteria are of limited use in arriving at ethical judgments. Similarly, there is a fresh sense of proportion in our conceptions of historical time. In contrast to previous exaggerations of the future that virtually excluded the past, we are beginning to respect the weight of history as it molds current options, and to regard its riches as the primary stuff of a textured consciousness. These shifts in perspective on space and time should enable a more reasoned assessment of the American place in a revolutionary world as a major nation, dominant still in many areas, but no longer in ascendance toward supreme power and influence everywhere.

With its stress on mutuality and proper proportion governing relationships between organisms and their surroundings, the conservative idea of balance informs all ecological visions. It is the basis of proposals for scaling down material expectations to fit the realities of limited resources and productive powers. It animates a series of experiments with Eastern religions, and informs a spate of therapies designed to reduce personal anxiety and restore a moderate balance between mental and physical activity, between occupational ambition and genuine leisure.[19] The conservative moral caveat adds value and meaning to private life, as people rediscover pleasure in lasting personal relationships. Based on a deepening sense of the moral and intellectual equality of men and women, family ties become more secure, or at least the value of familial bonds takes on a new urgency. And the shared role of parenting assumes fuller significance, yielding larger satisfactions, especially among middle class, college-educated men and women.

In illustrating what seem to me the seminal values of the spiritual and moral caveats of conservatism, I have resorted deliberately to a plain vocabulary, one obviously out of intellectual fashion. I have done so out of a conservative conviction that the idea of sin, as Karl Menninger suggests, ought not be absorbed into the categories of crime or disease (however often they overlap). Although moral norms change somewhat historically, and the nature and degree of offenses remain subject to fruitful dispute, the notions of individual and collective sin display remarkable consistency. Within the edges of disagreement, we acknowledge the existence of a traditional core of sins—excessive pride, unbridled sensuality, gluttony, sloth, envy, greed, avarice, preoccupation with material possessions, waste, theft, dishonesty, and violence in its many forms: war, murder, cruelty, rape, exploitation, slavery. These are plainly sins, pathologies of the soul that transgress the laws of God and/or received moral norms. The value of naming them is simply this: sin implies "guilt, answerability, and, by derivation, responsibility."[20] And its public recognition creates the possibility of confession, atonement, and reparation.

But I shall not insist on a particular mode of discourse, especially one not completely my own: in this diverse culture, people grope toward common understandings by way of different vocabularies. Calling attention to the need for moral restraint in more cosmopolitan terms, Arnold Rogow argues for a renewed cultivation of the superego, which he defines as "the *conscience and sensibility* of the Western mind, a conscience and sensibility that place a supreme value on human life and dignity, that attach importance to the intelligence of man and its ability to reason through to a right conclusion, that accept the inevitability of self-denial and frustration in private and social life, and that encourage in everyone respect for others and an awareness of the things that are *not* done."[21]

Similarly, there are more sophisticated (if less graceful and less powerful) ways of delineating the need for spiritual regeneration than the traditional imagery of Christianity affords. Commenting on the breakdown of cultural images and symbols—their loss of power, if not their disappearance—Robert Jay Lifton probes the idea of "communal resymbolization." The experience of spiritual desolation, a sense that we live precariously in the wake of holocaust—postmodern, postindustrial, post-Christian, indeed, survivors of everything—only reinforces our need to mend the life of the spirit. Lifton approaches the problem through a framework of "shifting modes of symbolic immortality" that express "man's need for an inner sense of continuity with what has gone on before and what will go on after his own limited biological existence." Exploring several paths to symbolic immortality, Lifton suggests that individuals may seek it *biologically,* through formation of families; *socially,* through creative works that survive physical death; *naturally,* through identification with nature; *transcendentally,* "through a feeling-state so intense that time and death disappear"; and *theologically,* in the idea of spiritual conquest of death.

More than a denial of death, the process of communal resymbolization aims principally at re-creation of an adult self. Whereas old people, living on the rim of death, need some immediate sign of continuity, and the young yearn for the intensity of transcendental experience, adults tend to seek more moderate spiritual reassurance. Immersed in "everyday tasks subsumed to cultural principles," adults keep the idea of individual death at a distance, often at too great a distance.[22] The spiritual, moral, and traditional conservative caveats I have proposed come together here to imply the need for a reaffirmation of spiritual longing and a cultural sanction for expressing spiritual energy that is balanced and given shape by the restraining power of a firm moral outlook—a vision of the self as a carefully fashioned sonnet rather than as sprawling free verse. Indeed, in a culture so affected by the allure of perpetual youth that stimulates all sorts of consumption designed to distract us from the facts—and pleasures—of aging, and to deceive others concerning the marks of age, such a turn toward redefining the periods of life would be most welcome.[23]

There are two further objections worth mentioning before moving along to the political dimensions of conservatism. Insofar as they discount the importance of the sociopolitical causes and remediations of public issues, the conservative caveats I have advanced may yield only a collection of pious, and hence politically distracting, hopes. Insofar as they preserve and express conventional wisdom, these caveats are not uniquely conservative.

Both objections are valid to a degree. It would be foolish to deny that a significant portion of our cultural malaise issues from the prevailing capitalist organization of production, the system of distribution, and the increasingly specialized and bureaucratized occupational structure of a technologically sophisticated society. An important fraction also may be traced to dominant, often conflicting notions governing the conduct of social and political activity. Whether brought on by the movement of large historical forces or by the conscious activity of groups, change in these realms obviously affects major cultural institutions and symbols—sex roles, family structure, schools, and the like. Because these figure importantly in the formation of personality, the quality of individual and social life depends significantly on politics, as I have assumed throughout earlier discussions of communism, democratic socialism, and liberal capitalism.

Rather than undermining the role of politics, the spiritual, moral, and traditional conservative caveats indicate a need to define political limits, and then respect them. They help us recognize the rhythms of culture as longer, deeper, and less accessible to rapid political alteration than socialists and liberals generally have assumed. It was possible, to take an obvious instance, for women to become enfranchised in a century and a half. Though consuming only a relatively brief historical moment, this battle was long and intense when measured out in individual lives. And it will take far longer for the sensibilities of women—and men— to incorporate the idea of moral, intellectual, economic, and political equality of persons as a *felt* assumption. When men and women come to live more as equals, they will encounter spiritual issues in different forms, no doubt, but the largest spiritual challenges and mysteries will remain, along with the largest moral challenges. Resolution of all major public issues probably would have a similar effect. Recognition of this fuller perspective seems to me a great advantage, negating as it does the extremes of communist utopias and a reactionary conservatism that ends in political quietism, or worse, in disquieting political activism. It reminds us that the deepest spiritual and moral aspects of the crisis of American (and Western) culture are not susceptible directly to political action and social engineering: they do not lend themselves to political solutions, however much they affect personal and public life. And it reminds us forcefully of the need to preserve, and where necessary to create, sufficient social space for individuals and groups freely to pursue their own spiritual consolations, and to define their moral resources.

It is true, of course, that the caveats discussed here are not uniquely conservative. Surely such notions are absorbed into the sensibilities of such liberal and Left literary critics as Lionel Trilling and Irving Howe, who have explored the conservative pressures in literary modernism. (Such conservative awareness, one ought to add, often saved the most distinguished critics from naive liberal and radical posturing. Beginning in the late 1930s, their commitment to the study of modernist literature helped them discover complications of social reality which others saw only later.) Though not unique to conservatism, then, conservative styles of reflection are uniquely valuable just now. The need to seek spiritual expression and discover moral direction requires formulation in terms other than the prevailing liberal rhetoric, the fashionable accents of apocalyptic discourse, and the kind of pidgin Marxism now flourishing in crevices of the academy. Moreover, the conservative reservations I have discussed express a growing public mood that affects attitudes toward elusive cultural issues and informs more precise political judgments. Anyone interested in democratic political change, then, must be concerned with the growth of conservative moral sentiments. Let me enlarge these related points briefly.

What I have termed the dialectical style of conservative reflection provides a useful supplement to radical modes of inquiry. Over the past century and a half, the habit of ideological unmasking, the practice of "ruthless criticism of everything that exists," as Marx put it, has yielded enormous advances in our understanding of social and psychological processes. But the other side of this activity needs to be remembered as well. Unless balanced by the formation of new beliefs, or the reconstitution of old ones, a stripping away of illusions may leave the critic with nothing except an abstract faith in a new social order that promises to do away with cultural crises by doing away with culture as we have known it. Such activity may destroy the "wardrobe of the moral imagination," to borrow Burke's memorable phrase.

Pushed to its limits, as it is too frequently, this critical process emits great nonsense and enforces a debilitating cynicism: the unmasker unmasks everything and is left with only the last illusion of a false utopia. Dismissing all of the past as bourgeois, merging cultural into sociopolitical categories, he grows to hate his present society, his culture, his fellow citizens, and, of course, himself. This drift into a brutal reductionism debases language and fuels *ressentiment:* marriage is perceived as nothing but a form of prostitution, education a mere mask for privilege, childhood only a form of servitude, and so on. All hope comes to reside in the thin, distended, overloaded category of liberation, of freedom considered only negatively, as flying. The quieter dialectical style of conservative reflection, with its accent on continuity—upon the concrete variety and richness of past and present life—is less abrasive. It preserves more, reminding us of the importance of spiritual and moral values, and of the need for civility, even when these overlap complexly with unjust social arrangements.

The conservative vision, then, is a useful corrective to the critical spirit of modern radicalism, though evidently not a replacement. It serves also as a ballast to the facile optimism of much of the prevailing liberal rhetoric. As we have had occasion to observe, this liberal rhetoric of accommodation became spiritually flat and morally flaccid, in part because of its unchallenged status and in part because its political practitioners and intellectual protagonists too often failed to give sufficient weight to the full range of cultural concerns. Taking the crisis of culture too lightly, they could not foresee the importance of conservatism in politically hard times. Indeed, they did not foresee leaner times at all. Promising more than they could deliver politically within the constraints of advanced capitalism—and probably more than they could deliver within the limits of any available social system—many postwar liberals were unprepared for the widespread disenchantment and cynicism that set in after the period of reform in the 1960s.

Of course, nobody came to the seventies well prepared. We might have been less disoriented, I shall propose in the concluding chapter, had socialist ideas and conservative caveats been given closer attention. But let us turn first to the political crisis, where the conservative vision also has been neglected.

Conservatism and the Crisis of Politics

Throughout these reflections—from the initial characterization of the related American crises through the discussions of communism, democratic socialism, and contemporary liberalisms—I have employed several of Kirk's canons as conservative caveats, often without articulating them fully. I wish now to bring them together and assess their value as perspectives on the sociopolitical crisis. It is, of course, difficult to keep the interrelated crises straight, since we inhabit both symbolic contexts simultaneously: leading attitudes permeate cultural and political spheres at the vague level of mood, if not so obviously at the more complex level of political movement. The moral caveat that we explored as a response to the crisis of culture offers an especially good example of such free movement. And it provides a convenient point of entry into neo-conservative views of our sociopolitical troubles.

The connections seem evident, even if the details remain hazy: observing the reordering of sensibilities expressed in the dominant cultural project of self-realization, many social commentators sense the lack of a firm moral response stressing balance, restraint, and moderation. As they become convinced of this general need, critics accustomed to imagining themselves as liberals or even as persons of the Left tend to drift toward more explicitly conservative interpretations of human nature and of the most significant cluster of social values: authority, liberty, democracy, equality, and merit. Though the confusing thickets of American ideology make the path from such critical reappraisals to an acceptable political strategy a crooked one, there has been a steady outpouring of neo-conservative thought in recent years, mainly in the form of essays in political philosophy which edge toward political statement and policy recommendations.

Much of this commentary is associated with a group of intellectuals gathered around *Commentary* and *The Public Interest.* Most of the main contributors are persons of some importance. Many fought in the political and cultural wars of the sixties, having served primarily in the academic theater. Daniel P. Moynihan, the best known member of *The Public Interest* company, has occupied high posts in the Nixon and Ford Administrations, and holds a chair in government at Harvard. Samuel P. Huntington, an editor of *Foreign Affairs,* also teaches at Harvard. Daniel Bell, Irving Kristol, and Seymour Martin Lipset, anti-Stalinist veterans also of the great ideological wars of the thirties, combine highly visible academic, intellectual, and public roles. Some of them, like Bell, remain committed to left liberal policies. Together, these leading lights of *The Public Interest* have articulated an important critical tendency in the debate over political philosophy and public policy. Rather than attempt a history or critique of this group, I intend only to borrow from their work, for it contains some of the most skillful applications of conservative caveats to the sociopolitical crisis.[24]

A number of leading neo-conservative themes turn up in Huntington's "The Democratic Distemper," the featured essay in *The Public Interest*'s Bicentennial issue.[25] Huntington sets out to link the liberal and Left politics of the sixties to the subsequent political crisis. In his view, the "democratic surge" produced an enlargement of governmental activity and a corresponding decline in governmental authority. The renewed interest in democracy brought on a distemper which threatens the governability of American society.

To rehearse the argument quickly: Huntington recalls the sixties as a time of intense democratic sentiment, an episode of "credal passion" comparable to those of the Jacksonian and Progressive eras. Previously marginal groups—minorities, students, women—

enlisted in the political ranks, changing their formations significantly. Their vigorous modes of political activity, such as demonstrations and single issue causes, were aimed primarily at enlarging the conception of equality in social, economic, and political life.[26] In response to the new politics, governmental activity multiplied, especially in the welfare sector. This "welfare shift," which Huntington regards as more or less permanent, raised expectations: those who began to receive more also came to demand more. And it upset a delicate balance between the bureaucratic, regulatory output functions of government, and the political and presidential input side.

Huntington is concerned primarily about the high social costs of the democratic surge. In his view, this surge accounts largely for the ubiquitous decline of authority in the seventies. Citing challenges to all existing sources of authority—the family, schools, churches, political institutions, business, and government—Huntington suggests that this neo-populist eruption of the egalitarian spirit adversely affected the political process: newly active citizens failed to understand the subtleties of democratic give and take. As a consequence, social forces overtaxed political and governmental capacities for response. Increased participation led to greater ideological consistency—and to polarization among groups. When the state proved unable fully to satisfy multiple, conflicting demands, large numbers of people became distrustful of the major political parties, processes, and governmental institutions. Having lost their sense of potency, people withdrew into apathy and cynicism.

Once set in motion, this pattern of unrealistic expectation and disenchantment further erodes the legitimacy of the state and of leading political institutions. Increased government benefits contribute to rising budgetary deficits and bring on endless rounds of inflation, thereby weakening confidence in the economy and adding pressures for indiscriminate growth. The decline of all modes of authority thus may end in a crisis of legitimacy: the party system begins to disintegrate; the presidency, once the principal source of major change, loses its moral authority, making it harder for any sitting president to piece together an informal governing coalition. The cycle is vicious: as the intricate play of balances that normally contributes to continuous democratic government comes apart, the rejection of authority gathers centrifugal force. Those who govern lose their capacity to elicit sacrifices from people, and social problems that seemed merely large begin to appear insurmountable.

Thus a period of democratic surge—especially in a "highly educated, mobilized, and participant society"—brings on distemper. The cure, however, does not reside in the additional doses of democracy that democratic socialists customarily recommend, but rather in a "greater degree of moderation in democracy." Though Huntington fails to offer very specific prescriptions, assuming as he does that the disease will subside more quickly and with fewer aftereffects if left alone, he manages to propose two applications of the conservative moral caveat. He reminds us that as a mode of constituting authority, democracy has limitations and hence ought to have limits. Many involved in the democratic surge of the sixties sought to brush aside the claims of tradition, talent, expertise, and experience in favor of participatory democracy as the sole mode of reaching legitimate decisions. In the process, it became evident once again that at a certain point in the ascendance of egalitarian sentiments, ends and means become hopelessly entangled. Institutions become less effective and less efficient when we forget that democratic procedures do not always serve democratic purposes.

Huntington proposes also that engagement and involvement in a democratic system need to be balanced by a certain degree of "apathy and non-involvement." In normal times, there is a useful slack in the political rope: the broad American "consensus favoring democratic, liberal and egalitarian values" works rather well so long as nobody takes these commitments too intensely. But periods of credal passion, which tighten the political rope, need to be followed by a return to moderation. Heating up, to change the figure, requires cooling down or the fragile machinery of democracy will burn out. This is so especially in America, with its unique combination of democratic institutions and its "exclusively democratic value system." As previously marginal groups move from the social peripheries toward the political center, taking up the slack upon which democracy depends, every group must practice a larger measure of "self-restraint." To extend the life of this fragile system, Huntington prescribes "a more balanced existence" —a regimen including mild exercise, surely, but long periods of rest as well.[27]

Despite Huntington's casual treatment of crooks within government, and their contributions to the decline of political authority, there is much to admire in his neo-conservative reading of current public dilemmas, and some old lessons to ponder. Complicated by the sheer complexity of social life and by the continuing realignment of sensibilities, the political crisis compels us to reassess dominant values as a prelude to formulating any viable public philosophy. Neo-conservatives contribute significantly to this process by challenging prevailing interpretations of the most important cluster of social goods—authority, liberty, democracy, equality, and merit—and by insisting on the need to make difficult choices among conflicting values.[28] They also offer refreshing though by no means novel insights into the complex relationships between values and institutional vehicles. And finally, they illuminate less sophisticated conservative moods that will affect central patterns of public discourse and shape democratic options in the coming years.

First, the problem of values. Since politics concerns itself largely with the distribution of competing and scarce social goods, the initial problem is to estimate their relative abundance or scarcity. Influenced by an acceptance of traditional moral notions, a pessimistic assessment of human nature, and a comparatively weak commitment to egalitarian ideals, conservatives generally take scarcity or relative deprivation as the essential moral, material, and psychological framework for exercises in public philosophy, even in times of affluence. They assume that there is probably not enough of any social value to go round, and surely not enough material goods, space, psychic satisfactions, or status to meet everyone's desires. Now anyone concerned with political philosophy, even in nontechnical ways, knows this, but conservatives give the point special emphasis.

These presuppositions concerning relative scarcity constitute perhaps the most important corrective to the liberal rhetoric that pervaded American public life so thoroughly in the postwar years.

Caught up in the mystique of abundance, many liberal thinkers slighted the importance of all but minimal fiscal, moral, and psychological restraints. If conservatives tended to ignore the claims of groups demanding redistribution of wealth, status, and power, liberals subordinated the idea of redistribution to the promise of more of everything as a means of satisfying as many wants as possible. Recognizing that the political crisis stems in part from indifference to the need to set limits on material and psychic desires, neo-conservatives stress the search for principles of internal—and external—restraint. Thus, for example, Huntington's interpretation of the democratic distemper proceeds from a perception of the decline of authority, and the accompanying rise of self-indulgence. And his prescriptions depend heavily upon a reallocation of duties and responsibilities based on a general resurgence of the idea of moral economy.

Authority: Although a precise and generally acceptable characterization of the notion of authority eludes conservative thinkers (as it does everyone), they have called attention to its visible decline throughout society and to the multiple consequences of its neglect by social commentators. Those who distend the notions of egalitarianism and democracy run the risk of regarding all modes of personal and institutional authority as disguised forms of oppression and repression. Such blurred vision leads to public and private effects that are disastrous. It erodes social order. It inhibits the search for principles governing legitimate and tolerable sources of authority, and hence frustrates the quest for positive notions of freedom. And it subverts the idea of merit.

Liberty: As I have implied, the conservative tradition in America is happily ambiguous in its conflicting interpretations of liberty. Philosophical conservatives tend to insist upon positive notions of liberty apprehended as a dependent function of modes of authority and legitimate social hierarchies. That is, they define freedom in limited ways, as a consequence, say, of learning to respect moral limits or of learning to accept familial authority in some spheres, and governmental authority in others. In contrast to such views derived from traditional, corporate notions of freedom, libertarian conservatives accentuate negative conceptions. Recovering seminal ideas of nineteenth-century liberalism, libertarians regard the absence of externally imposed restraints as the essential condition of freedom.[29] Neo-conservatives seek a balance, an untidy synthesis, and rightly so, I believe, for a highly mobile yet clearly stratified society requires an ambiguous mix of these central conceptions of liberty. They are theoretically incompatible and incomplete, but they are absolutely essential elements of a dialectical idea of liberty.

Democracy: Conservatives, as our discussion of Huntington illustrates, also propose useful caveats concerning democracy. Because they emphasize such multiple ways of constituting authority as tradition, expertise, experience, talent, and even wealth, conservatives of various persuasions call attention to the limits and limitations of popular democracy. Opposing simplistic ideas of participatory democracy that gained currency in the sixties, conservatives favor strengthening representative modes that reflect public opinion as it forms slowly through discussion and debate, trial and error, rather than those modes that mirror popular whims of the moment.[30] Criticizing the realities of interest group democracy, conservatives lament the neglect of moral principle that characterizes much of the political process in America, even after Watergate. They worry especially about the consequences of the condescending liberal rhetoric of accommodation that creates disturbing cycles of ideological boom and bust. By adding to the already ample stock of cynicism, this by-product of liberal capitalist democracy weakens confidence in the entire range of social values.

Equality: But the philosophical root of the democratic distemper, most conservatives would claim, is to be found in unwise and confused conceptions of equality. At least in principle, conservatives declare their faith in absolute equality of moral being, and therefore, in absolute equality before the law, equal rights to political participation, and absolute equality in the application of certain rights to liberty and the pursuit of property. That is to say, the idea of capitalist democracy in America represents an uneasy synthesis between equal political rights and a notion of equal opportunity that guarantees—and preserves—vast economic inequalities. Conservatives usually adopt some version of the old liberal doctrine of equal opportunity, defending the right of individuals to express their talents and ambitions in a competitive market, unhindered by arbitrary and demeaning social impediments. Few, I take it, would dispute the idea of equality of opportunity as a minimum notion of equality, and no one would deny the difficulties of defining it, much less of ensuring it in social life. This minimum definition serves as a point of contrast to the historical trend toward ever wider acceptance of the notion of equality of result. Although conceived frequently as a logical extension and radicalization of the notion of equal opportunity, the idea of equality of result represents in some ways a retreat from it. Equality of result—the idea that outcomes ought to be roughly equal, despite inputs, luck, quality of performance—functions as a rhetorical cover for two social facts: the unwillingness of most Americans to assume the economic, social, and political burdens of adopting full equality of opportunity as the basis of social policy, and their reluctance to bear the moral costs of clarifying the concept of equality.

Let us consider this issue more closely. If we adopt the familiar metaphor of life as a race for social goods (or even as a dash to find a quiet spot) and declare ourselves partisans of equal opportunity, as many conservatives do, the central problem becomes one of deciding what each entrant needs to compete fairly.[31] Though most people favor providing more than the formal right to enter, conservatives concerned with ideological coherence and purity oppose even public education—or they reject the need for more than minimal instruction in basic skills. Beyond such rigorous positions, however, the terrain becomes difficult. Acting principally through the state, the community assumes responsibility for transforming the formal right to enter the race into the substantive right to be equipped as adequately as possible, or as fully as possible (the doctrine of maximum feasible access). This invests a complete version of equal opportunity with the status of a de facto social goal, always to be approached, though never to be attained fully.

Instead of acknowledging the limited and ambiguous character of equal opportunity, however, we have drifted toward the seemingly more radical notion of equality of result for several reasons. First, in a free society the goal of complete equality of opportunity is theoretically unattainable. People develop new desires un-equally in an endless parade. And since desires require formulation and expression, individual differences in strength, intelligence, imagination, and a range of abilities ensure permanent inequality of articulated desires, and hence permanent inequality of both opportunity and outcome. Should all material wishes be sated—as now seems impossible—the idea of relative deprivation would persist along other dimensions, ensuring real and perceived inequalities of result.

Second, it has become increasingly clear that the state lacks the fiscal resources and probably also the intellectual and technical resources to guarantee full equality of opportunity. This is evident when we recall the vast inequalities perpetuated by differences in the cultural wealth of families that nearly all citizens wish to protect from direct incursions by the state. Thus, if the idea of equal opportunity were taken seriously, and pressed toward its full meaning, the state would need to provide every child with nutrition, medical care, and education equal to that given by the wisest and most favored families.

Third, even if it were possible, many who profess egalitarian convictions do not really favor providing full equality of opportunity because under the best of circumstances, where intelligence is fully discovered and fairly cultivated, and then directly correlated with achievement and reward (surely not our case), it leads quickly to inequality of result. Over time, a genuine meritocracy might emerge. But a social order in which each person clearly deserved his differential place would offend the egalitarian sensibilities of Americans, and deprive us of important sources of consolation. The alternative means of achieving full equality of opportunity would be to assign limited opportunities for, say, education or for access to scarce medical technologies by lot. Since this, too, would offend American sensibilities, I think there is collective wisdom in public resistance to sterile schemes for doing away with real and alleged social injustices that fail to provide for an ambiguous and indeterminate mixture of merit and luck.

The most rigorous alternative to conceptions of equal opportunity is for the entire community to furnish each child an equal start by agreeing to level down, break up the family structure, rear everyone in a similar environment, and compensate for inequalities of birth (due to such factors as the mother's level of health care and*nutrition), intelligence, strength, and ability. In this way, as Socrates noted, the idea of equality of result might take on clear significance. But few really want to charge the state with the responsibility for arranging a dead heat in every generation. And so we vacillate—wisely, though not always so fruitfully as on the question of liberty.

The conservative caveat on the puzzling social value of equality, then, ought to be this: since no conception of equality covers all cases, neither full equality of opportunity nor full equality of result constitutes an unambiguously desirable social goal. Neither goal, as Huntington suggests, can be pursued passionately for long periods without bringing on a case of democratic distemper. But neither can be ignored for long periods, or else the structure of privilege becomes hopelessly lopsided, a tendency Huntington treats too casually. Such opportunities as are provided equally to everyone need perhaps to be defended in terms of other social values. Equal political rights, as well as the right to security and dignity, and hence to some basic share of society's wealth, are based on the assumption of the dignity of personhood, and upon recognition of the partially arbitrary and imprecise character of every social calculus of opportunity and reward. Some portion of the social product, this is to say, belongs to everyone.

The conservative vision reminds us further that despite the value of equality as a social idea, there is also merit in discovering the relationships between degrees of inequality and actual differences among people—an empirical problem—and in candidly discussing acceptable and even desirable sorts of inequality. For example, we may treat victims of discrimination on grounds of race or gender unequally in order that they may exercise equal political and civil rights. Or we may favor equal access to opportunities to seek unequal rewards, and then, when rewards become too unequal, we may endorse unequal treatment of individuals and groups as a way of restoring more equal opportunity. And so on.

Finally, the conservative vision indicates that efforts to achieve either equality of opportunity or equality of result in contemporary America require interventions on the part of the state that threaten to distort seriously the balance among such other important values as liberty, authority, and merit. Both meanings of equality may be used to rationalize the vast proliferation of state bureaucracy and intervention in private life, for in America only the state, and primarily the federal government, has been able to take the lead in enforcing even minimal conceptions of equal opportunity, as the long struggle for formal civil rights and equal educational opportunities for people of all races and both sexes suggests. In theory, conservatives tend to favor as few governmental intrusions as possible (especially actions that benefit poor people), and in political practice, they probably support fewer intrusions than they ought to.[32]

Whatever decisions are taken to reduce inequality, then, ought ideally to expand the scope of liberty and equality. They ought to be compatible at least with the essential conditions of freedom—or entail only minimal sacrifices—and represent acceptable trade-offs which optimize both liberty and equality. In education, for example, involuntary busing probably should be avoided as a means of achieving racial balance, whereas vouchers that may reduce inequality while preserving choice constitute a more desirable model of public intervention.[33] Above all, the conservative vision should help us remember that state interventions affect those groups most directly whose lives are most vulnerable to its ministrations: lower income people—the working poor, welfare recipients, a disproportionate percentage of minorities—whose members presumably benefit from initiatives on the part of the state, and other inequitably taxed blue and white collar families with modest means whose children represent the leveling-down side of the equation. (In the case of busing, both groups may be drawn into battles that divert attention from the inadequacy of schools serving all working class people, black and white.) The least obviously affected are the very rich, who are subsidized through generous tax policies, and upper middle class, highly educated parents able to provide their children with the best head start, one that begins in the home. This set of advantages becomes comparatively greater as efforts to reallocate shares of a limited part of the social stock of income and wisdom by raising up and leveling down certain sectors of public education continue to produce largely unimpressive results.

This conservative reading of the dominant web of social values supplies the philosophical and ideological underpinnings for current critiques of the left liberal side of the main split in postwar American liberalism. It reminds us of the main faults of welfare liberalism and of the least attractive probable consequences of enacting democratic socialist assumptions. Having discussed both at some length in previous chapters, I will be content to summarize the strongest conservative caveats here, before bringing these reflections to a close.

First, left liberals have neglected older wisdom concerning the 7 idea of abundance. They simultaneously overestimate the chances of producing material plenty and underestimate the importance of relative deprivation as the inescapable framework of hard choices and the basis of large—and perduring—inequalities.

Second, having misconstrued the fiscal, psychic, intellectual, and moral materials at their disposal, left liberals pushed the growth of the welfare state to the edge of its useful and desirable limits in many areas. Government is too big and it threatens to become unmanageable: there are at the moment spending proposals before Congress totaling nearly $900 billion. Bureaucratic organizations charged with solving major social dilemmas tend to be unwieldy, wasteful, arbitrary, and in any case ill equipped to deal with problems better handled primarily by individuals and such mediating structures as families, local communities, churches and voluntary associations—or in some instances left alone. Nor are governmental bureaucracies in an essentially capitalist society apt to effect a significant redistribution of wealth and income. The increasing reliance on big government to bring about social ends subverts such values as liberty, and it generally distorts a balanced perception of the entire web of social values. Until the advent of ecological causes, however, left liberals advocated mere economic growth as a solution to conflicting claims, while minimizing the importance of the more realistic options of improving the effectiveness and efficiency of government, and of debating its proper scope. More important, having advocated growth, frequently on no grounds at all, they lack principles for limiting it or discriminating among its kinds and directions. And they lack also coherent criteria, institutional means, or a public mandate to redistribute additional increments of wealth effectively, as the experience of the sixties reveals.

Third, instead of enhancing authority, advocates of a growing welfare state may contribute to its decline. Their successes fuel inflation and threaten to increase economic insecurity among large sectors of the population. Their ideological pretensions, especially the current readings of popular democracy and the idea of equality of result, escalate public demands and expectations. But their performance—both the limited successes and the larger failures—creates a disparity that bankrupts political ideas, even the idea of politics, and adds to public cynicism. In effect, left liberals pursued egalitarian illusions to meet the demands of certain highly visible groups while avoiding a hard examination of the structures of privilege which made their welfare state too restricted for the poor it was supposed to serve and too expensive for the middle and lower sectors of society to bear. They went too far in proposing enlargements of the public sector, because they could not go far enough in the direction of what I shall call a conservative democratic socialism. Inadvertently breaking down the capacity for full moral response, left liberal proponents of the welfare state weaken the willingness of people to exercise voluntary restraint. And since their public solutions to social issues so frequently fail (as in the case of the War on Poverty), or worsen already bad situations (as in the instance of the Job Corps), they unwittingly raise the chances of our having to resort to authoritarian, external constraints to ensure a kind of order based more on sheer power than on genuine authority. A decline in liberty and a slackening of democracy, together with an erosion of the ideas of merit and authority, constitute the price of hitching egalitarian illusions so tightly to the star of an expanding welfare state.

In summarizing the main caveats so boldly and only alluding to the consequences of ignoring them in political affairs, I have neglected important differences among the several strains of conservatism. Thus, for example, neo-conservatives generally begin by accepting current realities—especially the long term prospect of large corporations and big government—and base their interpretations of the political crisis and their prescriptions for ameliorating it on modest changes, timely reforms. Rather than lamenting the loss of small government and competitive capitalism, such critics as Irving Kristol rush to the defense of corporations, arguing that they are neither so corrupt (and purely capitalist) as radicals imagine, nor so inefficient as some libertarian conservatives maintain.[34] Taking moderately conservative stances and seeking, above all, balanced views, these critics point out the dangers of state capitalism (or state socialism) on the one side, and the undesirable economic implications of breaking up conglomerates on the other.

Drawing on ideological reserves of older modes of liberalism, political figures such as Governor Jerry Brown of California and even such Senate moderates as Edmund Muskie are asking why liberals "can't . . . start raising hell about a government so big, so complex, so expensive and so unresponsive that it's dragging down every good program we have worked for."[35] This moderate political conservatism—or, if you will, "new liberalism"—is in part a response to popular sentiment against excesses of the welfare state. It issues mainly from the dilemma engendered by rising disparities between the costs of government and its revenues, a dilemma that establishes the framework of a new fiscal conservatism. Figures like Brown, however, also emphasize the conservative moral caveat, arguing that the dominant liberalism leads to a sort of moral vertigo—false expectations that further erode the individual's sense of initiative and responsibility. Neither the neoconservatives nor the "new liberals" thus far have challenged corporate capitalism from socialist or older conservative/right-wing points of view, though Brown periodically calls for sacrifices from the very rich and from well-paid state functionaries, as well as from less well-off citizens. His version of the "new liberalism" seems compatible with a kind of ascetic egalitarianism, a deemphasis on consumption, along with a leveling down (and up) of wealth and income, and an increase in liberty encouraged by more balanced, responsible, and restricted government.

Finally, the emergence of moderate conservatism is strengthened politically by the resurgence of older laissez-faire conservatives associated with the right wings of the Republican and Democratic parties. Here the main accent falls on the evils of big government as it moves beyond prudent limits, and on zealous attempts to regulate the private sector. (Among careless social critics and political rhetoricians, Washington now rivals Moscow as an urban center of evil.) Using a kind of corrupt Rousseauistic logic (if that is not a redundancy), conservatives on the Right suggest that government hampers free and "natural" enterprise, at times by giving unfair advantage to the largest corporations, but generally by restricting the uninhibited play of market forces. If neo-conservatives and new liberals wish to redefine the role and scope of government in order to alter trends toward an unmanageable welfare state, hard-line representatives of the far Right lobby for drastic reductions in governmental activity and spending, especially in the welfare sector, though usually not in the defense sector, or in other subsidies to the rich.[36]

These crucially important differences in outlook coalesce into what seems to me the dominant mood of moderate conservatism —a mood that is coming to reshape the contours of our political rhetoric. Should this conservative mood turn into more than a passing fancy, as I think it already has, it may be expected to redefine the range of political choice: one dominant axis of political discussion will turn on whether merely to reform the welfare state or attempt to dismantle it. Insofar as ideology loosely influences political behavior in America, these conservative limits will define choices within the new center of our politics.[37] This articulation of conservative limits should reduce the chances of a rapid democratic transition to democratic socialism, at least along the lines conventionally imagined by its advocates. Problems of transition lead back to questions concerning the desirability of socialist ends and the suitability of socialist vehicles. My conservative reading of the web of social values only highlights and reinforces the reservations concerning democratic socialism expressed earlier. Indeed, many of the conservative caveats have been incorporated into democratic socialist thought for decades: its present form, though flawed by the expectation of abundance, represents a series of conservative revisions of earlier socialist dreams. The core issue, of course, concerns how far these conservative perspectives ought to be pressed.

I asked earlier whether democratic socialism is democratic enough, whether there is enough democracy in America to bring it about, and finally, whether democracy is sufficient to ensure a good society. Let me review these questions in the light of conservative caveats.

The conservative vision suggests that democratic socialism may be too democratic in theory, and insufficiently democratic in practice: its proponents seem to rely too heavily on democracy as a cure for social ills, and as an antidote to authoritarian tendencies in their socialist schemes for reorganizing the political economy. Advocating enlargement of the welfare state despite their recognition of its faults, democratic socialists contend that the cure for social problems and political indifference on the part of governors is more democracy, greater participation. Huntington advances the hypothesis that too much involvement leads to bouts of democratic distemper. Perhaps. But I would suggest further that even if democratic socialists are right theoretically in prescribing more political, economic, and social democracy as a counterweight to the increasing size of economic and governmental units—and the expanded power these institutions could be expected to have under democratic socialism—they usually overestimate the willingness of people to devote a large portion of their time and attention to politics. Although political activity surely releases spiritual and moral energy, providing a full experience for some, it has not been the choice of enough people to ensure complete democratic control of capitalist or socialist institutions. And I see no reason whatever to predict a significant change, though levels of citizen participation may be expected to rise appreciably in the coming decades. However one evaluates the activity of the sixties—from intense to moderate, from widespread to limited, from successful to fruitless —it clearly was of a far lower order than democratic socialists recognize as necessary for the establishment and maintenance of a just society. And even this recent period of intensity yielded to a time of political exhaustion. Democratic socialists, I think, need to offer more than the conditional concession that socialism cannot prosper without extensive democracy. We know this. They need rather to entertain the probability that democracy would be limited severely under socialism, and argue their case within more modest limits.

Conservative caveats also illuminate the inadequacy of a strategy of gradual, democratic transition to socialism based on support of every left liberal scheme to enlarge the welfare state. The drift of democratic opinion into moderate conservatism calls into question all the old premises of democratic socialist politics. The idea of taking "advantage of every contradiction within the welfare state to win whatever gains are possible here and now" needs to be reassessed.[38] For the question of whether there is enough democracy in America comes down to a matter of whether the conservative content of much democratic opinion can take socialist directions, especially if democratic socialists continue to support left liberal causes as a matter of course. Thus, there might not be enough democracy of the right sort to achieve the goal of democratic socialism in America.

Finally, my assessment of conservatism and the cultural crisis suggests that the socialist emphasis on democracy and equality—indeed, the entire socialist reading of the main social values—is at best a limited response to the deepest aspects of our troubles. Democracy—and socialism—may not even be adequate to offset aspects of the cultural crisis brought on by a disparity between values and institutions: the disorientations in family structure, education, work, organized religion, and leisure. It lacks a firm vision of authority and an acceptable sense of hierarchy that Americans consider equitable.

Though elements of the conservative vision seem as vital as they are neglected generally on the Left, they comprise important fragments at most. Conservative readings of the dominant social values do not yield an attractive theory of social justice. Nor do they add up to an acceptable definition of the public interest. Taken whole rather than as caveats, none of these overlapping visions provide adequate assessments of American capitalism. And none in my judgment offers a fully viable politics of reform or restoration.

The connections between conservative values and capitalist institutions are tenuous at best. Though associated historically with capitalism—a point of some importance—modern democracy and the modes of freedom developed in bourgeois societies do not appear inseparably bound up with a capitalist organization of production. Nor do alleged links between wealth and virtue seem more secure now than they did to Socrates. Within conservative ranks, there is considerable disagreement and ambivalence on these points.[39] Kirk's third and fourth canons, which I excluded from the previous discussion, underline the need for hierarchies and classes in an orderly society: these constitute visible expressions of a deeper, internalized sense of authority. But Kirk goes on to identify private property as the sole economic basis for a just social order. Surely there are important connections between forms of ownership and freedom in society, and conservatives properly remind us of the dangers of concentrating all principal modes of economic and political power in the state. But it is by no means evident that the institution of capitalist property, especially as it has evolved in America, forms the soundest social basis for order and freedom. Quite to the contrary, as some philosophical conservatives have noticed, advanced capitalism subverts modes of social authority and order—and hence of positive freedom—through its ceaseless promotion of rapid change. It also generates a structure of power and privilege that deprives even the nineteenth-century interpretation of equal opportunity of much of its practical significance: all the efforts at reform in the postwar period have not succeeded in changing significantly the distribution of wealth and income. But conservatives who criticize capitalism do not posit very interesting alternatives: Kirk observes vaguely that in the second half of the twentieth century conservatives must resist the "idea of a planned society, through restoration of an order which will make the planned society unnecessary and impracticable."[40] He does not, however, venture to predict the shape or timing of this restoration, nor is he able to wish away the fact that some planning has become a necessary means to social survival.

Libertarian conservatives, on the other hand, posit an impossible alternative, maintaining that competitive capitalism ought to be restored on the ground that it diffuses power maximally and therefore optimizes liberty. It also promotes corporate capitalism, as our history reveals, including the large state that libertarians find so offensive. Moreover, the idea that business comprises the main arena for proving a person's moral and social worth now seems quaint—or at least incomplete in a society rapidly approaching its postindustrial phase.

Moderate philosophical conservatives such as Huntington and Kristol accept our mixed economy as a point of departure—and as a generally desirable destination. This in my opinion leads to overemphasis on the moral and political sources of what Huntington terms the democratic distemper, and to general—indeed, to overly general—prescriptions which lack complete ethical appeal. Injunctions to practice restraint and to lower expectations must be linked at some point to a clearer analysis of privilege than most conservatives have been willing to advance. What sacrifices are to be made? Who is to make them? How are they to be enforced? Even in the preliminary stages of investigation, I think this requires both conservative caveats and socialist analyses of corporate capitalism. For in addition to redistributing duties and responsibilities, and adding to their stock, we shall have to allocate income and wealth more equitably.

Conservatives who take a benign attitude toward capitalism and a hostile view of the welfare state often fail to use the insights of their tradition to full advantage. Too few conservatives establish connections between Judaism and Christianity and democratic socialism: they are compatible, at least. Conservatives too frequently slip into reactionary political stances, denying, for example, the partial though genuine achievements of the Kennedy and Johnson Administrations in civil rights, education, health, and housing, rather than granting them and then imagining ways to improve and humanize economic and governmental institutions. Thus far, conservatives have called attention to excesses of government without proposing an acceptable mean. The danger in the conservative moral caveat is that it will be used politically to squeeze the bottom one-third of society—the twenty million families with incomes under $10,000—without ever evoking a full-scale debate over entitlements. Taken whole, conservative visions can justify the most egregious forms of self-interest; they can be marshaled in defense of morally repulsive forms of social injustice, including arbitrary modes of racial and sexual discrimination.

But these manifestations of right-wing sentiment are not endemic to conservatism: they merely form one politically likely consequence of temperamental conservatism. Nor do they constitute the central political difficulties that American conservatives typically encounter. Because of their reservations concerning popular democracy and the egalitarian thrust, conservatives find it hard to develop positive domestic programs capable of attracting majority political support. Because conservative sentiments do not translate easily into viable programs, people in this tradition often seek to influence centers of decision informally. Though not entirely unsuccessful, American conservatives do tend to be frustrated chronically in their attempts to enact unpopular agendas. This creates the most subtle danger in conservative outlooks: the tendency to begin by hoping for a resurgence of faith and end by accepting a resurgence of fate. Calling attention properly to the limits of those liberal and radical notions of perfectibility that are to be approached through manipulation of people and control of the environment, conservatives easily can come to minimize the importance of manageable variables, and edge toward a kind of social fatalism, a disposition to believe, a priori, that little can be changed profitably.

They may feel beleaguered—even cornered at moments—and with good reason. In his introductory essay to the Bicentennial issue of *The Public Interest,* Daniel P. Moynihan laments the erosion of liberal democracy in America and its precipitate decline in the world. Protected by the essayistic form—which offers the leisure to collect thoughts and compose feelings—Moynihan expresses his lament with grace and moderation.[41] In his public role as chief United States representative to the United Nations, however, Moynihan vented an anger that anyone so thoroughly isolated from the ways of the world may be expected to harbor. These embarrassing public performances suggest that philosophical and ideological conservatives—in contrast to pragmatic conservative politicians—ought to restrain themselves when moved to seek power and wield influence, especially on matters having to do with foreign policy. Because they stand so far to the right on a world political spectrum, conservative ideologues (especially Christian ones who have been twice–born and ought to know better) customarily take the least defensible positions on foreign affairs.

The resurgence of political rhetoric concerning the renewed Soviet threat to global peace among some neo-conservatives and

right-wing academics, publicists, and political figures is disturbing, to say the least. Such dark pronouncements, which are accompanied inevitably by calls for larger allocations for defense, do not,
however, issue exclusively from conservative circles: the disasters
of American foreign policy have been genuinely bi-partisan ones
for more than two decades now. Nevertheless, one hears little else
than militant anti-communism from conservatives, and nothing
else on foreign policy from right-wing spokesmen (who are as
tedious and simpleminded as Maoists on this score).

Though these several reservations prevent me from adopting
any conservative vision as the basis of a dominant political outlook, they do not obscure the enormously valuable insights in this
rich tradition. At its best, conservatism is a style of reflection that
needs to be exercised continuously to prevent stereotypic vision
and political sclerosis. In a culture marked by rapid change, then,
this vision may be most useful as a perspective on the most radical,
practical possibility—which, in our case, I think, is democratic
socialism. Thus, if liberals ought to reconsider becoming democratic socialists, and democratic socialists need to adopt elements
of conservative vision, conservatives might find it profitable to
entertain socialist ideas as a balanced response to their nostalgic
views of earlier, competitive forms of capitalism—and more important, as an alternative to what American capitalism might become in the next decades if we do not take charge of its potential
directions.

5 / Crooked Paths

As long as men are poor, a poor society cannot be too poor
to find a right order of life, nor a rich society too rich to have
need to seek it.

—R. H. Tawney, *The Acquisitive Society*

Is there a crooked path? Though none seems visible at the moment, I think it reasonable to suppose that there will be at least
one—and perhaps several—paths through our present crises.
These reflections on socialist, liberal, and conservative themes
should illuminate the futility of communist and reactionary maps.
I trust that my remarks also illustrate the continuing vitality of
ideology as a central mode of social inquiry. But they cast only a
pale light on the social terrain of the present, and a still paler light
on the intermediate future. One thing, however, is evident: this
terrain surely will be rough, if not impassable. And political paths
through it will be hard and unfamiliar.

The reasons for this are plain. The collapse of the old paradigm
of unlimited plenty imposes new economic imperatives and somewhat narrower political and social options. It may be possible to
decide collectively whether to press ahead for maximum growth,
to pursue a policy of slow growth, no growth, or even intelligent
growth. But the scope of choice seems far more restricted now
than it did a decade ago.[1] Gatsby's vision of the green light has

been extinguished: the long term prospect of ecological limits, the pressing claims of other nations to more equitable shares of the world's wealth, and the need for American capitalism to make its way on a leaner diet of expensive energy all increase the likelihood that the production of goods, services, desirable space, and even intangible values will be far less than people desire. How much less, of course, is a crucial matter which concerns everyone, especially those who live below minimal standards of material decency. Whether the GNP dips by a few percentage points or grows by an average of 2–3% annually, as seems most likely, or even by 4–5% from now until the end of the century, a majority of Americans will have to strike a new balance between expectations and economic rewards by accepting the notion of limits, and adjusting to the prospect of living with less than they had learned to anticipate in the postwar years.[2]

As the idea of limits becomes a commonplace of social thought, it may add somewhat to the badly depleted stock of *civitas*, strengthening the general willingness to forgo a measure of private gain for the public interest. Far from settling hard questions concerning division of the relatively scarce supply of social goods, however, such a welcome turn would provide no more than a minimal framework for approaching them in a humane and realistic spirit. Nor would a resurgence of *civitas* take us very far toward a public philosophy that justifies old and new patterns of production and distribution. Indeed, it seems safe to assume that in the next half-century American life will be marked by continuous, probably heightened, conflict of all sorts, partly as a consequence of relative scarcity. There is ample reason to believe that the Europeanization of American politics, to borrow Richard Rovere's phrase, will proceed apace. A perceptible decline of consensus is evident everywhere—in the faltering, and increasingly ideological, two-party system, in imbalances of power among the three main branches of government, in the left liberal cast of the powerful media (an informal fourth branch), and in the right-wing bias of the military and intelligence estates (a potential fifth branch). Each of these centers of fragmentation contributes to polarization of opinion along Left and Right sides of the spectrum.

The near certainty of heightened conflict and the persistence of relative scarcity will make politics and government—the public household—even more crucial instruments for settling disputes concerning entitlements, rights, and responsibilities than they have become in the past several decades. The private sector's demonstrated inability to produce plenty on its own virtually ensures its escalating dependence upon the state as an agency of accumulation and legitimation, even though the rate of growth of the public sector must slow in the next decades. To the extent that democratic institutions can be preserved and improved, the private sector will rely heavily upon the processes of democratic politics. Whatever becomes of democracy (and its fate seems unclear at best), economic and social life will be affected more and more by political decisions. Politics will intersect personal life in more decisive ways, even though public cynicism may be expected to persist at disappointingly high levels.

Confronted with the problem of how to produce a relatively scarce stock of social goods, and allocate them fairly between the public household and private consumption, between present consumption and investment for the future, between the poles of wealth and poverty, we shall need to engage in more sustained and sophisticated exercises in the public philosophy. And we shall have to do so even in the absence of a unifying outlook or of bright prospects for establishing one. There are fates worse than diversity, and ours in any case is inescapable: whatever else can be said about American culture, only feeble-eyed or thoroughly alienated observers see homogeneity; only reckless prophets foresee it; and only fools seek it. The condition of cultural diversity, as well as the increasingly political character of economic matters, compel us to debate major social values continuously, to refine their meanings, and to discover acceptable tradeoffs among them. In an era of limits, the inherited tension between liberty and equality—difficult enough in flush times—becomes complicated by the need to consider other values that no longer can be taken lightly: order, authority, democracy, and civility. And values must be related to the complex world of institutional vehicles in fresh ways, inasmuch as the old equations between private property and freedom, public ownership and slavery (or liberation) no longer work, if they ever did. Considering the sheer complexity of such a task, we shall have to move into the future cautiously, recalling the largely negative and inappropriate examples of radical departures elsewhere in this century, as well as the uneven performance of our own major institutions. The only viable paths will be crooked ones, and these inevitably are slow.

In what ways, we may ask, is the bourgeois legacy of liberalism, conservatism, and socialism still useful in charting crooked paths? Though these reflections do not establish grounds for a definitive answer, they do, I think, permit some tentative formulations. Above all, it is important to remember that none of these orientations in itself constitutes a path, nor do they all together: only those who elect to live in delusional ideological worlds can sustain such a fiction, especially in America, where ideology has never held a firm rein on political behavior. At best, then, these perspectives serve as compasses that indicate possible ways through unchartable territory and equip us to make choices, to change course as often as circumstances require, and to endure the consequences of difficult decisions. Moreover, these ideological orientations are incomplete, vague, contradictory, and overlapping. Many find them significantly responsible for present crises and judge them inadequate as guides into a more difficult and vastly different future.

Yet they are all we have to go on in the realm of political choice, despite technical advances in the social sciences. Because their inadequacies have been the subject of intense scrutiny, we periodically lose a sense of their considerable strengths. Liberalism, conservatism, and socialism represent the bountiful resources of past experience and thought. They express our most humane moral and political aspirations. They describe our best achievements. And they offer cautionary wisdom concerning persistent utopian and reactionary heresies. These extremely supple perspectives admit new combinations of thought. And they generate conflicting orientations which evoke distress when we long for coherent direction, and relief when we contemplate the disastrous consequences of having elected a single guide toward the future at any point in the past.

Even apparent—and genuine—deficiences may be turned to

some advantage. As we think about the public realm and act politically in it, most of us choose to emphasize one perspective . or some combination of the three dominant ones. But we also must accept the limitations of each facet of the bourgeois tradition in order to appreciate the value of the whole, or else contemplate the grim alternatives of chaos or some authoritarian ideology, which represent refusals of serious political thought. Liberal, conservative, and socialist perspectives do overlap. Each is partial and vague. Each contains loose ends. And each guides individuals and groups along different, frequently incompatible political courses. But in a diverse, complex, and largely impenetrable social world that still admits some small degree of rational choice, only a tradition rich enough to entail such frustrating characteristics will do.

In what follows, I should like to press these general observations on the bourgeois tradition a bit further, and then reiterate the reasons why a conservative democratic socialism strikes me as the most sensible American direction for the next several decades.

Socialism, Liberalism, and Conservatism

I began these reflections with the intention of examining democratic socialism critically, and with the hope of defending it as the most reasonable secular perspective on the current American crises of culture and politics. Instead of drawing a straight line, however, I proceeded to construct a vicious circle. Suggesting that utopians shed communist fantasies and democratic socialists reconsider their dependence on left liberal political strategies, I then proposed that liberals entertain the option of adopting democratic socialism, and argued further that both liberals and democratic socialists ought to review their perspectives in the light of conservative caveats, only to recommend finally that conservatives might find it useful to assume elements of socialist vision.

There are, I believe, solid social reasons for pursuing each recommendation. The advent of a new era of scarcity, the emergence—or perhaps I should say, the persistence—of moderate conservatism as a main center of ideological gravity in a badly divided polity, and the tendency of the cultural impulse of self-fulfillment to spread beyond reasonable bounds, all compel people in each tradition to reexamine their most basic stances.[3] We must review and refine our various readings of major social values, reconsider our commitments to institutional vehicles, and scrutinize our usual approaches to politics. Taken literally, however, my proposals amount simply to a presumptuous fantasy of musical chairs—not merely because the players will refuse to cooperate in quite the ways I have in mind, but because serious people already engage in such activity on their own terms. This is how the entire tradition of liberal, conservative, and socialist thought sustains and renews itself, even, I think, at a time when many people have grown skeptical about the value of any ideology.

In a narrow sense, then, my proposals only call attention to what anyone who thinks about public matters in a sustained fashion does as a matter of course. But they do so, I trust, in an ultimately hopeful way. It is the essence of exercises in public philosophy, at least in our time, to borrow freely from liberal, socialist, and conservative facets of the bourgeois tradition in a search for political orientation that can yield periodic successes at most. This constant borrowing not only ensures a high level of confusion. It accounts also, I believe, for the marked degree of anxiety and irritability that informs so much debate: beyond the usual differences of interests, values, and goals that divide Americans, there is a sense that none of the basic perspectives quite fits, or that several positions on any vital question from capital punishment to busing may fit, depending upon the argumentative context, one's mood, and the considerations excluded from a crowded consciousness at a given moment.

Although these difficulties may induce cynicism, frustration, and doubt about the value of dominant perspectives—and the usefulness of the entire tradition—they need not bring on despair. Taken in a broader, hyperbolic sense, my modest proposals imply more hopeful conclusions. Liberalism, socialism, and conservatism are all reasonable points of departure. Though none is sufficient, each remains indispensable in some areas. And each interpenetrates the others to form a rich, evolutionary, and vital tradition of political thought. Let me illustrate these contentions with some examples, drawn mainly from earlier chapters.

Each of the major perspectives constitutes the basis of reasonable responses to the central problem of ideology—the need for a plausible and compelling vision of the future which connects visible trends toward various modes of economic and governmental collectivism with a growing desire for individual autonomy and a felt need for community. Beginning with liberal assumptions concerning the centrality of liberty and the largely experimental character of truth, to take a convenient example, we may derive a reasonable reading of the other principal values: political equality as an end in itself and as an essential condition of democracy, which in turn promotes equality of opportunity, modifies error, and ensures relatively peaceful amelioration of differences. This arrangement encourages merit insofar as equal opportunity prevails. And it establishes a constantly emergent if not always calm order stabilized primarily by the authority of consent. Using these central assumptions, it is reasonable for liberals to propose a defense of various modes of capitalist enterprise, and then proceed to defend a powerful state that offsets irresponsible power conferred upon individuals and economic institutions by virtue of their excessive concentrations of wealth. Similarly, we may begin with democratic socialist or conservative—rather than liberal— premises and derive reasonably coherent views of the best way to assess values and arrange institutional vehicles.

As I have observed in these reflections, socialism, liberalism, and conservatism break down at crucial points. None of them is sufficient—indeed, any one of them pursued exclusively very probably would yield disastrous results. But each remains indispensable. None furnishes materials for resolving the cultural crisis, especially its deepest religious aspects, though each contains important (if generally negative) clues to its amelioration. Every facet of the tradition illuminates major aspects of our political troubles. Take democratic socialism as an example. With their important analyses of capitalist political economy, democratic socialists expose patterns of privilege that become increasingly intolerable and socially divisive in a time of relative scarcity. They suggest that the ways of advanced capitalism systematically, perhaps needlessly, frustrate realization of dominant liberal values—and many conservative values as well. And democratic socialists offer by far the clearest perspectives on American foreign policy, which liberals and conservatives, proceeding from their capitalist premises, have botched so thoroughly throughout the postwar years. In a world turning rapidly toward various forms of socialism, liberal and conservative observers could do worse than consult socialists who retain their commitment to democratic norms without sacrificing their appreciation of the high aspirations and narrow options confronting people throughout the second, third, and fourth worlds, and in much of Western Europe as well.[4]

Similarly, the related conservative traditions in America have been a source of insight into obsolete liberal projections of economic plenty and the inadequacy of liberal assumptions about the capacities of a growing, beneficent welfare state to meet nearly all needs. Reminding us of the importance of tradition and the costs of precipitate change, philosophical and neo-conservatives stress moral vision above all. They have argued steadily the need to establish a fresh balance between rights and entitlements on the one side, and duties and responsibilities on the other. Whereas democratic socialists (and to a lesser extent, liberals) advocate some redistribution of wealth and political power, neo-conservatives generally support redistribution of responsibility in order to shore up the neglected values of personal liberty, authority, and merit.

In the previous chapter, I suggested that we might have come into the seventies somewhat less disoriented had socialist ideas and conservative caveats been given closer attention over the past forty years. But liberal perspectives are important, too. Though I have concentrated on the liberal default throughout this study, it should be remembered that a society characterized by multiple points of view requires a liberal conception of truth; the liberal values of tolerance, free inquiry, and free expression; and the liberal matrix of representative democracy operating within a constitutional framework. One might go so far as to suggest that a large socialist or conservative presence can be tolerated only in an essentially liberal society. Both socialist and conservative perspectives tend to deliquesce into varieties of authoritarianism unless permeated with liberal values, as socialists of democratic persuasion and conservatives of liberal persuasion have insisted for many decades.

In the American context, of course, the excesses of liberalism—not those of conservatism and socialism—thus far have provided the largest cause for concern: liberals, after all, have virtually owned the ideological atmosphere and the political turf for the past half-century. Yet within the ambience of liberal procedural assumptions, which a vast majority still accept or at least grudgingly abide by, there has been a fruitful interpenetration of socialist, liberal, and conservative outlooks. Current varieties of democratic socialism have been shaped decisively by liberal values. And as I have implied all along, socialist values are being reshaped once again by conservative caveats. Each facet of the bourgeois tradition continuously modifies and enriches the others. Elements of socialist vision regularly supplement left liberal perspectives. The dominant strain of American conservatism, which I call libertarian with some hesitation, incorporates key assumptions of nineteenth-century liberalism. And "new liberals" borrow freely from conservative and left liberal repertoires.

Taken together, these commonplace observations indicate the enormous strength of the bourgeois tradition of socialism, liberalism, and conservatism even as we approach the edge of what promises in many ways to be a postbourgeois age. A full sense of the range of our political thought and its dynamic possibilities will be necessary for the impending debate over the directions of American society and culture. This sense of range may serve first of all as an antidote to widespread cynicism about the value of political discourse and its relevance to the possibilities for public action. Of the many sources of cynicism among intellectuals and among wide sectors of the population, none is more potent than the basic rhetoric of exposure—the construction of ideological notions followed by continuous revelation of the large disparities between aims and performance, aspiration and achievement. Taken too simply as a dominant habit of thought, this important pattern of ideological acceptance and debunking leads to a debilitating form of antiintellectualism often practiced by intellectuals —namely, a refusal of serious political thought which erodes confidence in received traditions and renders them useless, except as dispiriting caricatures.

Ironically, then, cynics begin by misusing the only ideological traditions capable of renewing serious political thought and secular hope, and quickly become unable to use them in any constructive way. By recognizing merits and deficiencies in each facet of the bourgeois tradition—and accepting the lasting strengths as well as the limitations of the whole—we may minimize the disposition to become cynical. And we may begin simultaneously to define the terms on which public debate needs to proceed. The obvious failure of liberalism, socialism, and conservatism as separate guides to the creation of a just society does not imply that these old categories have lost all meaning and utility. Nor does the even more unnerving recognition that each perspective harbors internally conflicting values which may never be resolved or enacted, considering the narrowing options in the social world. They rather confirm the need to discover new, more complicated combinations by recycling ideological materials at hand.

Instead of abandoning old labels, we must break them down and use differentiated versions of notions implicit in the dominant tradition. The idea of abundance, for an example, is rapidly giving way to a paradigm of relative scarcity in the ecological and economic realms. This also directs our attention once again to the importance of the ideas of economy and restraint in moral and political affairs. At the same time, the notion of abundance may remain preferable in other areas. We can love one another generously. We can enlarge the dimensions of status and achievement and hence bestow merited praise more lavishly. There is an abundance of human energy: though oil and coal may have to be husbanded, the stock of raw human intelligence should continue to rise under the impact of relatively high birthrates, improved medical care, better standards of nutrition, the spread of secondary and higher education, and the like.[5] When invoking conservative caveats under our new conditions, then, it is not necessary to do so across the board, and in a tight-lipped spirit.

Even in the realm of economics, we may pursue growth in one sector while opposing it in another, favoring, say, more social services to raise the general level of health and education, and fewer plastic goods; or more expenditures to conserve resources and improve the environment, and fewer military ones ($1500 billion in military spending since 1945 seems a high figure on any calculus of danger). We may be conservative on fiscal matters, liberal on civil rights, and socialist on the issue of distributing

wealth. Or we may divide the available possibilities further, taking conservative positions on some fiscal matters though not all;
taking liberal stances on most civil rights issues without favoring
either free access to handguns or excessive judicial leniency toward incorrigible criminals. And so on. It is possible to embrace
the liberal (and socialist) metaphor of linear progress without losing a conservative sense of the circularity governing the most
fundamental rhythms of life.

The price of such strenuous activity includes more sophisticated
public debate. It requires also a willingness to live with greater
ambiguity, and a capacity to tolerate more intense disagreement
and confusion in the public realm than we have been accustomed
to. We must be willing to think (and do) more to achieve less—
as individuals, as members of multiple interest groups, and as a
whole society. This stoic realization compels us to expect as a
matter of course large discontinuities between the complexities of
individual vision and the comparatively simple political choices
that emerge from the collective process of analysis and debate.
And it compels us to adapt to a greater disparity between the
relative simplicity of individual perception and the actual intricacies of social processes. Finally, the new contexts of public debate
demand of us the courage to give up what now appear overly
ambitious illusions of older variants of socialism, liberalism, and
conservatism without relinquishing their capacity to help us continuously redefine the productive tensions between aspirations
and performance in every important dimension of social life. Otherwise, unqualified values will become ever more irrational factors
in political debate. Though high, the price of exercises in public
philosophy comes to less than the costs of accepting naively obsolete ideological versions of socialism, liberalism, and conservatism.
And it comes to much less than yielding to the costs of apocalyptic
and utopian fantasies, or lapsing into a cynicism engendered by an
inability to agree upon a single public philosophy.

Socialism with "the Old Crap"

It is important periodically to appreciate the value of the bourgeois tradition as a whole—its achievements, limitations, poten-

tialities, and grim alternatives—even if no individual can claim to understand fully either its intricacies or those of its opaque referent—the entire social world. But we should not neglect our responsibility for tending the several parts of the tradition on this account: if we do, various argumentative webs will come apart under the combined weight of events and new insights—as they must in a culture of rapid change—without being rewoven into more convincing designs. This labor is endless, but the exercise is beneficial, and the results, though inefficiently achieved, are often salutary. In the course of these reflections, I have included my own preference for the democratic socialist facet of the bourgeois tradition.[6] Despite many reservations concerning socialist readings of the interplay of values, the dubious character of socialist vehicles, and the flawed political strategy of an essentially peaceful transition elaborated on the expectation of nearly limitless abundance, I believe that a democratic socialism which absorbs the major principles of philosophical liberalism and the telling spiritual, moral, and traditional conservative caveats offers the most humane guide to the American crises of politics and culture in the opening decades of our third century.

This is not an easy position to maintain, considering the usual verdicts on the historical fate of conservative revisions of democratic socialism. In the *Communist Manifesto,* Marx and Engels flatly dismiss the possibility of "bourgeois socialism" as naive, suggesting that the "socialistic bourgeois want all the advantages of modern social conditions without the struggles and dangers necessarily resulting therefrom. They desire the existing state of society minus its revolutionary and disintegrating elements."[7] Though this formulation is too simple, we should be wary of any temptation to substitute a desire for social peace and progress for unrealistic projections of them. Neither Metternich, the *"socialiste conservateur,"* nor a succession of modern socialist reformers have registered smashing political successes, especially in America. No group on the Left has. Though some American socialists have absorbed conservative caveats into their outlook, many cling to older, more rigid formulations. Those who work mainly within conservative traditions usually bristle at the idea of taking socialist options seriously. And there remains considerable coolness toward such a notion among a decisive majority of citizens.

Still, the idea of a conservative democratic socialism strikes me as on the whole preferable to other American alternatives. It is certainly preferable to unrevised versions of socialism held by various left-wing sects. Its roots in the intellectual tradition of Christian socialism help to clarify facets of the cultural crisis.[8] — Though unconvinced that this clumsy name will catch political fire, I believe that conservative democratic socialism should be at least an important element in the looming debate over public philosophy in America. Suitably revised in the light of contracting material options and the increased importance of the polity, its leading themes may even figure crucially in the next decades.

To illustrate this contention briefly, let us return to the central ideas of rising prosperity and democratic demand which commentators from Marx to Harrington have taken as preconditions to a mature socialism in technologically sophisticated nations. More than a century ago, Marx predicted that without abundance, "one can only generalize *want,* and with such pressing needs the struggle for necessities would begin again and all the old crap would come back again." In his attempt to redeem the socialist past by projecting it onto the firm ground of an abundant future, Michael Harrington invoked Marx's admonition once again in the early 1970s.[9] The absence of either abundance or democratic demand, it has been claimed widely, nullifies the promise of modern socialism to reconcile the escalating claims of individuals to the old dream of community. Abundance has remained the connecting tissue.

This assumption of impending plenty bends democratic socialist thought in curious directions, which, over many decades, have established certain blind spots. Rising productivity, most socialists have contended, forms the material basis for greater democracy. This second precondition of democracy permits a rise in the popular demand for socialism. Taken together, these preconditions provide a point of departure that leads democratic socialists to base their short and even medium range strategies on a left liberal politics designed to augment the welfare state. Despite strong ambivalence about the immediate value of the welfare state, and doubts about its compatibility with socialist ends and institutional means, democratic socialists have consistently followed the logic of their argument along a tortuous political route.

I have argued that disintegration of the paradigm of abundance turns this difficult path into an obstructed one. Suppose, however, that we begin with the more plausible assumption of relative scarcity as the framework for any American version of socialism —not, of course, the sort of misery that concerned Marx and Engels in the early 1840s, but a lower degree of material productivity (under advanced capitalism or democratic socialism) than Harrington and others in this tradition have assumed would be the case. This now seems not only a necessary assumption but perhaps a salutary one as well. For it encourages us to consider a number of old and new lines of inquiry in a more concerted and less self-conscious way. Beginning with the hypothesis that only a return of relative scarcity can bring us collectively to a serious encounter with socialism by establishing conditions for an implosion of moral energy and a focused perception of choices, we could reassess major social values, modifying them in the light of conservative caveats, and adopt a more experimental attitude toward institutional vehicles than socialists usually have advocated. Moreover, this could be done in a fresh spirit of inquiry, not in one of disappointment where every revision seems somehow a concession to grim realities and a departure from communist purity. These reconsiderations in turn should allow a new look at received strategies of transition. And they should suggest wider political options than now appear to exist. In any case, such a departure from orthodoxy seems worth a try, for if there is to be a decent democratic socialism in America, I think it will contain a good deal of what Marx calls the "old crap." Let me illustrate this contention without making any pretense of exploring the issues exhaustively.

Values: If there are to be fewer scarce goods to go around than most of us assumed until only recently—if, indeed, many groups already feel the pinch with varying degrees of pain—then the question of entitlements and the problem of distributing sacrifices becomes a public issue of more than usual importance. The general consequences are evident. Discussion at all levels takes on greater intensity as the scope of apparent choice contracts and the material costs of bad philosophy rise. Thus, people move in two directions at once: first, toward a reconsideration of first principles

—general examinations of such major values as equality, order, authority, democracy, merit, and social justice; and second, toward more precise, textured, and sophisticated articulations of the differentiated and interrelated meanings of the general values in the present circumstances of American life.

Neither consequence of scarcity is novel: Aristotle and Socrates distinguished among kinds of equality and modes of liberty, as have all the other major and minor political philosophers in the Western tradition. But renewed emphasis on difficult tradeoffs engendered by the decline of the idea of abundance alters the terms on which socialists may contribute fruitfully. Reassessing the socialist idea, Leszek Kolakowski concludes that people in this tradition share general values but lack the hard knowledge to prevent clashes among them in social life.[10] I think Kolakowski steps too casually over prior questions of value. The advent of relative scarcity implies inevitable clashes among such general values as equality and liberty that no additional knowledge of social forces can forestall. Indeed, further knowledge will be necessary merely to avert clashes that may split the polity into warring factions and bring on an overtly authoritarian regime.

The new paradigm of relative scarcity should convince serious socialists that choices among social goods will be more difficult to arrive at and defend than even the most pessimistic commentators previously supposed. Since the old safety valve of a postcapitalist future marked by abundance has been shut off, it is no longer plausible to attribute present injustices *merely* to unfair patterns of capitalist distribution or to inadequate and wasteful modes of capitalist production. Nor is it plausible to base hopes of equity largely on a future promise of plenty under a rationalized capitalism or a rational socialism. Neither the old socialist criterion, "from each according to his ability, to each according to his work," which sanctions the work ethic, nor the communist criterion, which only loosely relates voluntary contributions based on ability to free consumption based on need, constitute adequate principles of distributive justice. Both may be necessary. Neither is sufficient.[11]

But our new conditions and prospects create unprecedented opportunities for socialists with something to say. By highlighting doubts about the justice of capitalism, the demystification of visions of abundance augments the potential appeal of certain socialist biases concerning more equal distribution of wealth, income, and power. The number of people who still perceive a close fit among individual ability, opportunity, perseverance, and the structures of reward under capitalism dwindles each year, as the numerous polls on public confidence in the leaders of American institutions indicate. And I see no reason to expect other than a persistence of the crisis of legitimacy in the near future, however much surface opinion fluctuates in response to dramatic public events and to rapid swings of the business cycle. Socialists conceivably may benefit from this trend toward pessimism, though I do not regard advancing it an appropriate political goal: disenchantment fills the air now, and too much of it only reinforces the vicious cycle of cynicism which may yet undo us all.

Socialists should rather contribute positively by participating in the national reexamination of basic values and specification of particular meanings. A large part of this agenda consists merely in ordering explicit meanings and articulating various implicit meanings we now assign to general values. The harder task is to supply good reasons for continuing present practices or changing them. But the full value of a distinctively socialist presence will be measured in terms of a willingness to take intellectual risks (and political gambles). There must be a disposition to modify old readings of values—in some cases, to adopt discarded ones—and back away from simple formulas. Since I have indicated in previous chapters that a contemporary rereading of socialist values in the light of conservative caveats seems the most sensible direction, let me offer only a general summary here, along with a few suggestive examples. Indeed, conservative revisions are aspects of a recurrent historical process, as indicated by the separation of democratic socialist from communist values, a complicated transaction which has taken up more than a century thus far. Though a contemporary conservative realignment of socialist values appears under way in America—at least among careful socialist thinkers—it should assume added clarity, force, and direction when pressed self-consciously within the paradigm of limits, and the attending strictures this imposes on exercises in public philosophy.[12]

Conservative revisions of socialist readings of the dominant cluster of social values accentuate the need for balance and moral economy. Such revisions may begin anywhere, but a usual place is with a reassessment of the idea of equality which some socialists and many critics of socialism regularly push into exaggerated shapes. In examining the conception of equality, it is necessary to bear in mind the multiple kinds, such as equality of being (or the equal right to political and civil liberties), equality of opportunity (or access), equality of outcomes (or result); and then to delimit the range of important inequalities, from natural differences in age, sex, strength, temperament, and intelligence, to conventional disparities of wealth, power, and status. Though these natural and social categories overlap in complicated ways, their approximate separation advances inquiry into inequalities which should—or must—be endured, and into those in need of redress. The next step consists in elaborating specific socialist critiques, especially of social inequalities based directly on unearned wealth (say, large inheritances), but also of inequalities of income that confer excessive power on the haves and, especially in a time of relative scarcity, deny the have-nots a fair chance to participate in public decisions and to lead a decent life marked by a guarantee of security, adequate diet, food, clothing, housing, medical care, education, useful work, and refreshing leisure.

Certain modes and degrees of inequality are intolerable because they prevent enactment of the vital senses in which people ought to be more or less equal—for example, the equal right to a secure life and the equal right to live well. But rights to basic equality and liberty also entail responsibilities, a side which some socialists have neglected on the grounds that those with systematically abridged rights owe little or nothing to the present system. If everyone is entitled to a *minimal* standard of life, everyone also must be responsible, insofar as he or she is able, for contributing some useful service to the community. And the community— primarily the public household in our present case—has charge of establishing opportunities to participate and of enforcing penalties for refusing to do so. Moreover, both liberty and equality entail other restrictions; or rather, different liberties and different dimensions of equality carry specific restrictions. In a world of scarcity, one person's equal right to a minimal standard of living may compel another to forgo the liberty of amassing—and transmitting —a great fortune.[13] This does not mean that liberty and equality cannot be expanded simultaneously in some areas, as socialists always have hoped. It does suggest, however, that in order for both to be optimized we may need to socialize the scarcest material resources. That is to say, we may need to call upon the state to distribute a basic portion of wealth and income far more equally, and then develop genuinely meritocratic criteria for allocating the rest.[14]

In the American context, tradeoffs between liberty and equality are becoming more complex. Entitlements to less unequal rewards and liberty cost more, and the price surely will rise. Moreover, ratios of exchange are harder to agree upon, especially if we reject the supremacy of the economic marketplace as final arbiter of a person's capacity for making money, of his intelligence, ability, perseverance, and luck—and thereby his entitlement to consume, in some instances, to consume conspicuously while others go without necessities. Hence, in the absence of a small, easily identifiable caste of governors possessing wisdom and espousing acceptable norms—or even just ones—we must rely more than ever on democracy as the chief mode of arriving at provisional social truths and values, and of resolving conflicts in a relatively peaceful fashion.

Representative political democracy rests on periodic consent, especially the right of the people to elect and dismiss public officials. But legitimate consent requires intelligent participation. Such participation, of course, presupposes an equal right to enter into public affairs, though not a right to equal influence. This right of entry reinforces the need to ensure fair terms of entry—the preconditions to a secure and decent life for everyone. And it demands vigorous efforts to reduce arbitrary concentrations of power that render participation by others virtually hopeless. Democracy presupposes further a degree of order which derives largely from the authority of continuous consent, but also from a hierarchy of other kinds of authority rooted in talent, ability, virtue, and demonstrated achievement.[15] Without a considerable stress on merit—which entails a widening of equal opportunity for its discovery and cultivation, and allowances for its consequences in the form of some inequalities in income, position, status, power, and influence—there can be no judicious balance within the cluster of democratic socialist values. And there can be no socialist theory of distributive justice, or at least none with potential appeal in the American context.

Each of these values, then, is an end in itself. Each is dependent also upon the others for its justification. And they all ultimately arrange themselves into an implicit theory of justice. Moreover, in an era of limits, the whole cluster requires conservative tempering if the several values are to be realized as completely as possible in social life. Whether a tolerable balance can be achieved through socialist vehicles is, of course, the next question. In any case, there seem immediate advantages to pursuing this conservative range of readings. Conservative revisions can reduce public objections to exaggerated formulations of socialist ends which have become materially impossible in addition to remaining morally repugnant to a majority of Americans. Their acceptance by people on the Left can help to deprive right-wing ideologues of an unearned and specious moral cover for their reactionary sentiments. Finally, conservative revisions should bring democratic socialist values closer to the mainstream of American values, and hence closer to the mainstream of democratic politics and public policy.

Vehicles: The problems are even stickier here, and the socialist alternatives to present arrangements less obviously desirable, so it is not surprising to find older radical formulas giving way rapidly to more experimental attitudes. I would propose only that socialists now take a fully experimental attitude toward institutional vehicles. The minimum conception of socialism as public ownership and flexible planning—and the corresponding elimination of private ownership of decisive industries and the market—has long since been discarded as a sufficient guarantor of a humane social order. Neither public ownership of industries and services nor the introduction of indicative (not to mention command) planning constitute desirable goals in themselves. Both may compound the potential dangers in excessive concentrations of economic and political power. Their value in any case is relative. It rests in part upon the degree to which public ownership and planning can be used to facilitate major socialist values, especially the reduction of excessive concentrations of wealth and poverty, and the democratization of decisions concerning production and apportionment of goods, services, and other values. But only in part: in the best imaginable circumstances, socialist modes of ownership and planning seem more flawed than ever.

Indeed, powerful critiques of received notions of institutional vehicles have led many to wonder whether public ownership of the crucial means of production and planning are even *compatible* with socialist values. Democratic socialists have argued regularly that social ownership and democratic planning (rather than mere public ownership and command, or even indicative planning) ought to be the principal long term structural aims. Though vague, such formulations express the democratic intent of replacing modes of capitalist ownership with a variety of other forms, and of deepening democracy as a counterweight to new and potentially unjust shares of power that surely would collect at the highest levels of government in the absence of a strong private sector.

We need even more supple approaches to the problem of forms of ownership. In America, a variety of such forms seems the most realistic, and perhaps the best hope. Considering the dominance of large corporations (and their alliance with powerful sectors of organized labor), I think it wiser and more realistic to work toward further democratization of power and redistribution of wealth through a multiplicity of schemes of ownership and control than to favor dismantling this essential economic infrastructure under the auspices of the state. Among the most obvious possibilities are profit-sharing plans within various enterprises; the extension of employee-owned pension funds throughout the private sector; a larger measure of employee democracy within corporations; public representation on corporate boards; flexible planning of such major factors as resources, income, profits, and investment conducted by blue ribbon, quasi-independent public panels; urban and rural cooperatives; a stronger small business sector to offset the power of what Galbraith calls "the planning system"; and introduction of competitive public enterprises.[16] Employed in varying combinations, these modes of ownership and control might have the cumulative effect of gradually redefining those property rights which now contribute most to inefficiency, ineffectiveness, and gross injustice in the economic, political, and social spheres. Such redefinitions might effect gradual redistribution of wealth and power without risking serious erosion of liberty by concentrated state or corporate control.

There is reason to believe that a fairly rapid introduction of mixed modes of ownership and control would be supported by large numbers of Americans. According to a national poll conducted by Peter D. Hart Research Associates in August 1975, 41% of Americans favor making "major economic adjustments" and trying "things which have not been tried before"; 37% advocate minor adjustments; and only 17% wish to maintain the system as it is and allow it to "straighten itself out." Two-thirds would support a program of employee ownership of the majority of stock "in the companies for which they work." A similar percentage of those polled also believe that people "don't work as hard as they could, because they aren't given enough say in decisions which affect their jobs." Coupled with the collapse of an older faith in private ownership as the only acceptable mode, these results suggest that a democratization of economic functions, including some forms of social ownership, has become a major item on the American agenda.

But balance among vehicles will be the key to any American socialism. In the Hart poll, 81% opposed the traditional socialist idea of "government ownership of all major companies."[17] Peter Drucker adds to the case for balance, arguing that we are drifting into a kind of socialism primarily through changes in the private sector rather than through a political movement to institute full public ownership. Drucker notes that through their pension funds, "employees of American business own today at least 25 per cent of the equity capital in American business." Public employees own another 10%, and in a decade workers in both sectors may hold at least 50%.[18] As in the case of public ownership, employee ownership through pension funds does not resolve the critical problem of control. But it does establish another sort of opportunity for economic democratization, which suggests that a workable democratic socialism in America depends upon a mixture of vehicles of ownership and control in both the state and independent (or private) sectors.

Relative scarcity and malfunctions in capitalist economic mechanisms make socialist biases concerning production and distribution more relevant than ever. And the growth of state interventions in the economy—as well as the imminent introduction of large scale, noncoercive planning—bring socialist vehicles into the center of our public life, somewhat ahead of public opinion. It is part of the critical responsibility of socialists to indicate and even predict misuses of these tools, for now that socialist proposals concerning ownership and planning fit into the mainstream of American political thought, they are liable to expropriation by people intent on using such vehicles to pursue other ends. But such criticism of proposed reforms needs to be tempered by realistic estimates of political options within American capitalism, and especially by a more modest view of the medium range possibilities of socialism than even the most chastened socialists have been accustomed to taking.

Socialist contributions to experimentation in the area of political economy can be most significant when we do not regard the modalities of mixed ownership merely as stopgap measures along some path to a fully socialist society, whatever that might mean in America. Thus, for example, in his appraisal of stances toward American planning and further government involvement in the economy, Harrington concludes that democratic socialists ought to oppose public ownership "when it takes the form of simply socializing the losses of a given economic function and privatizing the profits. Positively," he goes on to suggest, "the counterproposal should urge that the entire function be nationalized—that all of the railroads be taken over, for example, or that health care be financed publicly, through income tax revenues, and not by means of a private, corporate intermediary."[19] Well, perhaps. But not on the grounds that such a step brings full socialism closer. Counterproposals should depend upon the circumstances, the estimated consequences, and the available alternatives. It may be wise to nationalize all railroads—for this would add somewhat to the balance of mixed modes of ownership in transportation—but it would be an unmitigated disaster to nationalize health care completely. Similarly, however desirable it may be to press for a strong public sector within broadcasting, it would seem reckless to advocate nationalization of the entire industry rather than extend limited public assistance should one of the major networks fall into serious financial trouble.[20] Once a major social function is wholly nationalized, only a massive and costly failure can lead to reversal of the process.

Harrington, of course, knows the risks well, but remains willing to run them, with the proviso that democratic safeguards accompany all transactions of this sort. This, of course, is the catch, as I have argued throughout these pages. Regarding economic collectivism as inevitable in any event, Harrington believes that only full socialization of such functions can prevent it from becoming authoritarian. I think we should rather entertain the more moderate probability that the convergence of many tendencies toward collectivism—further interpenetration of economic, political, and governmental spheres, and large scale planning—will contain both authoritarian features and democratic possibilities, regardless of the dominant form of ownership and the dominant mode of political control. If this is a more realistic, though hardly less vague, expectation, we might do well to regard mixed and varied modes of ownership as permanent possibilities rather than as arrangements to be endured until the entire economy can be socialized in democratic ways. Though untidy, such a mixture of forms of ownership may be most conducive to an optimum balance among socialist values—and to an optimum balance among liberal and conservative values as well.

The Problem of Transition: One thing leads to another. Conservative modifications of values, and an even more flexible approach to the vehicles of ownership and planning in the light of the new preconditions of relative scarcity, open the way for reexamination of the dominant images of transition and the customary political biases of American socialists. Though such speculative ventures may add to the current swirl of confusion on the Left, they strike me as on the whole well worth pursuing.

As nearly everyone now concedes, any transition to democratic socialism in America will be longer, more difficult, and more circuitous than was assumed even a few years ago. And the destination seems less fully imagined than ever. The only difference—and it is a crucial one—is that a modest form of socialism now seems a genuine political possibility in America. If these assumptions are

correct, many of the received images of transition—and their at-
tendant difficulties—need to be recast. Most of them should be
abandoned. For more than a century, socialists have worried about
the problem of establishing some political and moral consistency
between a politics of the short run and an overall strategy for the
long haul. This desire for consistency is evident in the debates
between proponents of reform and advocates of revolution. In
America, this old debate seems resolved, or perhaps it is only
inactive for the moment, until a new quorum of "revolutionaries"
stirs up the issue once again. But the difficulties of reform as a
strategy of transition remain in effect. Despite the problems and
uncertainties of such a politics—slow progress and potential inconsistencies between immediate goals which strengthen unjust
elements of capitalism, and elusive structural reforms which provide momentum toward socialism—democratic socialists have favored reforms steadily. And as I suggested earlier, they have clung
to a strategy of progressive enlargement of the welfare state
through a coalition politics aiming at alliances among working
people, minorities, women, students, the underclass, and middle
class professionals.

Though disagreeing about the feasibility of an independent socialist party, most politically astute democratic socialists favor
using the left wing of the Democratic party (along with a politics
of radical pressure) in the absence of a viable alternative. But I
have argued also that this left liberal connection has frayed badly
over the last decade, and further, that the prospects for a majority
coalition disposed favorably to left liberal programs seem uncertain, considering the complexity of present issues and options:
disillusionment with politics and government; the likelihood of
greater relative scarcity, especially in the public sector; the near
certainty of continuous inflation; and the consequently wider divisions of immediate interest and opinion among, say, trade unionists, the underclass, and public employees that pull elements of the
imagined coalition in diverse directions. In a context of relative
scarcity, there is a seemingly permanent tension between the political goal of a full employment welfare state and organized labor's economic objective of increasing wages through free collective bargaining.[21] New coalitions nevertheless are taking shape,

and old ones are being reworked. But if they are to include crucial elements of labor—and they must—they need to be organized around such traditional liberal themes as full employment through policies to stimulate reasonable growth in the private sector; honesty and efficiency in government; and a comparatively narrow range of governmentally administered social benefits that cover all people. New coalitions must stress conservative caveats, especially as these illuminate such cultural themes as the imbalance between individual rights and responsibilities, integrity in government and business, and the like.

There are possible advantages here, too. If previous articulations of the idea of a transition which included a distinct socialist ideology, a mass movement, and an organizing socialist party have become obsolete, however, old political roads that have led nowhere may be abandoned.[22] The very conception of a transition from one identifiable political economy to another—even a long, leisurely transition—has become suspect and perhaps an impediment to political vision and political participation. When viewed in the framework of permanent limits, of conservative revisions of values, and of a desirable mix of forms of ownership, differences between advanced capitalism and socialism converge steadily, without disappearing. Just when politics is assuming larger import in American life, then, socialists may have to give up the idea of a complete transition from one social system to another in favor of more neutral conceptions of slow change that ultimately may add up to a "transition," or what will appear in retrospect to be a transition.

The opportunity to lay aside myths of transition should encourage socialists to explore a wider range of contradictory positions and proposals unimpeded by excessive moral baggage (which beyond a certain weight becomes moralistic), and by unreliable, old maps of a changing political terrain. Consider, as an example, political attitudes toward the welfare state. Instead of endorsing all worthy (and many dubious) proposals to enlarge the scope of the welfare state merely on the grounds of the defensible moral claims of many contending groups, or on the grounds of consistency with longer range anticapitalist aims, socialists need to participate more fully in the search for acceptable limits to public spending. It may be necessary to criticize the welfare state for its continuing inability to meet socialist ideals, but these critiques ought to proceed on less sure terms than they have in the recent past. In an era of limits, everyone must be concerned with efficiency, reasonable growth, and restraint in consumption as well as with the issue of redistribution. In the absence of clear, "final" socialist alternatives, people on the Left should participate also in the hard choices—the continuing need to cut back the defense budget, surely, and to restrict lavish consumption by the very rich through far steeper tax schedules and tighter inheritance laws, but also to economize in sacrosanct areas of health, education, assistance to the poor, and other public services. Those of us on the Left cannot afford the luxury of demanding greater accountability from public officials without also attending to the problems of efficiency in both the state and private sectors. Such issues, which only recently seemed primarily a matter for nonsocialist bureaucrats and politicians to worry over, at least as long as capitalism prevailed, now affect everyone in more complicated ways.

Socialists, then, should feel free to take forceful positions on the excesses of the rich as well as conflicting positions on the hard tradeoffs between the public sector and private consumption within, say, the bottom 80% of the population (where nobody is that well off).[23] In addition to obvious drawbacks, there are several advantages to a more open and supple approach to issues. A greater willingness to assume contradictory political stances that cannot be assimilated into even the most subtle socialist political algebra of class analysis, or justified by coalitions of the imagination, would complete the integration of socialists into the political process. It is no longer merely a matter of whether to participate in "bourgeois" politics—that issue, happily, is dead—but whether to participate as equals who may possess distinctive insights, but whose ethical leverage must be earned continuously, rather than assumed on the basis of some special vision or theoretical insight into future possibilities which exposes the moral rot of present arrangements. This redefinition of status forces socialists to be more alert and even more sympathetic to conservative directions of democratic thought in America, and to the changing political options which, for the moment, have gravitated largely toward the center on matters of national import.

Of course, even if democratic socialists move further in these directions than they have already, there still would be sufficient reason to endorse many left liberal social programs. But such support would no longer derive from a political logic confined by attempts to discover short range objectives in the light of one theory of transition or another—a futile exercise which often deprives socialists of ethical appeal. There is at least some awkwardness in those democratic socialist discussions of the welfare state which begin with a withering critique, go on to offer faint praise, and propose massive extensions of its programs, only to conclude with a resolution to limit its scope and democratize its conduct, once this Rube Goldberg machine has served its purpose. Instead, support of additions to the welfare state would derive mainly from a series of moral imperatives which, suitably modified by conservative caveats, form the core of what remains politically appealing in socialist visions. Socialism, as Stuart Hampshire remarks, is "not so much a theory as a set of moral injunctions, which seem to me clearly right and rationally justifiable: first, that the elimination of poverty ought to be the first priority of government after defence; secondly, that as great inequalities in wealth between different social groups lead to inequalities in power and in freedom of action, they are generally unjust and need to be redressed by governmental action; thirdly, that democratically elected governments ought to ensure that primary and basic human needs are given priority within the economic system, even if this involves some loss in the aggregate of goods and services which would otherwise be available."[24]

Moreover, advocacy of left liberal programs would be provisional, subject to cancellation based on several criteria: the desirability of a conservative balance among the cluster of socialist values; the acceptability of various vehicles of ownership; and an interplay of planning and market mechanisms. In some instances, socialists may even wish to attend openly to their own immediate interests without resorting to elaborate ideological charades; this would add to their credibility and encourage a simpler, more direct political discourse. Thus, for example, socialists might support a minimum guaranteed income only if it were connected to a strictly imposed set of responsibilities on the part of recipients able to work. They might favor fuller legal and governmental regulation of corporations and also lobby for harsher punishment of criminals, even ones from groups disadvantaged by conventional inequalities and injustices.[25]

In a word, revisions of values, vehicles, and inherited conceptions of transition may help socialists participate in public life in more realistic and appealing ways in the late seventies and eighties. At the moment it seems to me that the best chance of moving toward the old precondition of a democratic majority disposed to socialist ideas is not through a party of socialists or a coalition of tiny socialist groups, though such organizations surely serve other significant educational and social purposes. It is rather through public engagement of new configurations of liberal and conservative sentiment in the institutional context of more obviously "socialist" imperatives—especially the need for planning, the need for experimentation with various forms of economic ownership and control, and the need for a large public household, occasioned mainly by the inadequacies of the private sector and by the more sophisticated level of social services than Americans have come to expect. Those of us in the socialist tradition may help to shape more just options, of course, but we can no longer do so from privileged historical or moral vantage points.

The preceding discussion will strike some radicals as a final solution to the problem of the Left, one last step beyond Eduard Bernstein that eliminates tensions between vision and power by revising the socialist idea out of existence.[26] But the *idea* of socialism—at least as it emerges from characteristic patterns of the radical imagination—is already dead in America. In spite of its demise, however, the chances of enacting *socialist ideas* seem better than ever. A studied unwillingness to distinguish between the socialist idea and the ideas of socialism may put some people on the Left among the last to acknowledge the arrival of a conservative democratic socialism. In the past quarter-century, the leading ideas of socialism have taken hold rapidly. The ideological monopoly of capitalism has been shattered. New modes of ownership and control seem both desirable and possible to large numbers of people. The idea of planning has gained wide acceptance. And the goals of democratizing power in economic, political, and social life are thoroughly imbedded in American sensibilities. Despite such dramatic shifts, and the further possibilities they imply, socialists characteristically go to elaborate lengths to dissociate them from the idea of socialism.

Such reluctance, I believe, arises partly from stubborn habits of the radical imagination that connect vision and power in ways no longer appropriate to American circumstances. Beginning with a sense of powerlessness in relation to the might of capital and to projections of the completed socialist design, many on the Left have emphasized romantic vision as the chief means of rousing large numbers of people to a sustained politics of opposition. Such enthusiasm, it is assumed, provides energy that can be converted into radical political power capable ultimately of ending the reign of capital. But Americans have not responded to the whole socialist vision with sufficient enthusiasm, nor have they rallied to it in significant numbers (at least not in recent decades). And they show no signs of doing so in the immediate future. Recognizing this, as all but the silliest political dabblers must, many of us on the Left are drawn frequently to the gloomy speculation that socialism never will be enacted. Doubtless we are right, if by "enactment" we continue to imagine transitions along classical lines of violent revolution (needless to say), but also of parliamentary routes in which explicitly socialist parties grow large and vie for governing power. That is to say, there is scant reason to suppose that a decisive American majority will adopt the socialist idea, put the energy of its total vision under the direction of a small party (or a large Democratic party, for that matter), achieve state power, and then transform the institutions and sensibilities of capitalism into those of socialism. Even the most sophisticated scenarios of transition will fail to make political sense if they continue to flow from assumptions concerning vision and power so characteristic of the modern radical imagination.

In America, one is tempted to say, there never will be sufficient quantities of socialist vision to defeat the multiple powers of capital head-on. And so, we need to free the socialist idea from ingrained habits of imagination, and work at realizing the ideas of socialism. This seems a possible task, indeed one already under way. Though the socialist idea fails to elicit the sort of enthusiasm needed to energize a mass movement, it no longer evokes such deep fears and resentments either. Removed from the realm of metaphysical abstraction and dissolved into its constituent parts, the idea of socialism (not to mention the more obvious utopian heresy of communism) does not serve as an image of secular salvation or as a modern type of damnation, as it did from the late nineteenth century through the early cold war years. This change in the status of the socialist vision—especially its disaggregation and detoxification—represents a net gain for the American Left. (Almost anything would.) It does not mean, of course, that a vision of future possibilities has ceased to be essential, or that small, ginger groups of zealous visionaries do not meet some useful—if limited—political needs. With his usual flair for illuminating exaggerations, Leszek Kolakowski has remarked that "even the simplest improvement in social conditions demands the mobilization of such a huge amount of collective energy that if the full extent of the disproportion between results and effort expended became public knowledge the result would be so disheartening, and would so paralyze men's courage and strivings, that any social progress would be impossible."[27] Allowing for the utility of grandiose visions, I believe that demystification of the idea of socialism helps to transform the ideas of socialism into a set of practical options. The danger, of course, is that they may become a set of despised options. But socialist planning and socialist ownership (including more democratic control of economic, social, and political life) can be used now in the long battle to reduce racism, sexual oppression, gross economic inequality, destruction of the environment, the stultifying patterns of work, and the even more damaging patterns of unemployment. That is to say, the seminal ideas of socialism are becoming part of the American political repertoire.

Because these deep issues of exploitation and oppression cut across social systems (or so I assume in the absence of contrary evidence), socialism does not constitute a precondition to resolving them. In fact, the idea of final resolutions is probably an illusion. And it certainly lies outside the proper sphere of politics and government. Nevertheless, the ideas of socialism should be immediately useful in constructing a more humane social order. At some juncture, of course, the radical paradox of partial political power—what might be called the 35% paradox—may become as crucial in America as it is, say, in Italy or France. But it seems vastly premature to worry politically about problems that might be engendered by such successes. Should a sizable percentage of Americans come to favor reforms that require complete liquidation of the business system, extraordinary forms of political action will be on the agenda. By then, perhaps, models of successful majority transitions will be available. Though potentially not useful in more than marginal ways, considering the vast differences in history and culture between Europe and America, majority models of transition nevertheless are the only ones of conceivable interest to democratic socialists. In the meantime, democrats committed to enacting socialist ideas in America can attend to the more immediate tasks of participating in the remodeling of attitudes and institutions through a many-sided and multicentered politics of reform.

Operating in a social milieu characterized by a consciousness of material limits and chastened by a general recognition of the historical failure of the largest radical visions, serious Leftists, I have proposed, need to pursue a politics informed by a renewed awareness of conservative values. Such a direction seems to me crucial to any further political success of socialist ideas in America. Moreover, this conservative recasting may figure importantly in any spiritual resurgence of socialist vision. That is to say, the seminal political and social ideas of socialism—public ownership and planning—are quickly becoming the main genus of political economies in every part of the world. The character of the many evolving species of socialism, with their political, cultural, and religious dimensions—democratic and authoritarian, Christian and Zen—is rapidly becoming the central focus of interest.

Conservative revisions of democratic socialism, then, point to a narrow passage, a way of apprehending this facet of the bourgeois tradition not essentially as a consolation for the missed prize of communism but as a rich source of ideas and values of potential use in what figures to be a major effort to reshape the American environment to serve more humane purposes. But it is only one among several approaches to the continuing crises of politics and culture. Even if the sort of socialism I have proposed is the most hopeful approach—our best regulative political idea—it holds out no promise of full resolution of our crises. Indeed, our condition may be permanent insofar as the marks of confusion, disorientation, uncertainty, and continually hard—in some cases, impossible—choices that characterized earlier crises of more limited duration become accepted parts of our psychic and public life.

Though the grounds of hope are various, I should like to single out in conclusion the need for perspective. In an era of intense consciousness of limits, it is important to put away old illusions—illusions of total resolutions of our public troubles, and illusions also of the less grandiose ameliorations many of us hoped for only a short time ago. Collectively, we must learn to live with the deepest spiritual facets of the crisis of personality and culture, and to recognize that no single religious or political tradition can satisfy a majority of citizens. And we must acclimate ourselves to a political and economic realm of limited options. Such looming features of the total environment as large government, massive bureaucracies, escalating violence by terrorist groups, and persistently discouraging degrees of conventional inequality now seem permanent, or at least indefinite.

But we can hope to tame, manage, and soften the worst social injustices of racism, sexism, and capitalism in the next decades. This will require, among other things, careful examination of the limitations of ideology, social criticism, politics, and government—an examination that will lead to discovery of their genuine possibilities. Though the private sector and the state obviously will permeate the entire social atmosphere, they do not threaten by any means to exhaust our resources or our options. (We cannot afford 1984!) If, for instance, America assumes the character of a more mixed economy and achieves a more responsible and more democratic polity, the level of health of its citizens may rise appreciably, as it has over the past decades. There is every reason to work toward a condition in which the best possible treatment of disease becomes available to every sick person. But the right to good health, security, or any other social good implies a set of responsibilities. In the case of health, it entails responsibility for preventing disease (or should this fail, for seeking timely treatment). This labor of prevention and treatment remains largely a collective affair: only groups can engage in medical research, train doctors, deliver medical care, establish a clean public environment, educate people to seek proper nutrition, and regulate the food industry so as to ensure a decent supply at affordable prices. It appears (sadly so in some respects) that government will be the principal agency in efforts to ensure good health care. But even the most responsive and effective government cannot perform more than a fraction of the task. In the last analysis, individuals and families must assume responsibility for choosing the right foods (and avoiding others), taking proper exercise, and so on.[28] Similarly, this stress on personal responsibility is needed to establish a balance in the pursuit of other social goals.

In debating the future, then, it will be important to question the limits and limitations of government and to develop the resources of individuals and intermediate groups as fully as possible. Initiatives to reweave parts of the fabric of local and neighborhood life through decentralization of some economic, political, legal, and social functions surely are compatible with the continued existence—and perhaps the moderate growth—of large public and corporate sectors. Indeed, much of the fiscal thread for binding the torn ligatures of community will come from government. Such efforts at voluntary restoration of elements of community through strengthened mediating structures must unfold within a context of large economic and governmental units, and in the midst of political polarization on major issues. Matters will be worse if we do not proceed toward decentralization on a small scale. But a little decentralization should go a long way. Large economic and governmental organizations will not disappear, however fervently critics wish to restore the primacy of such arrangements as extended families, neighborhood governmental and legal institutions, community control of schools, and the like. Happily so. Such fashionable nostalgia for the virtues of decentralization helps us to remember the intimacy of extended families and the warmth of small, closely knit communities. But it also helps us to forget the oppressive, cloying, and unjust characteristics of such arrangements that earlier generations labored so diligently to modify. Moreover, since large bureaucracies are going to be with us for a long while, our central aim ought to be to humanize them, rather than to try to wish them away. Bureaucratic organizations are, after all, historically quite new in America—in their Model T phase, so to speak—and hence subject to extensive experimentation and improvement.

Even if we shed old illusions of a capitalism or a socialism of limitless abundance and accept a precarious existence in a mixed system marked by relative scarcity, there remains plenty of space for fruitful disagreement and considerable room for hope. Such an admission need not be made in a mood of resignation or even as a consequence of resignation, but rather in a spirit of determination to be resigned about what cannot be helped and energetic about the rest of our problems. America is, after all, still a comparatively new culture. As the nation comes of age (once again), we shall need to rely on our dazzling array of human resources, our capacity for self-examination, our openness and pragmatism, our preoccupation with religious values—and even on our past achievements in science, technology, productive ingenuity, and the civilizing arts. They are here, around and within us.

Notes

Chapter 1: Some Preliminaries

1. For an interesting survey of various uses of "crisis," see Randolph Starn, "Historians and Crisis," *Past & Present,* no. 52 (August 1971): 3–22. The formulations of sociopolitical and cultural crises in this chapter depend especially on the following sources: Irving Howe, "What's the Trouble? Social Crisis, Crisis of Civilization, or Both?" in Irving Howe and Michael Harrington, eds., *The Seventies: Problems and Proposals* (New York: Harper & Row, 1972), pp. 53–72; and Daniel Bell, *The Coming of Post-Industrial Society: A Venture in Social Forecasting* (New York: Basic Books, 1973), and *The Cultural Contradictions of Capitalism* (New York: Basic Books, 1976).

Howe offers the following distinction between sociopolitical and cultural (or civilizational) crises: "A social crisis signifies a breakdown in the functioning of a society: it fails to feed the poor, it cannot settle disputes among constitutent groups, it drags the country into an endless war. If local, a social crisis calls for reform; if extensive, for deep changes in the relationships of power. . . . Though it may coincide with a social crisis and thereby exacerbate its effects, a crisis of civilization has to do not so much with the workings of the economy or the rightness of social arrangements as it does with the transmission of values, those tacit but deeply lodged assumptions by means of which men try to regulate their conduct. At least in principle, a social crisis is open to solutions by legislation and reform —that is, public policy. But a crisis of civilization, though it can be muted or its effects postponed by the relief of social problems, cannot as a rule be dissolved through acts of public policy. It has more to do with the experience of communities and generations than with the resolution of social conflict. It works itself out in ways we don't readily understand and sometimes, far from working itself out, it continues to fester. A social crisis raises difficulties, a crisis of civilization dilemmas. A social crisis is expressed mainly through public struggle, a crisis of civilization mainly through incoherence of behavior." "What's the Trouble?" pp. 53–54.

2. In the characteristically bold strokes of a manifesto, Marx and Engels identify rapid change as a central feature of bourgeois society, distinguishing this epoch from previous ones: "All fixed, fast-frozen relations, with their train of ancient and venerable prejudices and opinions, are swept away, all new-formed ones become antiquated before they can ossify. All that is solid melts into air, all that is holy is profaned, and man is at last compelled to face with sober senses, his real conditions of life, and his relations with his kind." Karl Marx and Frederick Engels, *The Communist Manifesto,* in *Marx and Engels: Selected Works* (New York: International Publishers, 1968), p. 38.

3. Arthur M. Schlesinger, Jr., "The Velocity of History," *Newsweek,* July 6, 1970, p. 34.

4. John Lukacs, *The Passing of the Modern Age* (New York: Harper & Row, 1970), p. 5 (italics added).

5. Ibid. In thinking about socialism, liberalism, and conservatism as facets of the bourgeois spirit, I have found Lukacs' study particularly helpful. See especially Chapter 18, "The Bourgeois Interior," pp. 191–207. "The mathematicability of reality, the cult of reason, free trade, liberalism, the abolition of slavery, of censorship, the contractual idea of the state, constitutionalism, individualism, socialism, nationalism, internationalism—these were not aristocratic ideas. . . . bourgeois means something more than a social class: it means certain rights and privileges, certain aspirations, a certain way of thinking even more than of living." P. 195. In defining the main marks of the elusive bourgeois spirit—cultivation of the interior life in a generally urban metier of freedom, security, and the privacy of family—Lukacs notes the precapitalist origins of the term which extend back to eleventh-century France.

6. Remarks of Louis Harris, National Democratic Issues Convention, Louisville, Kentucky, November 21, 1975 (mimeographed). It may be that the pollsters overestimate the American public's pessimism and lack of confidence in its leaders and dominant institutions. In a survey of the limitations of polls, Seymour Martin Lipset notes that quite different readings of the public pulse follow from variant formulations of questions. For example, whereas few people express "high confidence" in leading institutions, few also express "hardly any confidence at all." Lipset wonders whether "the confidence glass" is "more full or more empty."

It is hard to say, of course, but Lipset's cautionary remarks should discourage critics from drawing firm conclusions from polls. At best, such crude devices, especially when used to explore subjects as sensitive as public moods, detect interesting straws in the wind. See Seymour Martin Lipset, "The Wavering Polls," *The Public Interest* 43 (Spring 1976): 70–89.

7. The Harris Survey, October 6, 1975. See also the NBC News Poll of January 4, 1976, which draws a similar, though somewhat less pessimistic, picture.

8. Daniel Yankelovich, "A Crisis of Moral Legitimacy?" *Dissent* 21 (Fall 1974): 526–533. A crisis of moral legitimacy occurs when "people who accept the normative rules of the political/economic system come to believe that the institutions are violating these rules for immoral reasons." P. 530.

9. Ibid., p. 528.

10. Hart Research Associates Poll, conducted for The Peoples Bicentennial Commission, taken during the week of July 25, 1975.

11. In *The Democratic Prospect,* Charles Frankel crisply summarizes the principal tenets of an open society, and the centrality of social criticism to its approximation: "The ideal of the open society proposes that men live under arrangements all of which are open to question. It holds that loyalty should be given to a social order precisely because it permits this process of criticism to take place. It insists that the process should be public, and that everyone is in principle qualified to take part in it. And finally, it assumes that criticism and judgment are the preludes to corrective action." Charles Frankel, *The Democratic Prospect* (New York: Harper & Row, 1962), p. 35.

12. The Harris Survey, October 6, 1975.

13. Robert L. Heilbroner, *An Inquiry into the Human Prospect* (New York: Norton, 1974), p. 22.

14. W. H. Ferry and the Ad Hoc Committee on the Triple Revolution, "The Triple Revolution," in Paul Goodman, ed., *Seeds of Liberation* (New York: Braziller, 1964), p. 396. Considering the nature of the document, it would be unfair to hold signatories to details. I use it here only to indicate basic assumptions about abundance in the sixties.

15. David Riesman, "The American Crisis," in David Riesman, *Abundance for What? and Other Essays* (Garden City, N.Y.: Doubleday, 1964), pp. 50–51.

16. As compared, roughly, with the current GWP of about $5.5 trillion produced by four billion people. These estimates, manufactured by the Hudson Institute, are reported in Norman Macrae, "America's Third Century," *The Economist,* October 25, 1975, p. 3. See also Herman Kahn and B. Bruce-Briggs, *Things to Come: Thinking About the Seventies and Eighties* (New York: Macmillan, 1972).

17. A high (and controversial) estimate of capital requirements for the next decade may be found in a special issue of *Business Week,* "The Debt Economy," October 12, 1974, esp. pp. 120–123. Edward F. Denison estimates the growth rate of Total National Income between 1929 and 1969 at 3.3%. See his *Accounting for United States Economic Growth 1929–1969* (Washington, D.C.: The Brookings Institution, 1974), p. 16.

18. For an interesting discussion of contemporary American capitalism as a system plagued by fiscal crisis, see James O'Connor, *The Fiscal Crisis of the State* (New York: St. Martin's Press, 1972). In one of the few preliminary attempts to suggest the implications of relative scarcity for classical formulations of socialism, Jack Jones observes that "the idea of socialism would . . . come to mean, in the advanced countries, a minimum or zero growth of the unnecessary, luxurious, and pernicious and the redirection of efforts toward improving *the basics,* including the natural environment and the situation of the domestic and foreign poor. Socialism would come to mean the control of the overproduction, overconsumption, overpopulation, overurbanization, overexploitation and pollution of the natural environment, and overeducation. All of these are hypertrophies with which neither capitalism nor classical socialism are able to cope." "The Idea of Socialism: The Ninety Degree Turn?" *Abraxas* 1 (Spring 1971): 274.

19. Reported in the San Francisco *Sunday Examiner and Chronicle,* October 27, 1974.

20. For an interesting discussion of such neo-conservatives as Irving Kristol, Nathan Glazer, Edward Banfield, Daniel Patrick Moynihan, and Robert Nisbet, see Lewis Coser and Irving Howe, eds., *The New Conservatives: A Critique from the Left* (New York: Quadrangle, 1974).

21. A historical review and summary of definitions of culture may be found in A. L. Kroeber and Clyde Kluckhohn, *Culture: A Critical Review of Concepts and Definitions* (New York: Random House, 1963). My principal debts in this area are to Philip Rieff, *The Triumph of the Therapeutic: Uses of Faith After Freud* (New York: Harper & Row, 1966), and Raymond Williams, *Culture and Society: 1780–1950* (New York: Harper & Row, 1966).

22. On this, see Bell, *Cultural Contradictions of Capitalism,* p. 13.

23. Daniel Bell, "The Revolution of Rising Entitlements," *Fortune* 91 (April 1975): 98–99, 98.

24. Rieff, *Triumph of the Therapeutic,* pp. 242–243.

25. William Simon provides a more sanguine view of the cultural crisis in "Reflections on the Relationship Between the Individual and Society," *Human Futures* (London: IPC Science and Technology, 1974), pp. 141–157. Simon questions the large model of individuals and society that informs the speculations of critics as diverse as Rieff and Bell (or in his example, as diverse as Hobbes, Durkheim, and Freud). Rather than assuming that individuals will engage in a Hobbesean war of each against all in the absence of social controls—and hence that brief periods of anomie must give way to a new, more authoritarian system of symbolic controls and remissions or to barbarism—Simon raises the possibility of benign adaptations to anomie, considered as a long term reality in a society of largely self-regulating individuals who are not "socially dangerous." P. 156.

26. Andrew Hacker, "We Will Meet as Enemies," *Newsweek,* July 6, 1970, p. 24. See also Hacker's *The End of the American Era* (New York: Atheneum, 1970). Roberto Vacca's *The Coming Dark Age* (Garden City, N.Y.: Doubleday, 1974) provides a recent example of dark prophecy. Jay Martin has written a splendid if rather melancholy Bicentennial essay on the American condition: "A Watertight Watergate Future: Americans in a Post-American Age," *Antioch Review* 33 (Spring 1975): 7–25.

27. François Duchêne, ed., *The Endless Crisis* (New York: Simon and Schuster, 1970), p. 26.

28. Jürgen Moltmann, *The Crucified God* (New York: Harper & Row, 1974), p. 17.

29. This alters somewhat earlier meanings of "crisis," an ambiguous term at best: rather than signifying a brief moment of truth or a decisive turning point, "crisis" in the past century has come to imply also "the continuity of organic processes but not steady equilibrium, decisive conflict but not 'total' revolution." Starn, "Historians and Crisis," p. 17.

30. See Seymour Martin Lipset and Everett Carll Ladd, Jr., "The Politics of American Sociologists," *American Journal of Sociology* 78 (July 1972): 85.

31. In a survey of American academics, Everett Carll Ladd, Jr., and Seymour Martin Lipset report that professors rank themselves last in terms of "relative policy influence" among fourteen elite groups—behind wealthy families, military leaders, union leaders, TV news, news magazines, etc. Reported in *The Chronicle of Higher Education,* January 12, 1976, p. 14.

32. J. P. Nettl, "Are Intellectuals Obsolete?" *The Nation,* March 4, 1968, p. 302.

33. William F. Lynch, *Images of Hope: Imagination as Healer of the Hopeless* (Baltimore: Helicon Press, 1965), pp. 23 ff. My discussion of hope is based on this neglected book.

34. Ralph Waldo Emerson, "The American Scholar," in *The Complete Essays and Other Writings of Ralph Waldo Emerson* (New York: Random House, 1940), p. 56.

35. Warren I. Susman, "History and the American Intellectual: Uses of a Usable Past," *American Quarterly* 16 (August 1964): 244. For a helpful discussion of distinctions between *ideology* and *myth,* see Willard A. Mullins, "On the Concept of Ideology in Political Science," *American Political Science Review* 66 (June 1972): 498–510.

Chapter 2: Communist Dreams—Socialist Prescriptions

1. Daniel Bell, *Marxian Socialism in the United States* (Princeton, N.J.: Princeton University Press, 1952, 1967), p. 3.

2. Acts 2:1, 3–4; 44–46. But note the early cold war commentary in *The Westminster Study Edition of the Holy Bible* (New York: Collins' Clear–Type Press, 1946, 1952), p. 192: "Some who had property *sold* it and used the money to prevent the starvation of destitute fellow Christians. This so–called 'communism' was simply sacrificial giving to relieve need." I prefer the plain text.

3. For a discussion of pre-Christian utopian visions, emphasizing the city as organizing metaphor, see Lewis Mumford, "Utopia, the City and the Machine," in Frank E. Manuel, ed., *Utopias and Utopian Thought* (Boston: Beacon Press, 1967), pp. 3–24.

4. E. Harris Harbison, "Socialism in European History to 1848," in Donald Drew Egbert and Stow Persons, eds., *Socialism and American Life* (Princeton, N.J.: Princeton University Press, 1952), I, 29–30.

5. For a brief account of the history of the term *socialism,* which was first used in the English Owenite *Cooperative Magazine* in November 1827, see Raymond Williams, *Keywords: A Vocabulary of Culture and Society* (New York: Oxford University Press, 1976), pp. 238–243.

6. On this, as on so many other aspects of socialist thought, G. D. H. Cole remains indispensable. See *A History of Socialist Thought: Communism and Social Democracy* (London: Macmillan, 1958), vol. IV, pt. II, pp. 846 ff.

7. See V. I. Lenin, *The State and Revolution,* in *V. I. Lenin: Selected Works* (New York: International Publishers, 1943), VII, 5–112.

8. Though notoriously vague, the idea of "scientific socialism" has been reified frequently by its advocates. See Iring Fetscher, *Marx and Marxism* (New York: Herder and Herder, 1971), pp. 302–311.

9. There is considerable confusion concerning the meanings of alienation and exploitation. For an interesting discussion of alienation considered in its broadest sense, as an inescapable human condition arising from the fact of conscious subjects separated from one another and from the world, see Walter Weisskopf, *Alienation and Economics* (New York: Dutton, 1971), especially Chapter 1. Marx's notion of alienation is narrower. According to him, the several modalities of alienation—alienation from self in the process of work, from the product of work, from others, and from solidarity with the species—are conditioned by various historical forms of class society that must cope with degrees of scarcity. Each historical constellation reveals a diminished form of human potentiality. Just as a stick appears bent in water, alienated man is mutilated by virtue of his existence in the historical media of precommunist societies. Marx infers man's true human nature—his unalienated potentiality—from a succession of historical moments. To enact his potential human nature as a social creature with individual characteristics, man must create a communist community. Nothing less will do. Since I regard this as impossible, I consider alienation, even in Marx's sense, incurable. See Bertell Ollman, *Alienation: Marx's Concept of Man in Capitalist Society* (London: Cambridge University Press, 1971).

Exploitation, in the Marxian scheme, refers to the ways in which inequitable shares of the surplus are systematically appropriated by classes in precommunist societies. To the extent that the organization of society into classes prevents individuals from enjoying the fruits of their labor, exploitation and alienation overlap. Exploitation is a dimension of alienation, but the terms are not interchangeable. The elimination of exploitation through socialist reorganization of society would reduce alienation, according to Marx. Only establishment of a communist community, however, can abolish it. On this, see Stanley Moore, "Utopian Themes in Marx and Mao," *Monthly Review* 21 (June 1969): 33–44.

10. Werner Sombart, "Capitalism," *Encyclopedia of the Social Sciences* (New York: Macmillan, 1930), III, 195.

11. For a fuller exposition of the ideas of socialism and communism, exploitation and alienation, see Peter Clecak, *Radical Paradoxes: Dilemmas of the American Left, 1945–1970* (New York: Harper & Row, 1973), esp. chaps. 2 and 8, and "Dilemmas of the American Left," *Social Research* 41 (Winter 1975): 467–491. I take up distinctions between *social* and *public* ownership later on.

12. Karl Marx, *Critique of the Gotha Programme,* in *Marx and Engels: Selected Works* (New York: International Publishers, 1933), II, 563. Note that in this context Marx uses the term "communist society" to cover all post-capitalist stages of the transition to communism, whereas contemporary Communist theoreticians use "socialism" to describe the present period in selected parts of the world.

13. Ibid. But the quid pro quo principle is only the dominant one. Both socialist and nonsocialist societies allocate portions of their surplus to guarantee minimal satisfaction of basic needs to those unable to work.

14. On this point, see Michael Harrington, *Socialism* (New York: Saturday Review Press, 1972), esp. pp. 49–52. " 'Dictatorship' . . . defined the class basis of a society, not its political forms, and it did not necessarily imply the repression of civil liberties." P. 51.

15. Marx, *Critique of the Gotha Programme,* p. 566.

16. For a lucid discussion of the utopian character of communism, see Leszek Kolakowski, "The Myth of Human Self-Identity: Unity of Civil and Political Society in Socialist Thought," in Leszek Kolakowski and Stuart Hampshire, eds., *The Socialist Idea: A Reappraisal* (New York: Basic Books, 1974), pp. 18–35.

17. Irving Howe and Lewis Coser, "Images of Socialism," in Irving Howe, ed., *Essential Works of Socialism* (New York: Bantam Books, 1971), p. 839.

18. Of course, it might be argued that redistribution on the basis of current (or even previous) levels of productivity could provide all Americans with "enough." The difficulty of distinguishing between needs and wants is obvious. Even if this issue could be resolved to everyone's satisfaction, the problem of compulsory work would remain. As long as the need for work persists, social morality must revolve around the problem of equitable relationships between obligations (and opportunities) to produce and corresponding entitlements to consume goods, services, status, space, leisure, etc.

19. Subsequent passages are adapted from Clecak, "Dilemmas of the American Left," pp. 475–476, 481–484.

20. The distinction between "dialectic of liberation" and "sociology of change" in the Marxian tradition is elaborated in Moore, "Utopian Themes in Marx and Mao." On the rise and decline of the new Left, see James Weinstein, *Ambiguous Legacy: The Left in American Politics* (New York: New Viewpoints, 1975), pp. 114–159. Alan Lawson has written a splendid review-essay covering several of the best books on the radicalism of the 1960s, "The New Left and the New Values," *American Quarterly* 28 (Spring 1976): 107–123.

21. Though reliable figures are hard to come by, the number of bombing incidents rose gradually in the early seventies and then leveled off. But bombings have become more destructive: 1,955 were reported to the FBI in 1973; 2,044 in 1974; and 1,012 for the first six months of 1975. Forty-six deaths, 209 injuries, and more than $40 million in property damages were reported to have occurred as a result of "bombing" and "explosive" incidents in the first half of 1975. The percentage attributable to left-wing terrorists is not available—and FBI estimates in any case would have to be considered less than fully reliable. See *FBI Uniform Crime Reports: Bomb Summary: A Comprehensive Report of Incidents Involving Explosive and Incendiary Devices in the Nation—1974; and January–June, 1975* (Washington, D.C.: United States Government Printing Office, 1975).

See also Robert Nisbet, *Twilight of Authority* (New York: Oxford University Press, 1975), especially Chapter 3: "The recipe for militarism in a society is basically twilight of authority in the civil sphere." P. 146.

22. Rubin, whose bad taste is rivaled only by his prose, records the latest episode in his odyssey in *Growing (Up) at 37* (New York: M. Evans, 1976).

23. For an interesting artifact of the late sixties, see Tom Hayden, *Rebellion and Repression* (New York: World Publishing, 1969). Compare this

with Hayden's more moderate and humane left liberal stance in the middle seventies as outlined in *Make the Future Ours,* Draft Program of the Tom Hayden for U.S. Senate Campaign, 1976: ". . . my discovery of the capacity of goodness in so many Americans gave me the strength to continue trying to persuade and organize instead of abandoning the process for extremes of despair. It made me a more patient person, believing that the good in all of us can be touched and liberated." P. 9.

24. See Clecak, *Radical Paradoxes,* chap. 7, pp. 233–272.

25. For a chilling account of the fate of children in many communes, see John Rothchild and Susan Wolf, *Children of the Counterculture* (Garden City, N.Y.: Doubleday, 1976).

26. Harrington, *Socialism,* p. 344. See also his "Leisure as the Means of Production," in Kolakowski and Hampshire, *Socialist Idea,* pp. 153–163.
Throughout, I draw many examples from the work of people close to *Dissent,* and especially from the writings of Harrington. I use him for purposes of illustration not merely because he is perhaps the best known spokesman for democratic socialism in America, and among the most able, but because he generally takes positions within the socialist spectrum fairly close to the center of American political thought and activity. He thus offers a convenient point of reference on the ideological landscape. But I do not pretend to supply a critique of his work here.

27. Ibid., p. 345. Harrington quotes from Sidney Hook, *Toward the Understanding of Karl Marx* (New York: John Day, 1933), p. 14.

28. Michael Harrington, *Fragments of the Century: A Social Autobiography* (New York: Saturday Review Press, 1973), pp. 226–246.

29. The rhetorical course of Soviet utopianism has fluctuated since the October Revolution. Reaching a high point under Khrushchev, who with characteristic ebullience predicted that "the present generation of Soviet people will live under communism," the idea has been soft-pedaled somewhat since the middle 1960s. Yet the notion of communism as the chief goal of social development remains central to Soviet ideology, even though it is represented as less imminent than in earlier years, and more the culmination of a long process of transition. The relatively unimaginative character of communist society as envisioned by Soviet theoreticians is shown clearly in Jerome M. Gilison, *The Soviet Image of Utopia* (Baltimore: The Johns Hopkins Press, 1974).

30. See David Caute, *The Fellow-Travellers: A Postscript to the Enlightenment* (New York: Macmillan, 1973).

31. See Robert N. Bellah, *The Broken Covenant: American Civil Religion in Time of Trial* (New York: Seabury Press, 1975), especially Chapter 5, "The American Taboo on Socialism," pp. 112–138.

32. See Howe, *Essential Works of Socialism,* secs. IV and V, pp. 407–850.

33. Ibid., p. 18.

34. Michael Harrington, "Welfare Capitalism in Crisis," *The Nation,* December 28, 1974, p. 687.

35. Harrington, *Socialism,* p. 118. See also Leon Samson, *Toward a United Front* (New York: Holt, Rinehart & Winston, 1935).
Among the factors most frequently cited in the continuing debate over American exceptionalism are the following: the absence of a feudal tradition, a democratic and egalitarian ethos, representative democracy, equal protection under the law, the open frontier, the presence of vast natural resources, affluence, the capacity of the two major parties to absorb elements of radical programs, fluid class lines, and a culturally heterogeneous work force composed of ex-slaves, rural emigrés, immigrants from Europe and Asia, colonized Native Americans, and Chicanos. The literature on the historical problem of the fate of earlier socialist movements in America has become nearly unmanageable. For a recent discussion, see John M. Laslett and Seymour Martin Lipset, eds., *Failure of a Dream?* (Garden City, N.Y.: Doubleday, Anchor Press, 1974).

36. See Tom Bottomore, "Socialism and the Working Class," in Kolakowski and Hampshire, *Socialist Idea,* pp. 123–133.

37. Kolakowski, "Introduction," in Kolakowski and Hampshire, *Socialist Idea,* p. 15.

38. Robert L. Heilbroner, "Economic Problems of a 'Postindustrial' Society," *Dissent* 20 (Spring 1973): 168.

39. Harrington, *Socialism,* p. 271.

40. See Gar Alperovitz, "Notes Toward a Pluralist Commonwealth," in Staughton Lynd and Gar Alperovitz, *Strategy and Program: Two Essays Toward a New American Socialism* (Boston: Beacon Press, 1973), pp. 49–109.

41. John Kenneth Galbraith, "Power and the Useful Economist," in Leonard Silk, *Capitalism: The Moving Target* (New York: Praeger, 1974), pp. 154–155.

42. The richest single collection of moderate critiques of democratic socialism from the Left is Branko Horvat, Mihailo Markovic, Rudi Supek,

eds., *Self–Governing Socialism: A Reader.* 2 vols. (New York: International Arts and Sciences Press, 1975).

43. Thomas C. Cochran, "History and Cultural Crisis," *American Historical Review,* 78 (February 1973): 10.

Chapter 3: The Liberal Connection

1. Quoted from Albert Fried, ed., *Socialism in America* (Garden City, N.Y.: Anchor Books, 1970), p. 265.

2. Socialists who align themselves politically with the democratic left tend to stress the gravitational pull of socialism and its generally salutary effects on liberalism. Other socialists emphasize the pull of liberalism and its corrosive effects on the development of an American socialism. See, for example, James Weinstein, "Notes on the Need for a Socialist Party," in James Weinstein and David W. Eakins, eds., *For a New America: Essays in History and Politics from 'Studies on the Left' 1959–1967* (New York: Random House, 1970), pp. 328–341.

3. Erazim Kohák, "Socialism and the Welfare State," *Dissent* 22 (Summer 1974): 440.

4. Irving Howe, "Notes on the Here and Now," *Partisan Review* 34 (Fall 1967): 581.

5. But as I maintain throughout, the bourgeois ethos is no mere reflex of capitalist economy. On this, see Robert L. Heilbroner, "Reflections on the Future of Socialism," in Robert L. Heilbroner, *Between Capitalism and Socialism* (New York: Random House, 1970), p. 80, *The Limits of American Capitalism* (New York: Harper & Row, 1966), and *Business Civilization in Decline* (New York: Norton, 1976).

6. Of course, the term "capitalism" is largely a nineteenth-century invention, and hence not used in its contemporary senses by Adam Smith, though he does employ the notion of capital in restricted ways. Oskar Lange provides a brief Marxian definition: "capitalism means an exchange economy with private ownership of the means of production, to which the further sociological datum is added that the population is divided into two parts, one of which owns the means of production while the other part, owning no means of production, is compelled to work as wage

earners...." "Marxian Economics and Modern Economic Theory," *Review of Economic Studies* 2 (Reprinted from German to English by Kraus Reprint Corp., 1935): 189 n. See also Raymond Williams, *Keywords* (New York: Oxford University Press, 1976), pp. 42–44.

7. A lucid discussion of the exaggerated claims lodged in such images of capitalism may be found in Henry M. Pachter, "Three Economic Models: Capitalism, the Welfare State, and Socialism," in Irving Howe, ed., *Essential Works of Socialism* (New York: Bantam Books, 1971), pp. 787–808.

8. On the history and character of "liberalism," see Leo Strauss, *Liberalism: Ancient and Modern* (New York: Basic Books, 1968), esp. chaps. 3 and 10. See also Robert A. Dahl, *Pluralist Democracy in the United States: Conflict and Consensus* (Garden City, N.Y.: Anchor Books, 1962); and David Spitz, "Liberalism and Conservatism," in R. A. Goldwin, ed., *Left, Right, and Center* (Skokie, Ill.: Rand McNally, 1967), pp. 18–41.

9. "Giving and Getting," NBC Reports, Monday, December 22, 1975. Of course, the issue of philanthropy is complicated by the tax advantages connected with it. But the figures are nevertheless impressive. Raymond Williams includes a useful, but I think needlessly pessimistic, discussion of the bourgeois ideal of service in *Culture and Society, 1780–1950* (New York: Harper & Row, 1958), pp. 295–338.

10. See James Weinstein, *The Corporate Ideal in the Liberal State, 1900–1918* (Boston: Beacon Press, 1968).

11. Henry David Aiken illuminates this dilemma by distinguishing two related liberalisms. The "corporate" or "pragmatic" variety conceives individuals as "systems of interest or belief," explaining behavior in terms of models drawn from the natural sciences, and calculating public policy in accordance with utilitarian principles. In contrast, "liberalism" proper treats individuals and groups as subjects capable of self-direction and self-evaluation: "man as human is to be understood as a being who intrudes upon the order of nature as an at least partially self-caused cause, responsible to himself and his fellow human beings for his conduct." This variant becomes more difficult to maintain than the "pragmatic" variety in the domain of advanced capitalism, where the state emerges as the central public agency of redress. "Violence and the Two Liberalisms," *Social Theory and Practice* 2 (Spring 1972): 50, 54.

12. David Riesman, *Abundance for What? and Other Essays* (Garden City, N.Y.: Doubleday, 1964), pp. 300–308. See also David Potter's classic post-

war text on the effects of abundance on the American character, *People of Plenty* (Chicago: University of Chicago Press, 1954).

13. There are, of course, differences between a large and growing state and a welfare state. The expansion of state activity can be documented with reasonable precision, whereas the categories of welfare—tax reform, health care, welfare payments, education, housing, urban renewal, transportation, energy, and conservation—and the effectiveness of amounts spent in these areas remain subject to debate. Indeed, much of the defense budget that is devoted to salaries can be construed as a form of welfare. Daniel Bell proposes a revival of the term "public household." The public household, he notes, "establishes the public budget—how much do we want to spend, and for whom—as the mechanism by means of which the society attempts to implement its concerns for 'the good condition of human beings.' " "The Public Household," *The Public Interest* 37 (Fall 1974): 65. But this formulation underplays the welfare role of the state in relation to capital. On the concept of welfare, see Williams, *Keywords,* p. 281.

14. Roger A. Freeman, *The Growth of American Government: A Morphology of the Welfare State* (Stanford, Calif.: Hoover Institution Press, 1975), p. xii. Though flawed by amateurish and gratuitous political judgments—especially the assumption that subpar performances by the private sector are attributable to liberal politics and a meddlesome government, and the fear that welfare expenditures have cut dangerously into the defense effort—Freeman's important study is a useful guide to understanding the recent growth and current dimensions of the American welfare state.

The beginnings of the modern welfare state in the West are usually traced to Bismarck. See James O'Connor, *The Fiscal Crisis of the State* (New York: St. Martin's Press, 1973), esp. pp. 150–178. For standard accounts of the growth of American government, see Solomon Fabricant, *The Trend of Government Activity in the United States Since 1900* (New York: National Bureau of Economic Research, 1952); and M. Slade Kendrick, *A Century and a Half of Federal Expenditures* (New York: National Bureau of Economic Research, 1955).

15. Source: *Statistical Abstracts of the United States,* 1975 (Washington, D.C.: United States Government Printing Office, 1975), pp. 280, 381. Real growth, calculated in 1958 dollars, climbed from $355 billion to $821 billion during the 1950–1974 period.

16. See Heilbroner, *Limits of American Capitalism,* pp. 65 ff.

17. Leonard Silk, *Capitalism: The Moving Target* (New York: Praeger, 1974), p. 43.

18. Michael Walzer provides the best contemporary democratic socialist discussion of the modern welfare state in "Politics in the Welfare State," in Howe, ed., *Essential Works of Socialism,* pp. 809–834. In subsequent comments on the American welfare state, I have drawn freely on Walzer's piece. For an earlier expression of misgivings concerning the welfare state as a path toward socialism, see G. D. H. Cole, "Socialism and the Welfare State," in Howe, ibid, pp. 768–786.

19. Bell, "The Public Household," pp. 32–33.

20. Eli Ginzberg and Robert M. Solow, eds., *The Great Society: Lessons for the Future* (New York: Basic Books, 1974), pp. 4–13.

21. Freeman, *Growth of American Government,* p. 161.

22. Ibid., p. 35.

23. Arthur M. Schlesinger, Jr., *The Vital Center: The Politics of Freedom* (Boston: Houghton Mifflin, 1962), p. xv (1962 Introduction). Schlesinger summarizes the perspective of a generation of postwar left liberal critics. On the conflicts within liberalism, see Zbigniew Brzezinski, *Between Two Ages: America's Role in the Technetronic Era* (New York: Viking Press, 1970), pp. 236–254.

24. But the confluence of self-interest explains much of the success of the liberal tradition from the first and second New Deals though the Fair Deal and beyond. "Public opinion polls taken in 1949 provided little evidence that the Democratic majority had been activated by a desire for programs as advanced as FEPC or national health insurance or even an objective as modest as Taft-Hartley repeal. The liberals, of course, supported the Fair Deal as a whole, but the Truman majority was made up primarily of groups with a much narrower view and much more limited goals." Alonzo L. Hamby, *Beyond the New Deal: Harry S. Truman and American Liberalism* (New York: Columbia University Press, 1973), p. 321.

25. Even in the ideological heyday of the New Deal, which Richard Hofstadter claims was politically bankrupt by 1938, there was a diverse collection of people representing a range of approaches to economic and social policy—supporters of traditional remedies such as economy in government and restoration of the private banking system; advocates of cheaper money; regulators and trustbusters from the Progressive era; proponents of a large degree of economic planning; and champions of government ownership. See Raymond Moley, *The First New Deal* (New York: Harcourt Brace Jovanovich, 1966). Also, William E. Leuchtenburg, *Franklin D. Roosevelt and the New Deal, 1932–1940* (New York: Harper & Row,

1963); and Richard Hofstadter, *The American Political Tradition* (New York: Vintage Books, 1948), p. 342.

26. For a discussion of the American two-party system as a set of shifting coalitions that cooperate in limited ways, see James L. Sundquist, *Dynamics of the Party System: Alignment and Realignment of Political Parties in the United States* (Washington, D.C.: The Brookings Institution, 1973).

27. Source: U.S. Department of Labor; Bureau of Labor Statistics News, Wednesday, May 5, 1976.

28. See, for example, the statement of such Nobel laureates as Gunnar Myrdal, Kenneth Arrow, and Linus Pauling calling for economic alternatives to policies favoring private corporate interests, especially in the areas of resource allocation and the establishment of humane social priorities. *Democratic Socialist Organizing Committee Convention Highlights* (New York: Democratic Socialist Organizing Committee, 1975).

29. John Rawls, *A Theory of Justice* (Cambridge, Mass.: Harvard University Press, Belknap Press, 1971), p. 303, and Norman Daniels, ed., *Reading Rawls* (New York: Basic Books, 1975).

30. Rawls, *A Theory of Justice*, p. 302; Daniels, *Reading Rawls*, p. 75.

31. For a Left critique of the 1975 version of the Humphrey–Hawkins bill, emphasizing its modest target of a maximum of 3% unemployment, its tendency to increase the role of the state, and its bias against unskilled and semiskilled workers, see H. Brand, "The Problem of Full Employment," *Dissent* 22 (Fall 1975): 321–325.

32. A. Philip Randolph Institute, *A "Freedom Budget" for All Americans* (New York: 1966), pp. 1–15. A prefiguration of the general outlines of the Freedom Budget and the *Full Employment and Balanced Growth Act* may be found in Franklin Roosevelt's celebrated economic rights speech of 1944.

33. Arnold S. Kaufman, *The Radical Liberal: New Man in American Politics* (New York: Atherton Press, 1968). John Kenneth Galbraith's progress from *American Capitalism* (1952) to *Economics and the Public Purpose* (1973), where he comes to accept the idea of socialism, exemplifies the pattern I have in mind here.

34. Michael Harrington, "Say What You Mean—Socialism," *The Nation,* May 25, 1974, p. 651.

35. See, especially, Robert L. Heilbroner, "Economic Problems of a 'Postindustrial' Society," *Dissent* 22 (Spring 1973): 163–176; and Michael

Harrington, *Socialism* (New York: Saturday Review Press, 1972), esp. chap. 12, "Beyond the Welfare State," pp. 270–307.

36. For a splendid overview of the fortunes of the planning idea in America since the 1930s, and a convincing projection of the range of its potential uses in the coming decades, see Otis L. Graham, Jr., *Toward a Planned Society: From Roosevelt to Nixon* (New York: Oxford University Press, 1976). Graham argues that the growth of government intervention in economic and social affairs during the thirties was not accompanied by widespread acceptance of systematic planning at the national level (though elements of planning have been introduced gradually in recent decades). The result was "the post-New Deal Broker State, a compromise system that contained the social programs demanded by contemporary liberalism but without the institutional capacity or political commitment required for coherent social management." P. 297. Though useful and durable, the broker state now must be superseded by a planning state which can be accepted in broad outline by socialists, liberals, and conservatives. There will be familiar differences of emphasis—important ones —resulting from differing ideological commitments, Graham predicts, but the planning state has been made imperative by the advent of an era of limits, by the size and complexity of institutions, and by the nature and degree of governmental intervention. Graham predicts sanely that the turn toward planning may make large differences in the long run, but in the short run "we will wake to the same problems, the same inadequate understanding, the same power groupings and habits and expectations in the society. . . . Those who fear ought to fear more moderately, and for the very long run. Those who hope, one reluctantly concedes, the same." P. 306.

37. See Walzer, "Politics in the Welfare State," pp. 822–834.

38. Between 1950 and 1973, social welfare expenditures under public programs have grown from $23 billion to $242 billion (or from 8.9% to 18% of GNP, and from 37.6% to 55.8% of total government outlays). Of projected 1974 spending, a total of $160 billion (or 66%) went to social insurance, public aid, health and medical programs, and veterans' programs. Of the rest, education received the largest slice ($72 billion, or 30%). Source: *Statistical Abstracts of the United States, 1975* (Washington, D.C.: United States Government Printing Office, 1975), p. 280. According to the Social Security Administration, the total public social welfare spending for fiscal year 1975 reached $287 billion: the federal share was 58% or $166.4 billion. Total estimated social welfare expenditures, including those from private sources, amounted to $389 billion, or 27% of GNP.

39. Andrew F. Brimmer, "Income Distribution and Economic Equity in the United States" (mimeographed). Paper presented at the Annual Meeting of the American Association for the Advancement of Science, February 23, 1976, p. 26.

40. Joseph H. Crown, "Taxes and Budget: Ford Plays a Demagogue," *The Nation,* October 25, 1975, p. 391.

41. See Barrington Moore, Jr., *Reflections on the Causes of Human Misery* (Boston: Beacon Press, 1972), pp. 150–193.

Chapter 4: Conservative Caveats

1. In discussing the libertarian and egalitarian stresses within every major ideological facet of the bourgeois tradition, I use the terms loosely to suggest what have become opposing and seemingly irreconcilable tendencies of thought in the current American context. Libertarian positions are often identified with extreme doctrines of individualism—with a nonviolent anarchism on the Left, and on the Right, with a kind of antitraditional conservatism that rejects the premodern feudal and aristocratic survivals in philosophical conservatism and accepts the idea of a free market as the principal key to maximizing personal liberty in society. I use "libertarian" in this context to refer to people who embrace the ends of individualism, distrust in varying degrees all functions of the state, believe for the most part in the free market as the *ideal* if not always the most practical vehicle of maximizing personal liberty, and remain suspicious of the state as an agency for redistributing wealth, and at least uncomfortable about the state as an agency for redistributing opportunity.

"Egalitarian" also identifies an emphasis that is by no means unified. In recent decades the egalitarian thrust toward further redistribution of wealth and opportunity has required its advocates—many of whom remain nervous about the large powers of the state and the power of dominant economic institutions as well—to embrace a growing state apparatus as the main vehicle for ensuring fair opportunity and a more equitable (that is, less unequal) distribution of rewards.

For an interesting discussion of libertarianism as a position distinct from liberalism and conservatism, and in the opinion of its advocates, superior to both, see Murray N. Rothbard, "Left and Right: The Prospects for Liberty," in Tibor R. Machan, ed., *The Libertarian Alternative: Essays in Social and Political Philosophy* (Chicago: Nelson-Hall, 1974), pp. 525–549.

2. Lionel Trilling, *The Liberal Imagination: Essays on Literature and Society* (Garden City, N.Y.: Doubleday, 1953), p. vii. Trilling notes also the dangers of confining conservatism to a collection of unarticulated sentiments, mere actions, or "irritable mental gestures which seek to resemble ideas."

3. Raymond English, "Conservatism: The Forbidden Faith," *The American Scholar* 21 (Autumn 1952): 393, 395. At the same time, it should be noted that the number of Americans identifying themselves as conservative in basic outlook has remained fairly constant, fluctuating between 50% and 60% since 1936: 53% in 1936; 51% in 1962; 59% in 1964. Source: Gallup Polls, cited in Roger A. Freeman, *The Growth of American Government: A Morphology of the Welfare State* (Stanford, Calif.: Hoover Institution Press, 1975), pp. 161–162. But these figures do not correspond with party identification, since for example, only about 21% of registered Americans identified themselves as Republicans three years after Watergate, according to a 1976 Gallup Poll.

4. For the most influential postwar view of the liberal tradition, on which I have drawn in obvious ways, see Louis Hartz, *The Liberal Tradition in America: An Interpretation of American Political Thought Since the Revolution* (New York: Harcourt Brace Jovanovich, 1955). See also Daniel Bell, "The End of American Exceptionalism," *The Public Interest* 41 (Fall 1975): 193–224.

5. A useful discussion of the political potential of conservative sentiments may be found in Kevin P. Phillips, *Mediacracy: American Parties and Politics in the Communications Age* (Garden City, N.Y.: Doubleday, 1975). It should be noted also that popular images of the academy as a hotbed of liberal and Left activity are at best only partly accurate. There are as many cold spots, though these are not found generally within disciplines directly concerned with social thought and public policy. The academic profession is more deeply divided than any other, according to surveys conducted by Everett Carll Ladd, Jr., and Seymour Martin Lipset, with social scientists and some humanists taking consistently liberal and Left positions on political, social, and cultural matters, and faculty members in such fields as engineering, the agricultural sciences, business administration, and health (excluding medicine and dentistry) adopting more conservative positions. Reported in *The Chronicle of Higher Education*, November 3, 1975, p. 2.

6. There is a considerable body of literature on the American political Right and its relation to conservative thought. The best overview may be

found in Seymour Martin Lipset and Earl Raab, *The Politics of Unreason: Right Wing Extremism in America, 1790–1970* (New York: Harper & Row, 1970). See also Robert A. Schoenberger, ed., *The American Right Wing: Readings in Political Behavior* (New York: Holt, Rinehart & Winston, 1969), pp. 280–298.

7. On the "projective" politics of the far Right, see Richard Hofstadter, "Pseudo-Conservatism Revisited: A Postscript (1962)," in Daniel Bell, ed., *The Radical Right* (Garden City, N.Y.: Doubleday, 1964), pp. 100 ff.

8. Karl Mannheim, *Ideology and Utopia: An Introduction to the Sociology of Knowledge* (New York: Harcourt Brace Jovanovich, 1936), p. 230.

9. Quoted from John P. Diggins, *Up from Communism: Conservative Odysseys in American Intellectual History* (New York: Harper & Row, 1975), p. 410. I found Diggins' study most helpful in designing this chapter.

10. English, "Conservatism," pp. 399–405. In this taxonomy, English loads the case for philosophical conservatism in familiar ways, compressing the range of meanings of libertarian, or liberal, conservatism, into a narrow economic calculus of profit and loss. See also Clinton Rossiter, *Conservatism in America* (New York: Random House, 1962), pp. 2–10.

11. English, "Conservatism," p. 399.

12. Ibid., p. 400.

13. Russell Kirk, *The Conservative Mind: From Burke to Eliot* (Chicago: Henry Regnery, 1953), p. 525.

14. Ibid., pp. 6–8. The quotation on the relationship between conservation and change is from Edmund Burke, *Reflections on the Revolution in France,* ed. William B. Todd (New York: Holt, Rinehart & Winston, 1965), p. 23.

15. Walter Lippmann, *Essays in the Public Philosophy* (New York: New American Library, 1956), pp. 109–110.

16. This is, of course, a central thrust of post-Christian morality. See Philip Rieff, *Freud: The Mind of the Moralist* (Garden City, N.Y.: Doubleday, 1961). Lionel Trilling explores and employs the ideas of Freud to illuminate the harsh terms of the moral life in an essentially post–Christian culture. See, for example, his brilliant little book, *Sincerity and Authenticity* (Cambridge, Mass.: Harvard University Press, 1972), especially Chapter 6, "The Authentic Unconscious," pp. 134–172. On the character, strengths, and dangers of American civil religion, and the Judeo-Christian

archetypes that inform it, see Robert Bellah, *Beyond Belief: Essays on Religion in a Post-Traditional World* (New York: Harper & Row, 1970), pp. 168 ff., and *The Broken Covenant: American Civil Religion in Time of Trial* (New York: Seabury Press, 1974).

17. See, for example, the differing views of Irving Babbitt, who argues for the sufficiency of ethical bases of authority, and T. S. Eliot, who insists on the need for religious sources.

18. Daniel Bell, *The Cultural Contradictions of Capitalism* (New York: Basic Books, 1976), p. 14.

19. Robert Bellah reports that among the various groups espousing "the new religious consciousness"—from charismatic Christian to Zen—self-discipline has become a central theme in the seventies. "Civil Religion: The Sacred and the Political in American Life," *Psychology Today,* January 1976, p. 63.

20. Karl Menninger, *Whatever Became of Sin?* (New York: Hawthorn Books, 1973), p. 20.

21. Arnold A. Rogow, *The Dying of the Light* (New York: Putnam, 1975), p. 14.

22. Robert Jay Lifton, "The Struggle for Cultural Rebirth," *Harper's,* April 1973, pp. 85, 90.

23. As the middle stages of life become more important demographically in America, they need, more than ever, to be conceived in spiritual dignity and moral balance. According to a 1976 Census Bureau report, 22,000,000 Americans are sixty–five or older (10% of the population); by 2030, if present birth trends continue, and other factors hold steady, there will be 45,000,000 persons over sixty-five (17%). An interesting division of adulthood into several stages of development may be found in Harold L. Hodgkinson, "Adult Development: Implications for Faculty and Administrators," *Educational Record* 55 (Fall 1974): 263–274. On the conservative political implications of the "graying of America"—the movement of the post-1940 "birth surge" toward the middle stages of life—see Phillips, *Mediacracy,* pp. 221 ff.

24. The "neo-conservative" label was affixed to *The Public Interest* intellectuals by Michael Harrington. Though some find this label unsettling and the jacket ill-fitting in places, one senses that most of these critics will grow into it in time. For a democratic socialist critique, see Lewis Coser and Irving Howe, eds., *The New Conservatives: A Critique from the*

Left (New York: Quadrangle, 1974). An early statement of the leading themes of the neo-conservative critique of the welfare state may be found in Nathan Glazer, "The Limits of Social Policy," *Commentary* 52 (September 1971): 51–58. See also Frances Fitzgerald's nicely written but thin and predictable left liberal critique, "The Warrior Intellectuals," *Harper's,* May 1976, pp. 45–64.

25. Samuel P. Huntington, "The Democratic Distemper," *The Public Interest* 41 (Fall 1975): 9–38. This is a condensed version of a longer piece Huntington contributed to a study sponsored by the Trilateral Commission, which includes a distinguished cast of supporting characters from business, labor, government, and education who are concerned about the prospects of capitalist democracy in America, Western Europe, and Japan. See Michael J. Crozier, Samuel P. Huntington, and Joji Watanuki, *The Crisis of Democracy: Report on the Governability of Democracies to the Trilateral Commission* (New York: New York University Press, 1975), esp. pp. 59–118.

26. Though Huntington recognizes that voter participation has declined over the past two decades, he bases his argument on the rise of other forms of participation—the vast increase in volunteer workers in political campaigns; the growth of such organizations as Common Cause, Nader groups, and environmental activist groups; the protest politics of the 1960s, including the resurgence of political activity among minorities, students, and women.

27. Huntington, "Democratic Distemper," p. 37.

28. The subsequent discussion of conservative readings of dominant social values is not abstracted directly from the work of neo-conservative intellectuals associated with *The Public Interest,* though it perhaps could be —despite lively disagreements among them—if one were to review carefully the contents of the first decade of that journal. I draw also on the traditions of philosophical and libertarian conservatism for this section.

29. In *Anarchy, State, and Utopia* (New York: Basic Books, 1974), Robert Nozick carries the libertarian idea of liberty to its extreme. This much heralded defense of the minimal state is an elegant (though I think overrated) philosophical articulation of a prevalent mood of disenchantment with government. Nozick claims to go beyond socialist, liberal, and conservative positions, and I am inclined to agree that he does, but the libertarian stress on the individual and the minimum state fits well enough with libertarian conservatism, though not with most varieties of philosophical conservatism. These themes also account in part for the wide and generous reception accorded the book.

30. For a recent treatment of the differences between public and popular opinion, see Robert Nisbet, "Public Opinion versus Popular Opinion," *The Public Interest* 41 (Fall 1975): 166–192: "More and more it becomes difficult to determine what is genuinely public opinion, the opinion of the people organized into a constitutional political community, and what is only popular opinion, the kind that is so easily exploited by self-appointed tribunes of the people, by populist demagogues, and by all-too-many agencies of the media." P. 192.

31. My discussion here presupposes acceptance of the fairness of differential rewards for differential contributions to society based on the cultivation of talent and the expression of ambition. But such presuppositions are under severe attack. John Rawls reminds us that even if advantages of intelligence and energy based on heredity could be distinguished thoroughly from social/environmental factors, there would be no reason to regard natural advantages as more or less arbitrary than social ones. Because of the impossibility of establishing full equality of opportunity, Rawls argues the case for equality of result as a desirable, fair, and potentially functional social norm. John Rawls, *A Theory of Justice* (Cambridge, Mass.: Harvard University Press, Belknap Press, 1971), pp. 73–74. For an excellent overview of the problem of equality and merit, see Daniel Bell, "On Meritocracy and Equality," *The Public Interest* 29 (Fall 1972): 29–68.

32. An interesting discussion of the inconsistencies between conservative principles and politics may be found in Diggins, *Up from Communism,* pt. 3, "The Dilemmas of American Conservatism, 1955–1974," pp. 339–456. See also David Spitz's splendid essay, "Liberalism and Conservatism," in R. A. Goldwin, ed., *Left, Right, and Center* (Skokie, Ill.: Rand McNally, 1967), pp. 18–41.

33. For an example, see the proposals of Milton Friedman. A general discussion of Friedman's views on conservatism and capitalism may be found in his *Capitalism and Freedom* (Chicago: University of Chicago Press, 1962). His ideas on social security reform are sketched in "Reforming Social Security," *Current* 142 (July-August 1972): 45–50.

34. Irving Kristol, "On Corporate Capitalism in America," *The Public Interest* 41 (Fall 1975): 124–141.

35. Senator Edmund S. Muskie, quoted in "Liberals Join Attack on Big Government," *Los Angeles Times,* October 27, 1975.

36. Ronald Reagan, representing the far edge of the respectable right-wing political attack on the welfare state, proposed a $90 billion cut in

federal spending in 1975—nearly one-quarter of current totals and the equivalent of the entire defense budget. But Reagan would cut mostly in the areas of health, education, and welfare, not defense.

37. Kevin Phillips traces the ideological shift away from liberalism since the middle sixties, noting that in 1974 approximately 40% of Americans who characterized themselves as "moderates" or "conservatives" were onetime "liberals." Among the principal reasons given for shifting away from liberalism were economic self-interest, advancing age, disillusionment with social programs designed to assist the poor and minority groups, and a growing conservatism in attitudes toward a range of issues such as busing, drugs, pornography, and treatment of criminals. Phillips, *Mediacracy,* pp. 202 ff.

38. Michael Harrington, "The Welfare State and Its Critics," *Dissent* 20 (Fall 1973): 452.

39. See Diggins, *Up from Communism,* pp. 443 ff.

40. Kirk, *Conservative Mind,* p. 539.

41. Daniel P. Moynihan, "The American Experiment," *The Public Interest* 41 (Fall 1975): 4–8.

Chapter 5: Crooked Paths

1. Though zero growth of goods and population ultimately will have to become the basis of public policy, it would be foolish to predict this juncture. For a balanced inquiry into the merits and drawbacks of proposals for zero population growth and zero economic growth, see Mancur Olson, ed., "The No Growth Society," *Daedalus* 102 (Fall 1973).

2. Estimates of economic growth for the next quarter-century vary widely, but the most sensible ones, in my opinion, run to about 2% to 3%. This rate of growth would yield an output of goods and services considerably above present levels. And if the average annual growth rate of about 3.3% which has characterized the American economy for several decades persists, GNP will more than double by the end of the century. Such predictions—depending as they must upon a cluster of other contingencies such as the size and composition of the work force, total population, international economic and political developments, income and tax

policies, *and* the shape of the public sector—obviously are hazardous. See Roger A. Freeman, *The Growth of American Government: A Morphology of the Welfare State* (Stanford, Calif.: Hoover Institution Press, 1975), pp. 185–190.

3. I have employed Daniel Bell's useful notion of a disjunction of realms—techno-economic structure, polity, and culture—as a heuristic device here. See his *The Coming of Post-Industrial Society: A Venture in Social Forecasting* (New York: Basic Books, 1973), and *The Cultural Contradictions of Capitalism* (New York: Basic Books, 1976).

4. Even such Western European nations as Italy, France, Portugal, and Spain may work out of the zone of the capitalist world in the next decades. In my judgment, the most balanced democratic socialist perspective on socialisms in the developing nations is found in Robert L. Heilbroner's essays. See, for an example, *Between Capitalism and Socialism: Essays in Political Economics* (New York: Random House, 1970).

5. Of course, higher education runs on fuel, too, and if its costs are high and rising, its benefits are still greater, even though the rate of economic return to individuals appears to be leveling off. See Paul Taubman and Terence Wales, *Higher Education and Earnings* (New York: McGraw-Hill, 1974).

6. I have stated this preference elsewhere at greater length. See, for example, *Radical Paradoxes: Dilemmas of the American Left, 1945–1970* (New York: Harper & Row, 1973), and "Dilemmas of the American Left," *Social Research* 41 (Winter 1975): 467–491.

7. Karl Marx and Frederick Engels, *The Communist Manifesto,* in *Marx and Engels: Selected Works* (New York: International Publishers, 1968), p. 59.

8. A number of American men of letters in the tradition of Christian socialism, from Melville to Reinhold Niebuhr and F. O. Matthiessen, have espoused facets of the sort of conservative democratic socialism that I have in mind here. For a discussion of Niebuhr's attempts to synthesize liberal, socialist, and conservative elements in the light of his Christian vision during the 1930s and 1940s, see Donald Drew Egbert and Stow Persons, eds., *Socialism and American Life* (Princeton, N.J.: Princeton University Press, 1952), II, 229–232. See also Reinhold Niebuhr, *Faith and History: A Comparison of Christian and Modern Views of History* (New York: Scribner, 1949).

9. The quotation from *The German Ideology* appears in Michael Harrington, *Socialism* (New York: Saturday Review Press, 1972), p. 29. This pas-

sage suggests the need for making the difficult distinction between *wants* and *needs*. Whether we define wants as the sum of preferences, or needs on the basis of criteria appropriate to a culture at a particular time, much of "the old crap" would recur under socialism, if not at the level of essential material requisites for life, then along other material, social, and psychological dimensions. As material productivity rises in America, the age-old concern with the satisfaction of physiological needs, to borrow from Maslow's hierarchy, lessens somewhat (though not nearly to the extent that most postwar American critics imagined), and attention focuses more on satisfying needs for safety, community, self-esteem, and self-fulfillment.

10. Leszek Kolakowski, "Introduction," in Leszek Kolakowski and Stuart Hampshire, eds., *The Socialist Idea: A Reappraisal* (New York: Basic Books, 1974), p. 15.

11. Both principles now operate, though in fragmentary and caricatured ways: wages are allocated partly on the basis of ability, and welfare is extended partly on the basis of need.

12. In the United States, *Dissent* is the most consistently intelligent journal of democratic socialism in my opinion, and though it is not a hub of expressly neo-conservative ideas, it does provide the best American examples of socialist thought being revised continuously in the light of conservative caveats. On the problem of values, and especially the matter of equality, for example, see two splendid essays, one by Michael Walzer, "In Defense of Equality," *Dissent* 20 (Fall 1973): 399–413, the other by David Spitz, "A Grammar of Equality," *Dissent* 21 (Winter 1974): 63–78. In the ensuing discussion of values, I draw on these sources freely.

13. Unless it can be shown that making fortunes is an indispensable element in producing the optimum—or even the maximum—of goods and services, a contention which socialists of all persuasions find dubious.

14. The distribution of income and wealth remains badly skewed. The richest 10% of the population receive 29% of personal income and own 56% of the national wealth. The poorest 10% receive 1% of the income and own none of the national wealth. Edwin Kuh, "Who Gets What and Why," in Leonard Silk, ed., *Capitalism: The Moving Target* (New York: Praeger, 1974), pp. 83–88. See also Andrew F. Brimmer, "Income Distribution and Economic Equity in the United States" (mimeographed). Paper presented at the Annual Meeting of the American Association for the Advancement of Science, February 23, 1976. Brimmer argues that after a postwar trend toward greater equality supported by the economic

expansion of the 1960s, the distribution of money income has become more unequal, beginning in 1970: "In general, over the last five years, income has been redistributed so as to favor whites vs. blacks; the better off vs. the poor; the newer regions of the country vs. the old; and the suburbs vs. both rural areas and central cities." P. 1. For a discussion of the conceptual and technical difficulties involved in measuring income inequality, see T. Paul Schultz, "Long-Term Change in Personal Income Distribution: Theoretical Approaches, Evidence, and Explanations," in Donald M. Levine and Mary Jo Bane, eds., The "Inequality" Controversy: Schooling and Distributive Justice (New York: Basic Books, 1975), pp. 147–169.

15. The problems here include establishing criteria for a just meritocracy; discovering ways to read existing hierarchies so as to distinguish between unmerited and just elements in their orderings; and deciding upon tolerable tensions between an ideal meritocracy (if that is not itself an inconsistent notion, considering the claims of equality) and the exigencies of actual hierarchies in society. On this, see Daniel Bell, "On Meritocracy and Equality," The Public Interest 29 (Fall 1972): 29–68.

16. I believe that indicative planning at the highest levels should be conducted by blue ribbon panels with a mixture of experts and interested citizens appointed by elected officials for terms sufficiently long to minimize the dangers of a politics of self-interest.

17. Peter D. Hart Research Associates, Inc., Highlights of a Survey Conducted for the Peoples Bicentennial Commission, August 1975 (mimeographed), pp. 2, 4, 5, 6.

18. Peter F. Drucker, "Pension Fund 'Socialism,' " The Public Interest 42 (Winter 1976): 3–4. Drucker notes also that the large employee pension funds "own a controlling interest in practically every single one of the 'command positions' in the economy"—including the 1,000 largest industrial corporations and the 50 largest companies in banking, retail, insurance, communications, and transportation. Pp. 3–4.

19. Michael Harrington, "Economic Planning—Promises and Pitfalls," Dissent 22 (Fall 1975): 316.

20. After all, billions have been poured into manpower training programs, the Job Corps, and other such programs over the last decade without remarkable results. It may be that some federal assistance would be spent better in shoring up essentially sound corporations. But on tough terms. These occasions would furnish the chance to tie some heavy strings

to the activities of companies in trouble: to demand greater efficiency, accountability, democracy, and consideration of a range of public goals— all under the threat of nationalization, which will become an increasingly meaningful threat in the next decades.

21. On this, see Peter Jenkins, "Dilemmas of Social Democracy," *Dissent* 22 (Fall 1975): 345.

22. Elsewhere in the West, received notions of transition are being modified drastically, especially where socialist forces command wide support. On the movement of the Italian Communist party toward a politics of coalition, see Ronald Radosh, "Chaos or the Communists? Italy Seeks a Coalition," *The Nation*, February 28, 1976, pp. 234–238.

23. About four-fifths, or 43,566,784, of the 55,712,000 American families (averaging 3.5 persons) have incomes of $20,000 or less—surely not a harvest of abundance; 42.4%, or 23,621,888, of all families have annual incomes between $10,000 and $20,000; 22.6%, or 12,590,912, receive between $5,000 and $10,000; and 13.2%, or 7,353,984, receive between 0 and $5,000. Adapted from Andrew Hacker, "Cutting Classes," *The New York Review of Books* 23 (March 4, 1976): 16.

24. Stuart Hampshire, "Epilogue," in Kolakowski and Hampshire, *Socialist Idea*, p. 249.

25. An interesting examination of the idea of corporate responsibility may be found in Christopher D. Stone's thoughtful study, *Where the Law Ends: The Social Control of Corporate Behavior* (New York: Harper & Row, 1975).

26. I am grateful to Richard Flacks for raising the important issues mentioned in subsequent paragraphs. My brief comments here do not do justice to his thoughtful criticisms. See Richard Flacks, "The Importance of the Romantic Myth for the Left: A Discussion of Peter Clecak's *Radical Paradoxes*," *Theory and Society* 2 (Fall 1975): 401–414.

27. Leszek Kolakowski, *Toward a Marxist Humanism: Essays on the Left Today* (New York: Grove Press, 1968), p. 145.

28. Health care is divisible by degrees, and so is sickness. Advances in medical technology raise such difficult questions as: what are to be the standards of premium, adequate, and minimally acceptable health care? Who is entitled to what, and on what grounds? For an overview that documents the general improvement in health care in the United States in the past several decades, see *Health: United States, 1975* (Rockville, Md.. DHEW Publication, No. 76–1232, 1975).

Index